THE EYE TEST

THE
EYE
TEST

A CASE FOR HUMAN CREATIVITY
IN THE AGE OF ANALYTICS

Chris Jones

TWELVE

New York Boston

Twelve
Hachette Book Group
1290 Avenue of the Americas, New York, NY 10104
twelvebooks.com
twitter.com/twelvebooks

First Edition: January 2022

Twelve is an imprint of Grand Central Publishing. The Twelve name and logo
are trademarks of Hachette Book Group, Inc.

The publisher is not responsible for websites (or their content) that are not
owned by the publisher.

The Hachette Speakers Bureau provides a wide range of authors for speaking
events. To find out more, go to www.hachettespeakersbureau.com or call
(866) 376-6591.

Print book interior design by Marie Mundaca

Library of Congress Cataloging-in-Publication Data

Names: Jones, Chris, 1973- author.
Title: The eye test : a case for human creativity in the age of analytics /
   Chris Jones.
Description: First edition. | New York : Twelve, [2022] | Includes
   bibliographical references and index.
Identifiers: LCCN 2021019906 | ISBN 9781538730676 (hardcover) | ISBN
   9781538730683 (ebook)
Subjects: LCSH: Problem solving. | Decision making. | Creative thinking. |
   Data mining.
Classification: LCC BF449 .J664 2022 | DDC 153.4/3--dc23
LC record available at https://lccn.loc.gov/2021019906

ISBNs: 978-1-5387-3067-6 (hardcover), 978-1-5387-3068-3 (ebook)

Printed in the United States of America

LSC-C

Printing 1, 2021

For my boys, who remind me.
And for Ana, who rescued me.

I am enough of the artist to draw freely upon my imagination.

Imagination is more important than knowledge. Knowledge is limited.

Imagination encircles the world.

—Albert Einstein[1]

---

1 This was Einstein's reply, in an interview published in the *Saturday Evening Post* in 1929, to the question: "Then you trust more to your imagination than to your knowledge?" A similar, widely seen quote attributed to Einstein—"Logic will get you from A to B. Imagination takes you everywhere."—while snappier, is probably not his.

Contents

A Note to Readers

You perhaps noticed a few pages back a footnote.

I am aware that some readers find footnotes cumbersome and interruptive. I have no idea what percentage; no hard data on footnote participation appears to exist. But a textbook titled *Stats: Modeling the World* includes the following footnote on its opening pages: "This chapter might have been called 'Introduction,' but nobody reads the introduction, and we wanted you to read this. We feel safe admitting this here, in the footnote, because nobody reads footnotes either."[1] The writers of statistics textbooks should seem to know.

To those of you who don't appreciate footnotes—everyone, apparently—I apologize. I use them either to explain sourcing or provide additional context that I struggled to fit into the narrative. Entirely without innovation, honestly. Worse, several of them cite myself. Readers who have closely followed my magazine work will recognize some of the people others of you will be meeting for the first time. I didn't want to pretend I'd forgotten the many creative men and women I've been lucky enough to meet over the course of my career or

---

1 David E. Bock, Paul F. Velleman, and Richard D. De Veaux, *Stats: Modeling the World* (Boston: Addison-Wesley, 2004).

the lessons they taught me, but those self-referential footnotes, while necessary, are deeply weird to me. Please feel free to skip them. None is essential to read, unlike the text itself, every word of which is sacred.

To those invisible few of you who do read footnotes: Thank you. They are a lot of work, and the people I cite deserve recognition for their labor. I use the Chicago style, because I like it best.

Whether you choose to read the footnotes or ignore them, I hope all of you enjoy this little book and find someone between its covers who inspires you to make or do something beautiful.

ENTERTAINMENT

There's No Accounting for Taste.

Not everything can be quantified, and it's foolish to think so. How do you measure something as limitless as the human imagination? Unfortunately, that means there is no "right" way to do creative things, and no guarantee we'll achieve what we want to achieve. You will receive no false promises here. But we can almost always improve our handiwork, and so our odds of success. That earned difference, the margin between where we are and where we can be, separates us from each other, and us from machines.

It was 2009, and Ryan Kavanaugh had just announced his plans to burn Hollywood to the ground. We met in the garden at the Chateau Marmont, because even revolutionaries have to acknowledge the Establishment's sometimes superior taste.[1]

---

1 I first wrote about Ryan Kavanaugh for *Esquire* magazine, where I worked from 2002 to 2016. Again, some of the people I met during that time reappear in these pages, usually after subsequent conversations and with the benefit of hindsight. The story on Kavanaugh, titled, imaginatively enough, "Ryan Kavanaugh," appeared in the December 2009 issue. Despite warnings from Hollywood friends who knew better, I was not as skeptical about him as I should have been. It took a few years for his plans to unravel, and a few years more for me to understand why they did.

Kavanaugh was in his mid-thirties but looked younger, or he dressed younger at least. He wore a skinny tie, dark jeans, and blue Converse sneakers. His ginger hair was spiked, and his eyes never stopped moving, on the lookout for the affection that had become inevitable for him. Less than a minute after we arrived, Baz Luhrmann, the colorful Australian director, emerged from the foliage and wrapped Kavanaugh in a long embrace.

"That was Baz Luhrmann," Kavanaugh said when we sat down, nodding at me to make the note. Earlier that day, the waiting room at Kavanaugh's West Hollywood office had been graced by another, less flamboyant, director. Ron Howard wore a baseball cap and hiking boots, and he sat like a school-boy, with his hands folded in his lap. A receptionist offered him a bottle of water. "I'm A-okay," he said, exactly the way you might expect him to say it.

Howard was waiting for Kavanaugh to finish yet another meeting, this one with an author whose book he wanted to make into a film. The deal was taking time to come together. The author had been making the Hollywood rounds, and he was telling Kavanaugh how many famous directors he had met. He wasn't some starstruck, moony-eyed simpleton; he had a property that was in demand, and he wanted to be paid. Kavanaugh, an expert negotiator, smiled and shrugged. He had dated Kate Bosworth and was not shy that he had. "I know a few famous directors, too," he told the author. One was waiting to see him *at this very moment.*

Kavanaugh was the founder of Relativity Media, and famous directors were waiting for an audience with him, or jumping out of hedges to hug him, because he was sitting on a reported (and disputed) $2 billion in liquid assets. Much of it had been raised from Elliott Management, a venerable New York–based hedge fund that had billions more cooling behind its initial investment; the studio had other big-money backers from as far afield as China. Even by Hollywood standards, Relativity's vault appeared bottomless, and Kavanaugh held the only key to its locks. He was suddenly very popular with people who needed money to make things, including more money.

Kavanaugh was accustomed to being the center of attention in crowded rooms. In his actual youth, he had earned a swash-buckling reputation in investment circles. People who later sued him had to admit that he was an unbelievable salesman. He had then remade himself as a financial middleman in slates of movies made by established studios. Now his billions in venture capital had allowed him to put up his own shingle in an industry ripe for cataclysm. He promised his investors, of which there never seemed a shortage, that he was going to do something that no other studio head in a century of filmmaking had done: He would make only hits.

Kavanaugh's timing was flawless; his message could not have found more receptive ears. He had set up shop in those awful, worried months after the 2008 recession. The credit squeeze, investor flight, digital piracy, the dismantling of bizarre German tax shelters, and a bunch of really bad movies had seen the usual coffers go empty. The Weinsteins were told to cut back to ten films a year.[2] New Line had vanished into the ether at Warner Bros., and Metro-Goldwyn-Mayer was on the verge of bankruptcy.

The heart of the problem was that movies had become increasingly expensive to make, compounding the pre-existing concern that even successful studios missed nearly as often as

---

2 When Harvey Weinstein was only a rumored rapist rather than a con-victed one.

they hit. "Nobody knows anything" is a Hollywood maxim, first asserted by William Goldman, the late screenwriter of *Butch Cassidy and the Sundance Kid*. Goldman's edict continued: "Not one person in the entire motion picture field knows for a certainty what's going to work. Every time out it's a guess—and, if you're lucky, an educated one."[3] No one set out to produce *Ishtar* or *Heaven's Gate*, but whether a movie became a hit, a flop, or most likely landed in the maw of the forgettable middle seemed to come down largely to chance. "Trying to understand how something is going to be received—you can never ever tell," Darren Aronofsky, the director of *The Wrestler* and *Black Swan*, has said. "You can never ever tell how a film's going to come out."[4] Now, with shooting budgets spiraling out of control, bombs had become more than a regrettable cost of a fickle business. They were big enough to destroy the studios that made them. And sooner or later, everyone made a bomb. Every Hollywood story was doomed to end badly.

Except at Relativity. Ryan Kavanaugh boasted over lavish dinners and the thump of his private helicopter's rotors that he had cracked the profitability code. Using analytics—the rational, quantitative decision-making systems that Michael Lewis had elevated with his game-changing book *Moneyball* in 2003—Kavanaugh would take passion and instinct out of the filmmaking equation. Mirroring baseball's new appreciation for getting on base, he didn't claim that he'd always hit home

---

3 William Goldman, *Adventures in the Screen Trade: A Personal View of Hollywood and Screenwriting* (New York: Warner Books, Inc., 1983). More on Goldman later. He's wonderful.

4 The same holds true, of course, for our other arts. On January 11, 2021, Finneas O'Connell, older brother of Billie Eilish and the co-writer of many of her songs, tweeted: "don't trust anyone who says they know what a 'Hit' is." (He's on Twitter @FINNEAS.)

runs, but he'd make box-office singles and doubles routine. The strange sorcery of art and its making would soon seem as arcane as any other witchcraft. At Relativity, Big Data would reign supreme.

When considering the merits of a particular script, Kavanaugh's army of quants plugged countless variables into their mainframes, which hummed away in their air-conditioned chambers. Those boy-wonder statisticians then toyed with their Monte Carlo model, evaluating different actors in different roles in different movies released on different weekends, comparing each of their theoretical combinations against reams of historical box-office data—divining patterns of what had previously worked, where and when.[5] The computer knew, for instance, that Natalie Portman drew reliably well in France, perhaps a holdover from her child-star turn in *Léon: The Professional*. It also knew that New Mexico offered generous film-tax credits and could stand in for Minnesota, the Middle East, and Mars. Cameras rolled only when the math made unassailable sense. And at Relativity, the math worked out surprisingly often. Kavanaugh's name began appearing on dozens of movies each year.

"I'm not in this for the art, you know," he told me. "I don't care about awards. I want to make money. I want to own a *business*."

He sometimes called films "widgets," as though he were making electrical appliances rather than expressions of human

---

5 The Monte Carlo method, in simple terms, relies on computer algorithms to experiment with different combinations of random inputs until the user reaches an acceptable probability for a desired outcome. In Relativity's case, inputs included actors in starring roles, directors, and release dates. Different combinations of inputs gave varying probabilities of commercial success. Putting Tom Cruise in a Steven Spielberg movie released on a July weekend, for instance, would yield the cinematic version of a lock.

emotion. He had helped make *Paul Blart: Mall Cop*, because Kevin James on a Segway killed in certain parts of the country. He had also helped produce one of my favorite movies, *The Assassination of Jesse James by the Coward Robert Ford*. It is languid, gorgeous, and artful, and that night in the Chateau's garden, I told Kavanaugh that I was having trouble with the contradiction. He rolled his shining eyes. He had expected to make money with both; he found it instructive that *Paul Blart* so dramatically outdrew *Jesse James*. "Do you know how many people saw *The Assassination of Jesse James?*" he asked. "You and seven other people. *Paul Blart* grossed nearly $200 million worldwide. I'll take *Paul Blart* all day, every day."

After that hard-negotiating author had left Kavanaugh's office earlier in the afternoon, he was accompanied to the door by Tucker Tooley, Relativity's then–president of production. On their way to the elevator, the author saw Ron Howard stand up, next in line. He stopped and grabbed Tooley's arm. "That was Ron Howard," he said.

Tooley agreed: Yes, that was Ron Howard.

"He wasn't *lying*," the author said.

Kavanaugh was not lying about Ron Howard's presence in his lobby. Many of his other promises proved less true. In the years after our meeting, Kavanaugh helped make more than fifty movies, placing bet after supposedly hyper-educated bet. Far from singles and doubles, some of them were absolute disasters. *The Warrior's Way* cost $42 million and brought in only $5.7 million domestically. Something called *Machine Gun Preacher*, starring Gerard Butler, earned precisely $538,690 in American box office against a $30 million budget.[6] Many of the

---

6 All box-office figures from BoxOfficeMojo.com.

others lost money. (Some of them were good films; most were not.) In 2012, Relativity lost $85 million. In 2013, it lost $135 million. In 2014, another $118 million went out the door.[7]

The losses weren't solely because his Monte Carlo model didn't work. In a tale as old as time, Kavanaugh also spent extravagant amounts on "non-production expenses," such as private jets, a hangar at the Santa Monica Airport, and, for a brief period, a pet wolf. In 2010, when Elliott Management pulled out what remained of its investment, Kavanaugh had to engage in a relentless hustle to find enough money to keep afloat. He really was, in hindsight, an incredible salesman, but more and more of his financing came in the form of loans rather than investments. When those loans came due by the tens of millions in 2016, Kavanaugh finally couldn't meet his fantastic debt obligations, and Relativity declared its first bankruptcy. Its reputation fatally wounded, Relativity filed for bankruptcy again in 2018, and Ryan Kavanaugh wasn't being hugged by famous directors anymore.

By 2021, Kavanaugh had reinvented himself for a third time, as the face of a digital-entertainment platform called Triller. He publicly blamed Relativity's collapse on his panicky financiers, who pulled out their money before he could make good. "I tried to make Relativity work," he said. "It was just too difficult. Everybody had their hand out."[8] But I'm confident that Relativity failed, ultimately, because it wasn't very good at its core business: making profitable movies. (Or, as one subsequent lawsuit, later dismissed, memorably maintained, "Kavanaugh's claimed penchant for picking successful movies

---

7 Benjamin Wallace, "The Epic Fail of Hollywood's Hottest Algorithm," *Vulture*, January 24, 2016.
8 Alex Ben Block, "How Triller Became Ryan Kavanaugh's Big Comeback," *Los Angeles Magazine*, April 16, 2021.

was exposed as nothing more than an alchemist's failed efforts to spin lead into gold."[9])

The studio's last quant-approved production was the ironically titled *Masterminds*. Relativity predicted that the film, based on the true story of a heist gone wrong, would earn $125 million in revenue; its delayed release fell nearly $100 million short of that promise.[10] Analytics might have helped the small-market Oakland A's become playoff contenders in *Moneyball*, but Kavanaugh couldn't afford to make any more bets. Regular old Hollywood luck had won out.

———

"Know your audience" is an adage older than "Nobody knows anything." Forgive me, but I've made some assumptions about *you*. This book is designed to encourage you in the truest sense: I want it to put courage into you. That probably means it will be shelved in stores and libraries under "self-improvement." That suggests that you, its readers, wish to do whatever you do better than you're currently doing it, which makes me think, in turn, that you believe you are capable of improvement. Otherwise you wouldn't try. If you're running low on optimism—these are strange, breakneck times—then let me be hopeful on your behalf: I hope that you will find in these pages cause for a renewed faith. Yes, there are once-in-a-generation talents who come along and do something completely original. They become the leaders of movements and make other people feel like imposters. But for most of us, creativity isn't an expression

---

9 Eriq Gardner, "Ryan Kavanaugh Is Lampooned as Relativity Investor Seeks to Keep Fraud Lawsuit Alive," *Hollywood Reporter*, April 11, 2018.

10 David Lieberman, "Relativity Tells Bankruptcy Court It Will Make Money on 13 of 14 Upcoming Films," Deadline.com, December 14, 2015.

of genius, especially early in our work. Creativity is a virtue that we need to spark and nurture and practice.

One of the great pleasures of my writing life has been talking to especially creative people about how they do what they do. (You're about to meet my favorites of them.) Even reticent subjects tend to open up when they're asked about process or craft. They are often particular people, and they love when someone else shares a whisper of their single-mindedness. It's permission for their mania. Ask an expert carpenter about his favorite tool. You will receive a fascinating, intimate, occasionally meandering education in the relative merits of his beloved Pulaski.

We also live in an age of direct access to formerly inaccessible people. Celebrities, too, are spending too much time online. If you want to know something about the finer points of their profession, ask on social media, and you'll be surprised how often they'll answer. The more you wade into the minutiae, the more likely the response, because obsessives find some of their deepest satisfaction in the weeds.

Jason Isbell,[11] a songwriter I admire, once wrote on Twitter that when choosing a new guitar or amplifier, he fiddles with the volume and tone knobs. He enjoys when an adjustment affects the sound of the instrument; the pitch or warmth produced by good ones will be altered by slight changes in the settings. I love music but am tone deaf, and I wondered whether someone like me might hear the same difference, or whether Jason's ears are different from mine in some fundamental way. I asked him how he became a good listener, and he was generous enough to reply.

---

11 "If We Were Vampires," off Jason's 2017 album *The Nashville Sound*, is one of the great sad love songs. His band is called the 400 Unit. He's on Twitter @JasonIsbell.

"I think it's like art criticism," he wrote. "If you look really hard at a million paintings, you'll know what makes a good one."

I liked that answer because it suggests that talent is learned, which is an optimistic position for any of us to hold: If we're willing to put in the time, we have a degree of choice over our fates. We can do what we dream of doing. I don't know how true that is, exactly. I don't think I could be a great musician no matter how many hours I spent trying to become one, because I have a tin ear. The same goes for something like palate for a chef, or rhythm for a writer. It's hard to imagine someone could launch a transcendent career in either of those professions from nothing, born out of some spiritual mud. Achievement has *some* preconditions.

Still, I believe that passion counts for a lot when it comes to creative work, because I've watched passion perform miracles. I've seen what motivated people can make happen, especially when their motivations are internal, almost inexplicable, as though an accident of birth. Such people improve with practice, but they also improve because of their faith in themselves and whatever it is they find divine. Almost universally, the biggest hearts in a room make *progress*: Maybe they can't leap from poor to great in their abilities, but they can lift themselves from poor to fair, fair to good, and good to great, because they care enough to be better than they were. Like you.

I want to give you a seat next to some of our greatest creators in a host of fields, for you to feel the same emotions I've experienced watching them work. I want you to see the world the way *they* see it, and to see the value of their diverse perspectives. And I want to share their gifts with you—right now, at this moment—because too often lately we've diminished the value of human beings, the potential of ourselves and each other, by overestimating the value of machines. We've dismissed the voices of smart, devoted people—minimizing the value of their experience—and sought to replace their testimony with colder, more clinical language: data, numbers, code. I'll repeat myself many times: Analytics have their place; artificial intelligence and algorithms have their place. They are useful when employed carefully and responsibly to help make certain decisions. Those numbers also bring joy to some people, but not to me, and not to that many of us, I don't think. I turn to people for joy and its uniquely human antecedents, like inspiration and desire. I will never tire of hearing talented makers talking about their work. It's like a medicine that might be prescribed to you when you're feeling hopeless.

———

Artists don't always like to think so, but their work is more often the product of slavish method than brilliant madness. Most popular songs follow something like the same structure: verse-chorus-verse-chorus-bridge-chorus-chorus. Most magic tricks have three parts: the pledge, the turn, and the prestige. Most paintings and photographs obey the Rule of Thirds or subscribe to the Golden Ratio. Most books have a traditional narrative arc, the way most movies have three acts. Most of our entertainments are, like bridges, feats of engineering: They succeed or fail based principally on how well they're structured.

In moviemaking, there are dueling foundational texts. One is *Story* by Robert McKee.[12] He's on the side—he called the side

---

12 The full title of McKee's book is *Story: Substance, Structure, Style, and the Principles of Screenwriting* (New York: ReganBooks, 1997).

to arms, in fact—that believes most movies tell stories that have been told before, and there are certain industry specifications with which novice screenwriters must become fluent. McKee now holds workshops and seminars to teach his narrowly pre-scribed storytelling methods; more than 100,000 people have attended them around the world, including sixty future Academy Award winners.[13] (Those are impressive figures in isolation, but they combine for a grim statistic: McKee's seminar attendees have a 0.0006 percent chance of one day holding an Oscar.)

Story is filled with lessons that read more like commandments, because they are written like them, in bold-faced type.

For instance: **The PROTAGONIST has a conscious desire.**

Or: **TRUE CHARACTER is revealed in the choices a human being makes under pressure—the greater the pressure, the deeper the revelation, the truer the choice to the character's essential nature.**

Or: **A STORY must build to a final action beyond which the audience cannot imagine another.**[14]

McKee never presents his findings as suggestions, as wisdom that writers *might* wish to consider; his rules are *musts*. An exaggerated, bombastic version of him was played by Brian Cox in the excellent 2002 film *Adaptation*, written by Charlie Kaufman. Channeling the real Robert McKee, Cox roared

---

13 This is according to his website, mckeestory.com.
14 These appear on pages 138, 101, and 140 of *Story*, respectively.

and prowled across the conference-room stage like a big-tent preacher. But as much as Kaufman sought to lampoon McKee, he also acknowledged that many of his rules are hard to dispute. Unlike Ryan Kavanaugh's exposed code breaking, McKee's divinations hold some significant truth. Just about every Pixar movie follows his prescriptions, for instance, and Pixar movies are pretty great.

In *Adaptation*, there is a character named Charlie Kaufman, a sweaty, perpetually hungry writer who's struggling to adapt Susan Orlean's *The Orchid Thief* into a movie. (It's all very meta.) Charlie has a twin, Donald—in the movie, not in real life—who decides he's also going to be a screenwriter. Donald attends a McKee seminar and breezily writes a cookie-cutter action film that sells quickly and for millions; Charlie suffers for his higher art, fighting to write much of anything. Desperate, he, too, searches out Cox's McKee for guidance and receives more iron-willed advice: "Find an ending," McKee counsels through the haze of his cigarette. "Don't cheat. And don't you dare bring in a *deus ex machina*."

Adaptation ends, of course, with an ironic *deus ex machina* in the form of a timely appearance by an alligator. It's as though the real Charlie Kaufman wanted to thumb his nose at convention, which he has done his entire career. He writes weird, heart-swelling movies like *Being John Malkovich* and *Eternal Sunshine of the Spotless Mind*, none of which follow McKee's principles. They abide by Charlie Kaufman's beliefs. The results are beloved by some, including me, but they have found more critical than financial success. They hit certain people hard, but he'll never reach the movie-going majority, and he hasn't been able to make as many movies as he might like. Kaufman isn't a very good commercial bet, and today's Hollywood isn't built to take such chances.

"Plays are alive and movies are dead," Kaufman once said. He expanded on his pessimistic thought in a later interview with the Writers Guild of America: "I love movies," he said. "I've always loved movies. It's been a big passion of mine my whole life. I just think that there's a very kind of one-route way of making movies in this culture. And there seems to be this mindset that it has to be this one thing, and this is the structure of it, and this is what has to happen to the characters. I think that, like in anything, like in any art form, the world opens up when you take that away."[15]

Kaufman's own work proves that breaking the rules can yield something beautiful—which returns us to William Goldman, whose *Adventures in the Screen Trade* provides the counterweight to Robert McKee's *Story*. Goldman's résumé is much more impressive than McKee's in terms of the actual writing of films. In addition to *Butch Cassidy and the Sundance Kid*, for which Goldman won the Academy Award in 1969, he won another for writing *All the President's Men* in 1976. He also wrote *Marathon Man* and *The Princess Bride*, both based on his own novels. He did all of it while ignoring the demands of studio executives and the opinions of marketers. *Butch Cassidy* feels purposefully unsettling in its construction, a film built around two halves rather than the conventional three acts; *All the President's Men* somehow makes two men talking on the phone and typing feel like a thriller.

When Goldman died in 2018, *Variety* published a laudatory obituary. Its writer, Peter Debruge, confessed that *The Princess Bride* was his desert-island movie: the movie he would choose

---

15 I watched this interview on YouTube. It's titled "Charlie Kaufman on His Latest Film & Why 'Movies Are Dead.'" It was posted by the official account of the Writers Guild of America West on the release of Kaufman's *Synecdoche, New York* in 2008.

to keep at the expense of every other movie ever made. ("By writing scripts he believed in, rather than the flavor of the day, the late, great William Goldman left a legacy that will endure for decades."[16]) Debruge also recalled that Goldman's fight to realize *Butch Cassidy* was made easier when MGM gave more of its attention to *Dirty Dingus Magee*, starring Frank Sinatra. Do you remember *Dirty Dingus Magee*? You do not. But if you saw *Butch Cassidy*, you remember it. You remember the cliff jump and the shootout and the easy chemistry between Paul Newman and Robert Redford. Unless you happen to be Bolivian, that movie might be the first thing you think of when you think of Bolivia.

Debruge is right, too, about *The Princess Bride*, which is flawless. Originally a bedtime story that Goldman told his daughters to lull them to sleep—not exactly what you want to hear in a movie pitch—the film employs the same narrative device. It's a story told by a grandfather (Peter Falk) to his grandson (Fred Savage), who asks that he skip the boring parts. The result is magic: a beautiful, fun, suspenseful, lovely film. It's a movie that any right-thinking person will defend to his or her death.[17]

But *The Princess Bride* did not do very well at the box office, in part because it confused its own studio. The marketers did not know what it was. Sometimes it feels like a romance, and sometimes like an action movie; sometimes it reads like a comedy and other times like a drama. In a way, it's the

---

16 Peter Debruge, "With One Line, William Goldman Taught Hollywood Everything It Needed to Know," *Variety*, November 16, 2018.
17 Rob Reiner was the director. Between 1985 and 1992, Reiner directed *Stand by Me*, *The Princess Bride*, *When Harry Met Sally...*, *Misery*, and *A Few Good Men* in succession. That's a remarkable streak of excellence. Goldman happened to write two of the films and mentored Aaron Sorkin through his writing of *A Few Good Men* as well.

perfect desert-island movie because it contains fragments of every movie. Unfortunately, most people want to know what sort of movie they're about to watch before they watch it, and *The Princess Bride* defies labels. Goldman refused to meet the expectations of our collective subconscious—the rules, McKee argues, to which all of us subscribe, however unwittingly. The joyous, unabashed originality that makes *The Princess Bride* great also made it hard to sell.

Of course, art should sometimes make us uncomfortable. It should surprise us and confound us and delight us. But it's not easy watching something that doesn't do what we think it's going to do, and not everyone wants to be challenged by their diversions. (Remember what Ryan Kavanaugh said to me about the total audience for *The Assassination of Jesse James*? "You and seven other people." Man, that was dispiriting.)

Take the 2014 movie *Chef*, written and directed by Jon Favreau. He's also the lead. *Chef* is no *Butch Cassidy*, but its more limited ambitions make it more surprising in some ways. The movie's structure is wholly conventional at first, setting us up for McKee's sacrosanct three acts. Favreau is a chef at a popular Los Angeles restaurant who quits after a public humiliation at the hands of a food critic: the so-called "inciting incident," and the end of act one. He goes to Miami to buy and refurbish a food truck with his best friend; he then embarks on a cross-country road trip back to Los Angeles with his friend and his son, whom he shares with his ex-wife. The trio of man-boys stop and make delicious food for people along the way, becoming closer with every mile and morsel.

Now, in most movies with *Chef*'s aspirations, the second act would end with a terrible setback—just when we think everything is going to work out for all involved, calamity strikes. That's the winning formula. Our hero's subsequent reckoning with the fallout, in some triumphant and satisfying manner, will complete our emotional voyage. (The best endings are surprising in the moment but feel inevitable in the afterglow.) So around the time our heroes reached West Texas, I expected something very bad to happen.

Don't get me wrong. I did not *want* something bad to happen. I liked everybody in the movie. It made me really want them to succeed; if you've seen it, you'll understand that it also made me really want a grilled-cheese sandwich. I was watching *Chef* during the COVID-19 pandemic, precisely because it seemed undemanding, and I felt zero desire to see something sad. I had real life for that. But I know what I know about screenwriting, and I knew disaster was coming.

In one scene, Favreau's friend, played with unfailing loyalty by John Leguizamo, is driving the truck at night. He looks sleepy; Favreau and his son have already zonked out in the back. Here comes the accident that ruins everything...But no, it's just an excuse for everybody to wake up and bond over jock itch. Earlier in the film, Favreau had bought his son his first chef's knife, which he wields a little too cavalierly. That's it! Chekhov's gun! The son is going to cut off his little fingers and...Huh. Actually, he's going to be totally fine. Okay, wait. Favreau's ex-wife is going to demand that her son return to her in Los Angeles immediately, leaving his father and their adventure behind—and *whoops, wrong again*. She's the most accommodating ex-wife in the history of cinema.

In fact, Favreau seems to be toying with his audience, giving us plenty of reasons for tension without any of the release. I got sweaty, waiting for the inevitable turn. That's the discomforting thing about *Chef*: The turn never really comes. After Favreau quits his job, nothing bad happens to him or anyone else. *Chef* has two acts, not three. He quits his job, and then he rebuilds his life the way he prepares a meal, following a perfectly ascendant trajectory until everything ends with dessert.

The credits rolled, and I sat on my couch stunned; I found the ending to *Chef* as surprising as the famous twists of *The Crying Game* or *The Sixth Sense*, or *Butch Cassidy*'s iconic freeze frame. Jon Favreau, intentionally or not, had used my entire movie-going existence against me, as though I'd been the victim of a long and elaborate con. Did I enjoy *Chef*? I did. Was I also unsettled by it? I was.

Too often today, we're implored to pick a side. It's always one or the other. I will confess I have thought so: I was as black-or-white in my approach to life as an adult can be and still function. You're either for art or you're for commerce. You're for anarchy or you're for the law. You're for analytics or you're for gut instinct (or, worse, willful wrongheadedness). I've stopped thinking that's true. I'd always thought I'd become *more* certain with age. Instead, I've become less. I've lived long enough to hear the counterargument to every argument. I see causes for allegiance in both sides of almost every debate, the way there are lessons to be learned from both the winners and losers of a fight. I have become a professional hedger. Welcome to my Kingdom of Doubt.

How would I write commandments, were I trying to write like Robert McKee?

FOLLOWING THE RULES too closely risks seeming *formulaic.*
BREAKING THE RULES, especially all of them, risks seeming *discordant.*

———

There is a songwriter whose name you probably don't know. You almost certainly have never heard his voice, although it is reputedly very good. It is virtually a guarantee, however, that you have heard some of his songs, and the odds are nearly as high that you have sung along to one of them, however embarrassed you might be to admit it.

His professional name is Max Martin. (His real name is Karl Martin Sandberg.) He is, of course, Swedish. At the time of this writing, he is approaching fifty years old. He has straight hair, which he usually wears long enough to fall past his shoulders, and sometimes sports a thick beard. If you saw a picture of him and were told he's a musician, you would guess he played heavy metal or experimental jazz. He is in fact an expert in pop, and most of his work has been performed by boy bands and young women, usually British or American. Paul McCartney is the songwriter with the most number one singles to his credit; John Lennon is second on the list; Max Martin is third and gaining. He is proof how often our entertainment echoes itself, because he has written so much of it, using the same principles. He is music's version of *Story*.

Martin began making his mark in the late 1990s, after he worked on *The Bridge* by Ace of Base, a wildly if briefly popular Swedish quartet whose infectious love songs drew comparisons to ABBA. He wrote all of the singles on 1999's *Millennium* by the Backstreet Boys, including "I Want It That Way." The Backstreet Boys decided against recording one of his proposed songs, so he gave it to Britney Spears instead: "...Baby One More Time" made her a star. He wrote "That's the Way It Is" for Celine Dion; "Since U Been Gone" for Kelly Clarkson; "U + Ur Hand" for Pink. He co-wrote a slew of singles for Katy Perry, including "I Kissed a Girl," her career-making debut. He helped write several of Taylor Swift's singles—"We Are Never Ever Getting Back Together," "Shake It Off," and "Blank Space," among others—and he either co-wrote or produced tracks for Ariana Grande, The Weeknd, Shakira, Jennifer Lopez, Ellie Goulding, Demi Lovato, Selena Gomez, Adele, Justin Timberlake, Ed Sheeran, Justin Bieber, and Lady Gaga.

None of those artists or their songs might appeal to you, but it's impossible to deny Martin's influence on the last two decades of commercial music. His singles have sold hundreds of millions of copies. The *New Yorker* described him as "the Cyrano de Bergerac of today's pop landscape, the poet hiding under the balcony of popular song."[18] The man can write a hook.

Martin is also largely, purposefully anonymous. Music fans prefer to imagine that their favorite artists write their own songs, and most artists are happy to give that impression. He has shown up to collect Grammy Awards—he has won five and been nominated for twenty-two—but he has sat down for precisely one English-language profile, for *TIME* magazine in 2001, when he was ascendant but not yet omnipresent.[19] (He was beardless at the time.) In that interview, he explained how Karl Martin Sandberg became Max Martin. It's a particularly Scandinavian tale that included public music education, the innately Swedish sense of melody, and classical training in the French horn. It didn't hurt that his older brother filled his childhood home with catchy glam metal. Max Martin heard it through his bedroom walls and fell in love.

Next, Martin found a mentor in a perfectionist producer

---

18 John Seabrook, "Blank Space: What Kind of Genius Is Max Martin?" *New Yorker*, September 30, 2015.
19 Jeff Chu, "The Music Man," *TIME*, March 19, 2001.

named Denniz PoP (not his given name, either; Dag Krister Volle died of cancer in 1998 at thirty-five), who apprenticed him during marathon recording sessions, starting with *The Bridge*. Martin learned the technical requirements of modern music making: how to mix, layer, and polish. He soon became one of those people who carried a Dictaphone around, because melody and chorus spilled out of him like breath.

When Martin writes a song, he also records it, with his own elusive voice; prospective artists hear his version of it, and then he compels them to record exactly that version. (His demos are not publicly available, but John Seabrook, who wrote the *New Yorker* piece, heard a recording of Martin singing "...Baby One More Time." Seabrook marveled: "The Swede sounded exactly like Spears." It's more true to say that Spears sounded exactly like the Swede. In effect, she'd covered him.) Denniz PoP was untrained and instinctual, but Martin's work was always less like alchemy. He had what his many admirers called "pop sensibilities," and from the beginning of his career, he subscribed to the shocking premise that it was better to appeal to a wide audience than a narrow one. ("Instead of making tracks for 5,000 people, why not make tracks for a million?" he once said.[20]) Really what he had discovered was a formula for writing earworms.

Most of Martin's songs could be described as ABBA with a groove and a slightly harder edge—a holdover from his brother's obsession with KISS and, later, his own affection for American R & B. He produces something like that sound again and again, and people around the world find themselves yodeling along to it. His songs are so catchy most listeners

---

20 John Seabrook, "The Doctor Is In," *New Yorker*, October 7, 2013.

don't realize they are often parroting nonsense. Martin speaks English, but for him, lyrics aren't words with meaning so much as additional opportunities to make pleasing sounds: "Melodic math," he calls it. That's why so many of his songs don't make a lot of sense upon closer listening. He chooses words that *sound* like they fit even if they don't. He never considered that a fifteen-year-old girl named Britney Spears singing, "Hit me baby, one more time," might conjure uncomfortable images of domestic violence or BDSM. (Her label changed his title to "...Baby One More Time," burying the "Hit me" part of it.) An otherwise admiring Seabrook notes that the verse and chorus of "I Want It That Way" cancel each other out.

Over time, Martin has nurtured an army of apprentices. Most of them are Swedish, but not all. (The best known of Martin's prodigies and co-writers is Dr. Luke—real name Lukasz Sebastian Gottwald—the Polish-American son, appropriately enough, of an architect.[21]) They often write in teams, assembling songs like pieces of a puzzle, or more like engines, with parts waiting on the shelf for installation. Someone lays down a beat, and someone else writes a chorus that they keep logged somewhere. A verse in need of it will come along sooner or later. The bridge is already waiting on a hard drive in Stockholm. Piece them together in the right combination, and suddenly Avril Lavigne has a hit record.

The continued success of Max Martin and the Scandinavian pop factory he oversees shouldn't be taken to mean that

---

21 Dr. Luke gained wider fame than his mentor in part because of his years-long legal dispute with the singer Kesha, for whom he wrote and produced hits like "Tik Tok." In 2014, she sued him to void her recording contract, alleging a litany of physical, sexual, and emotional abuse; he countersued for defamation and breach of contract. As of this writing, the case is ongoing.

anyone can do what he does. He is clearly gifted, custom-built from childhood to write music. Nor am I suggesting that every song should be written his way. No one would mistake his music for Great Art, the way we might think of Bob Dylan (or Charlie Kaufman's movies), or groundbreaking, like the Sex Pistols, Nirvana, or Billie Eilish. But he writes songs that people like to hear, and for students blessed with the right foundational skills, Martin's Method, perhaps more properly thought of today as the Swedish Method, has proved predictable, repeatable, and teachable.

I'm reminded of a teenage friend who bought his first guitar and announced to me that he wasn't going to learn chords; he was going to play "what sounds good." Well, we have agreed as a species that when it comes to stringed instruments, chords are what sound good. And for a couple of generations, at least, Max Martin has understood better than anyone else on Earth the order in which many of us wish to hear them played.

———

So if that's true—if our entertainments are often built with common components pieced together in prescribed ways—why did Ryan Kavanaugh fail so spectacularly? Why couldn't Relativity make appealing movies the way Max Martin writes number-one singles? I'd argue that Kavanaugh's computer mainframes contained the seeds of his inevitable destruction rather than the secret to his certain success. He put too much faith in the machine.

The problem with his model was its exactness: It was built on the logical but flawed idea that if one movie was successful, and he made a movie very much like it, he would find the same audience. Most movie studios subscribe to something like that belief, if not so extremely, which explains the modern dominance of sequels or films based on previously popular works—or better yet both, like the *Twilight* and *Harry Potter* sagas. It's hard to risk $100 million on a completely original piece of cinema, unless someone like Christopher Nolan is the person directing it; every movie represents a massive personal and professional gamble by its makers, and even the most vanguard studio heads seek to hedge their bets. Kavanaugh seemingly believed that he could *eliminate* risk by stripping almost anything that resembled human instinct from the process. He didn't trust his gut or anyone else's, because analytics had proved how often our guts deceive us. Hence, "widgets." Assembly lines don't run on feel.

But human audiences are infinitely more complex and variable than the movies or songs or books we consume. Many of our entertainments are simple machines; we are not. Most franchises eventually run out of steam, because most people don't want to see *exactly* the same thing each time out.[22] We want to see the same but different.

Max Martin's longevity has relied in part on his anonymity, on the fact that we never hear *his* voice. If he sang all of the songs he wrote, many of them likely wouldn't have become hits, because we would have tired of him by now. Not many artists can sustain a twenty-year career, and those who do often engage in stylistic self-immolation over the course of them, killing themselves to live. Madonna, for instance. Or the Grateful Dead, who lasted as long as they did by changing familiar songs just enough to keep them interesting, at least to stoned people.

---

22 The most die-hard *Star Wars* fans might be the exception. Their universe is not expansive enough to include change. Ask Rian Johnson.

Martin substituted the artists rather than changing his style, choosing new collaborators who sounded fresh enough to make his songs *seem* unconventional. Taylor Swift and The Weeknd have different voices; they do not present as inter-changeable artists. But they both sing songs written by Max Martin. Had the Backstreet Boys recorded "...Baby One More Time" after all, would it have become a monster hit for them the way it did for Britney Spears? Perhaps. Or maybe we were ready to hear someone new.

Those shifts in our desires are hard for even the most ad-vanced algorithms to quantify, never mind Ryan Kavanaugh's fairly simplistic Monte Carlo model. Your entertainment providers wish to keep you engaged, and they sensibly try to predict what you will like to watch or listen to based on what you have previously enjoyed. Netflix, YouTube, and Twitter all rely on secret formulas to track what you consume and then predict what you will consume next.[23] Netflix even makes sub-predictions about how confident they are in their matches. It can sometimes feel like a dating site more than a streaming service. *Oh, you liked* Ozark? *There's a 97 percent chance that you will enjoy* Fargo, *because it's also an offbeat crime drama that takes place in rural America with a lead actor who looks a little like Jason Bateman.*

If you're like most people, those recommendations have sometimes resonated with you, the way some couples paired by Match.com have ended up married. Data mining and predictive math lend validity to their suggestions; they're better aimed at your heart than a blind stab. (In 2013, Netflix

---

23 Algorithms themselves have value, like any other intellectual property, and they are protected by their owners from theft, usually with secrecy. That's understandable, but their opaque nature can sometimes, as we will see, hide a darker intent.

revealed that 75 percent of its collective viewing was spurred by its recommendations.) My purpose is not to deny the value of data. That's like railing against truth itself, and I believe in facts.

But how many times have algorithms made assumptions about you that are in the vague range of your tastes, yet not quite right? How often has your favorite show or movie or song led you to another that you didn't like at all? The way entertainment algorithms are sometimes fallible, the dependence on math in other fields can lead us down paths that are later proved incorrect, and we need to be mindful of those limitations. We also need to see the opportunity and know how to respond when the answer can't be a number. That doesn't seem like an outlandish proposition to me, but suggest that the analytics movement has sometimes threatened overcorrection, and you risk becoming a victim of the same *Us* versus *Them* mentality that plagues our society as a whole. You're either for data, fully and completely, or you're for fairy dust. What an unhelpful way of thinking. Smart zealotry is still zealotry.

Unlike the most fervent proponents of analytics, tech companies have been more willing to acknowledge their own blind spots, and they are constantly seeking to improve their abilities to understand you. Susan Wojcicki, the CEO of YouTube, wanted a recommendation model that was more predictive than reactive: "freshness" was her stated goal.[24] She wanted to Max Martinize her algorithm. Leaving the job entirely up to machines led to benign missed marks. Listen to Lord Huron, and you might have been recommended Mumford & Sons, two bands that are *not the same*. It also sparked the dangerous

---

24 Kevin Roose, interview with Susan Wojcicki, *Rabbit Hole*, "Episode Four: Headquarters." Podcast audio. May 7, 2020.

radicalization of viewers who binged their way from self-help videos to destructive ones, advocating white supremacy and right-wing violence. (The New Zealand government, for instance, specifically cited YouTube's role in the derangement of the Christchurch mosques shooter.[25]) In response, Wojcicki added more humans to the mix, relying on their experience and judgment. Under famed producer Jimmy Iovine, Apple Music did the same, hiring hundreds of music obsessives to curate content. "Curation was supposedly not hip—that's bullshit," Iovine said at the time. "When you listen to a radio station that was programmed purely by an algorithm, you will go comfortably numb."[26] Most of us don't like shock, but who doesn't enjoy a pleasant surprise?

Even with such carefully weighted combinations of machine filters and human finesse, our hearts remain sometimes elusive targets. That's because our favorite songs, say, are not the products of a purely aesthetic response. It's not just how the song sounds that matters, which is why songs that sound similar to something we love do not necessarily connect. We also respond emotionally, in ways that are difficult to pinpoint or predict; psychologists don't agree whether we're experiencing an actual emotional response, like a dopamine rush of good feeling, or more of an evocative response, tied to memory. Nostalgia can be a powerful motor for affection, but it's an intricate, almost mystical relationship: "Fortunately or unfortunately, even other humans cannot replicate our individual experience and autobiographical memory," wrote neurologist

---

25 The Royal Commission of Inquiry into the Terrorist Attack on Christchurch Mosques on 15 March 2019 issued its final report to New Zealand's Parliament on December 8, 2020.
26 Michael Rundle, "Apple Music's Jimmy Iovine: 'No One Will Be Able to Catch Us,'" wired.co.uk, August 7, 2015.

Dr. Lara K. Ronan, "and we are left with discovering our favorites through chance, serendipity, and luck."[27]

That gulf between our anticipated favorites and the realities of our affections—call it the Affinity Gap—was what swallowed up Ryan Kavanaugh and Relativity. His hubris might seem preposterous in hindsight; the emergence of analytics did not suddenly make our entire existence quantifiable. I marvel at how many people bought what he was selling, and I count myself among them. "You can't think of it as money," he told me. "You have to think of it as math." What a load of bullshit. Kavanaugh was trying to say that you have to detach yourself from the realities of existence to make optimal decisions— the way poker players would probably bet differently if they played with actual money instead of chips. Unfortunately, sooner or later someone will come along and ask to exchange your representation of money for actual money, in which case your math had better hold. Relativity's didn't. But in 2009, during the rise of analytics as an almost religious movement, Kavanaugh was confirming perhaps our strangest, most arrogant self-belief: that for every question there is one right answer, and it's always in us to know it.

He also committed a far greater sin: He took something about which we feel romantic and tried to make a virtue out of being anti-romantic. I believe that came across in his movies; consciously or not, we sensed the artlessness behind them. He thought he could skip the part when he opened your hearts and go straight to the part when you opened your wallets. He miscalculated.

There might be a soft science to creation, and certain patterns

---

27 Dr. Lara K. Ronan, "Why Is That Your Favorite Song?" *Psychology Today*, January 1, 2019.

of human behavior are predictable. But there is no equation in the world that fully captures *you*. Your favorite song is your favorite song because it gave you something you needed when you needed it. The reason you don't respond to similar art similarly isn't because the art has changed; *you* have changed. "Movies do not change, but their viewers do," Roger Ebert once wrote.[28] Your affections are a moving target.

That's why nobody knows anything in Hollywood or anywhere else: They don't know who *you* are. They know only who you used to be. I made a guess about why you're reading this book, and I want very much for you to enjoy it, so I've tried to remember my imaginary version of you, my dream reader, as I've written it. But I still can't trust that you will. We love what we love because we love it. All you can do is make something you would like, as well as you can. And then hope you're not a freak.

———

I met Teller the magician ostensibly because of a lawsuit, but the lawsuit was only a convenient excuse for me to meet someone I admired.[29] He was suing a Dutch antagonist, Gerard Bakardy, for stealing one of his signature tricks. Teller called the disputed trick "Shadows." (Bakardy called his version "Rose & Her Shadow.") The far superior magician of the two had been infatuated with magic since he was a child, and he

---

28 Roger Ebert, "What's Your Favorite Movie?" RogerEbert.com, September 4, 2008.

29 I wrote about Teller and magic for *Esquire*. The story was called "The Honor System"; it appeared in the October 2012 issue. I have followed him and his career obsessively since. I believe him to be one of the great American artists, which seems more obvious when you start to think of magic tricks as stories.

had invented "Shadows" when he was a teenager. He had performed it at virtually every show he had given since 1975; he and his oversize partner, Penn Jillette, still perform at the Rio in Las Vegas, with "Shadows" sitting at the heart of the show, a shimmering interlude between bullet catches. I first saw Teller perform the trick there. It nearly caved in my chest.

"Shadows" is a simple trick, small and self-contained. Lesser magicians use theatrics to baffle, employing puffs of smoke and showgirls to draw distracted eyes away from the secrets behind their illusions. When Teller performs "Shadows," it's just him, alone on a darkened stage, enveloped in a silence so total the audience can hear his footsteps. ("That's what makes it a very brave trick," I was told by no less an authority than the late Amazing Randi!) Teller walks across to an easel, on which a large pad of paper has been clipped. A single rose in a plain white vase sits a few feet in front of it. A spotlight casts the rose's shadow on the paper on the easel. In Teller's hands is a very large knife.

Teller cuts into the paper, into the shadow of the rose, attacking one of its bundles of leaves. The real leaves fall from the real rose. Teller casts a sidelong glance at the rose, as though learning of his power for the first time. Then he steps between the rose and its shadow, from one side of the easel to the other. This is what magicians call "a proof," whereby Teller proves that there are no wires running between the rose and the easel. He cuts into the shadow again, and more leaves fall from the actual rose. Finally, he completes his murderous handiwork. He cuts into the shadow of the rose itself, the flower, and a cascade of red petals falls to the stage.

The trick appears to be complete. In Bakardy's version, that was the end of it—an amateur who made the coin disappear but didn't bother trying to reappear it, which is the real trick.

(Penn described Bakardy's version of "Shadows" as the Byrds' cover of "Mr. Tambourine Man," while Teller was Dylan, performing a true original.) Teller isn't finished. We have yet to receive his prestige.

Admiring his mastery of the impossible, Teller "accidentally" pricks his finger with his knife. He shakes away the pain. Then he looks at the light. He raises his hand between it and the easel, so that his hand's shadow now falls where the rose's shadow once did. A small trickle of blood begins to run down the paper, as though out of his shadow, exactly where he cut himself. In a chilling final flourish, Teller smears the blood on the paper with his hand. The paper looks like a butcher's apron, with a thick streak of blood across it. Teller stares at the audience, and the lights go out.

My written account of "Shadows," like Bakardy's clumsy lift, does no justice to the experience of it, in the dark, the hairs on your arms rising with you out of your seat. Teller was trying to protect that *feeling*, the magic of that moment, with his lawsuit. He didn't care whether Bakardy had learned his method. Thinking that the method is the essence of a great trick rather than the means to give an audience something beautiful was Ryan Kavanaugh's mistake. Teller had performed the trick with three different methods over its lifetime. "The method doesn't matter," he told me, almost impatiently. The method was science, after all. It was knowable fact. It was the baseline. It was data.

Teller knew the value of artists, making art. There is an almost literal crackle in the room when he performs "Shadows," an electric current that passes from one stranger to the next. Some people jumped to their feet; some people recoiled; some people covered their eyes; some people lost their ability to blink. I even heard people crying around me, trying to hold back their soft sobs. The magic of Teller's magic is not what he does with his hands, with instruments, to objects. It's what he does with his imagination to *you*, no matter who you happen to be.

Teller's lawsuit was, at its essence, a stand less against theft than against the cheapness of imitation, of shortcuts. It was a fight to save something *special*, something human, against the mediocre output of mass production. You can't copyright an idea, but you can copyright your *expression* of an idea. "Shadows" follows all the usual structural rules of illusion. But within that time-honed framework, Teller found his own particular way to express his love of magic. That was the art of it, and the art was what he wanted to preserve, to capture and keep like a lightning bug in a jar.

I wasn't certain at first whether the lawsuit was real, or some elaborate con set up by a born deceiver. I could establish no firsthand connection with Bakardy; all of my knowledge of him came *through* Teller, and I sometimes wondered whether Bakardy was a make-believe foil for a man with no natural rivals. Bakardy and the lawsuit turned out to be all too real, one Teller won in the end. No magician had successfully sued another magician for theft, and the case set an important precedent for the industry of magic. But in the years since Teller's courtroom victory, I've found that "Shadows" has had less of an impact on me, however lasting it remains, than another trick I saw Teller perform. It was, at the time, new to him, and so new to the world. I have never stopped thinking about "The Red Ball."

Before Teller performs the trick, Penn walks out on the stage. The only visible prop is a park bench. Penn looks to the audience. "The next trick," he says on his partner's behalf, because Teller does not speak in public, "is done with a piece of thread."

Teller then appears with a red ball a little smaller than a soccer ball in one hand and a wooden hoop in the other. He bounces the ball. He throws it to a member of the audience, who bounces it and throws it back. Teller then begins walking around the stage, and the red ball somehow follows him, like a legless dog on a leash. It hops up onto the bench and rolls back and forth on it, too. Sometimes the ball gets drawn to one of Teller's fingers or the small of his back. He also has it jump through the hoop. All of which makes it impossible for Teller to be performing "The Red Ball" with a piece of thread. Penn is lying.

That's the real point of magic, Teller told me: "It's telling a beautiful lie. It lets you see what the world would be like if cause and effect weren't bound by physics." Magic works especially well when you *know* what you're seeing can't be happening, but some part of you hopes, or even believes, that it is. Good magic stokes a battle between your head and your heart; the best magic makes you want for your heart to win.[30]

I asked Teller where his own love of magic was born. He quoted, from memory, a passage in the play *Equus*. I've repeated it embarrassingly often since. *Equus* is about a lot of things, but at its center is a troubled boy with a blinding love of horses. The boy sees a psychiatrist named Martin Dysart, who tries to understand the boy and how his love turned into an affliction. Dysart is thwarted in his efforts and becomes disaffected in his former mission of "curing" troubled youth. He can't explain the origins of the boy's love, and it's hard to finish something without knowing how it began.

---

30 When I came to this conclusion in my original *Esquire* piece, Teller wrote me to say that he would be stealing the line. I don't think I've ever been so flattered.

33

A child is born into a world of phenomena all equal in their power to enslave, Dysart says. *It sniffs—it sucks—it strokes its eyes over the whole uncountable range. Suddenly one strikes. Why? Moments snap together like magnets, forging a chain of shackles. Why? I can trace them. I can even, with time, pull them apart again. But why at the start they were ever magnetized at all—just those particular moments of experience and no others—I don't know.*[31]

"I don't know," Teller said. "I don't know." His eyes filled with tears that he failed to blink away. It's not only our small favorites that are difficult to quantify. The grandest, most obsessive loves of our lives might be the hardest to put into words.

Teller didn't invent "The Red Ball," exactly. His version of the trick builds on the wisdom of a previous master, an ancient magician from Omaha, Nebraska, named David P. Abbott: the magician Houdini paid to see. Abbott did a trick with a floating ball painted gold, and he really did use thread to do it. He tied the string between his ear and the wall, which allowed him to pass a hoop over the ball—because the thread was horizontal, not vertical. Abbott had explained how to do the trick in a posthumous tome called *Book of Mysteries.* He had given away his method to anyone who bought his book; the effect was up to whoever cared to learn it.

That was a lesson all its own. Teller put those instructions on a music stand in his library and began working with a red ball, on the trick that would become "The Red Ball." He decided that his ball would roll rather than float. That would

---

31 *Equus* was written by the late Sir Peter Shaffer in 1973 and won the Tony Award for Best Play in 1975. Shaffer was inspired by true events: A seventeen-year-old stable boy in Suffolk blinded six horses; Shaffer then imagined how that might have happened. Love is hard to explain, but maybe only love could explain such a horror.

look easier to do to everyone but magicians, who would know that it was harder. He practiced the trick in a mirrored dance studio in Toronto, and at a cabin deep in the woods, and for eighteen months after every show on the empty stage in Penn & Teller's theater at the Rio.

"It's still the hardest-to-execute piece of magic I've ever tried," he said. It was, by any measure, a ridiculous, perhaps insane amount of effort for a few minutes on stage each night. Teller did not disagree. "Sometimes magic is just someone spending more time on something than anyone else might reasonably expect," he said.

In the dustier, lonelier strips behind the Las Vegas Strip, a man named Bill Smith has a workshop: Bill Smith's Magic Ventures. Smith doesn't invent tricks—he isn't an *ingeneur*, a conjurer of illusions. He builds the dreams of better magicians. He's built tricks for David Copperfield, Lance Burton, and even Penn & Teller. He knows all the secrets. I went to see him, and we found ourselves talking about "The Red Ball" and how wonderful it is. Smith said one of his greatest wishes was to know how Teller pulled it off. "That one has me fooled," Smith said. "There's no way he does that with a piece of thread."

Here's the truth about "The Red Ball." It's the same truth that allows a casting director named Allison Jones to create a legion of stars out of a thousand uncut gems, filling the credits of *Freaks and Geeks* and *Parks and Recreation* and *Arrested Development* with relative unknowns who almost universally become very known.[32] It's the same truth that explains how Daniel Day-Lewis turned his "lifelong study in evasion" into Oscar-winning turns as a painter with cerebral palsy, a psychotically

---

32 Elyse Roth, "How CD Allison Jones Discovers the Comedy—and Now Drama—Stars of Tomorrow," *Backstage*, January 24, 2020.

ruthless oilman, and an American president.[33] It's the same truth that saw Lin-Manuel Miranda spend ten years writing "In the Heights," and another seven writing "Hamilton"— seventeen years in exchange for two pieces of transcendent work.[34] It's the same truth that lies behind nearly every piece of art that has left you wanting for your heart to win.

There is no such thing as magic. There is the wisdom of elders and the experiences of others on which to rely. The past does hold its lessons. Even art has its historical patterns. But there remains no substitute for the acquisition of good taste, and there isn't a mainframe in the world that can replace or inspire desire. Ryan Kavanaugh thought he'd found a shortcut that got him around the hurdle of hard work, as though he could write code that mimicked affection. But the Affinity Gap doesn't exist only between your expected desires and your actual desires. It's the margin that also exists between standard creative work and extraordinary creative work—the sometimes fine but important difference that unabashed passion makes. All of us should seek to grow that distance—between what we, and others, and all these godforsaken machines, are capable of today, and what we alone might be capable of tomorrow—and there is only one way to cultivate it: *Sometimes magic is just somebody spending more time on something than anyone else might reasonably expect.* Teller lies about a lot of things, but he's never been dishonest about *why* magic: He does it because he loves it for reasons even he can't explain.

Penn isn't lying, either, by the way.

Teller really does that trick with a single piece of thread.

---

33 Peter Stanford, "The Enigma of Day-Lewis," *Guardian*, January 13, 2008.
34 Rebecca Mead, "All About the Hamiltons," *New Yorker*, February 2, 2015.

SPORTS

Love and WAR.

Too often, supporters of analytics conflate numbers with certainty—as the only acceptable answers to our questions. But when an answer is elusive, why should we all use the same method to find it? Instead, we should try to understand how we see differently, and what we see differently, and improve our own particular ways of looking at the beauty and chaos of the world. We should seek to pass the new Eye Test.

In 2012, Michael Lewis gave the commencement address at Princeton University, his alma mater. That speech is one of my favorite things he's written: a short, funny, moving meditation on the role of luck in our lives, including his own.[1] Lewis told the students about how he'd met the right people at the right time who gave him the right breaks, a series of fortunate events that culminated in an extraordinary professional career.

---

1 Lewis called his speech "Don't Eat Fortune's Cookie." He gave it on June 3, 2012. It's available online at Princeton's website and also on Princeton's YouTube channel. I was alerted to it on June 24, 2020, by my friend Seth Wickersham, after I'd tweeted some sentimental blather about realizing how lucky I'd been in my professional life. I read it immediately and realized how perfectly it fit here, in this book. That was all very lucky.

That was partly his doing, of course, but he was humble enough to acknowledge that his success wasn't entirely up to him. "Don't be deceived by life's outcomes," he said. "Life's outcomes, while not entirely random, have a huge amount of luck baked into them."

We might prefer to think that we're in control of our destinies—that if we make the right choices, and do good work, we will be rewarded. We especially like to think that way when things work out, because it's gratifying to believe that we've earned our way to the top. Sometimes that's what happens: The best man or woman wins, separated from the rest by an earned margin in skill and effort. The Affinity Gap is real. But it's also possible for two relatively similar people to follow the same sets of instructions and reach two different ends. That's because we don't live our lives in petri dishes. We build laboratories because the world doesn't behave like one. We might try to create our own private universes, but it's impossible to isolate our actions from one another and every other force that lies beyond our control. Strategy has only so much to do with outcomes. There are also those pesky matters of opportunity, privilege, and chance.

Lewis hoped Princeton University's class of 2012 might remember their own good fortune. "You are among the lucky few," he said. "Lucky in your parents, lucky in your country, lucky that a place like Princeton exists that can take in lucky people, introduce them to other lucky people, and increase their chances of becoming even luckier." Those mostly affluent graduates might have believed they deserved everything they had been given, and a few of them probably did. But it would be vanity for them to think that their lives—for any of us to think that any of our lives—are entirely up to any one of us, even if we follow the most well-reasoned guidance. We can almost always increase our odds of success; we can almost never guarantee it.

When I started at *Esquire* in the spring of 2002, I was a sports columnist. It took a miraculous series of happy accidents for me to land that job. My favorite sport was baseball, which I had covered previously for the *National Post* newspaper in Toronto. My first story for *Esquire* was about Barry Zito, a young, quirky pitcher for the Oakland A's. I'd met Barry on the beat and had fallen in something like love with him; I thought my affection for him would improve my chances of writing something good. I also knew Billy Beane, Oakland's rebellious general manager, and something of his innovative, analytical approach to evaluating baseball talent. I pitched a second story to my *Esquire* editor, who said that he'd like to read more about Beane. I called him up. Beane spoke to me while he was driving, his voice pure California. I don't know if he was driving in a convertible, but he sounded as though he was.

I asked Beane whether I could come spend time with him, learn about his work, and write about him for *Esquire*.

"I'd like that," he said. He then told me that another writer had recently started following him around. Beane said he'd feel like a heel, not incorrectly, if he talked to me just then— as though he'd undercut the guy who came first. "But not to worry," he said. "It probably won't amount to anything." I just had to wait a little while for the other writer to lose interest. "It's a matter of time," Beane said. "Then you can come on out."

Unfortunately for me, that other writer happened to be Michael Lewis, and his work amounted to a little something after all: *Moneyball* was published in 2003 to rave reviews, sold nearly two million copies, became the basis for a hugely popular movie starring Brad Pitt as Beane, made Lewis even more of a big deal than he already was, and forever changed how we look at the world around us.

I did okay and wrote some other things. But I've never forgotten that *Moneyball* began as something so small, it felt accidental. "I was going to do something little," Lewis has said. "By the time I thought I was going to do something big, I'd hung around so much it would have been socially awkward to ask me to leave."[2] Lewis lived in Berkeley, not far from the Oakland Coliseum. He noticed the A's were beating moneyed, big-market teams fairly routinely, and he wondered why and how. He asked if he could stop by. Beane had read Lewis's first book, *Liar's Poker*, and thought he might learn something, too. He agreed. The two men began their conversations as a kind of mutual curiosity society. Beane was a difficult subject, in that he didn't like to talk about himself, and it didn't seem as though much would come from their chats other than a friendship built on bilateral inquisition. Lewis couldn't write a book about baseball statistics; nobody would read that. He needed a protagonist, and Beane wasn't an obvious one—until he revealed something fundamental about himself that Lewis found irresistible.

When Billy Beane was eighteen years old, he faced a difficult decision between two pretty good options. Stanford University had offered him a full scholarship. The New York Mets countered with $125,000 and the chance to begin his professional baseball career. As in the movie, Beane sat at his kitchen table with his modest, middle-class parents and went with the Mets. He wasn't much of a ballplayer in the end. By twenty-seven,

---

2 Simon Kuper, "Inside Baseball: Michael Lewis and Billy Beane Talk *Moneyball*," Slate.com, November 13, 2011.

he had been long forgotten by the Mets and was miserable with his fourth team, the A's. He quit playing to become one of Oakland's scouts. Did a man who would become famous for his decision-making make a bad choice, in hindsight, when he picked baseball over education? In isolation, maybe. But none of our choices is truly isolated. Look how the rest of his life turned out. *Because* he never went to school, he was driven to improve himself—to be smarter, to do better—and worked his way up the front-office ladder until he became the team's general manager in 1997. "It's a huge advantage to him that he has some slight anxiety left that he didn't go to Stanford," Lewis has said. That's what made Billy Beane a good story: a man seeking corrections in himself accidentally corrects the whole world.

Moneyball was mostly celebrated upon its release, although neither man anticipated how celebrated it would become. I loved it when I read it. (I was asked to review it for *Esquire*, good for a little extra salt in the wound.) Like many of Lewis's books, it's curious and entertaining. I love the movie, too, even though Brad Pitt's hair is magnificent enough in it to make me feel insecure. Its director, Bennett Miller, has made three films, and all three are fantastic: *Capote*, *Moneyball*, and *Foxcatcher*. Miller is yet to miss.[3]

But the success of *Moneyball* remains something of a mystery to the man who occupies its center. Nearing twenty years later, Billy Beane doesn't want to take credit for starting the analytics movement. He was merely an early adopter, an exceptional thief of other people's bright, non-copyrightable ideas—most

---

3 Don't just take my word for it. *Capote* has a score of 90% Fresh on Rotten Tomatoes, the review aggregation site; *Moneyball* lands at 94%; *Foxcatcher* sits in third at a still-commendable 87%. My affection for Bennett Miller's movies has been scientifically validated.

notably from Bill James, who invented new baseball statistics to keep his brain from atrophying while he minded the boiler in a pork-and-beans plant. Beane doesn't regret being part of the book. "My life has changed in great ways because of it," he's said.[4] But he's uncomfortable with his position as a seer. He doesn't see *Moneyball* as the start of a revolution, and he certainly doesn't see himself as the first man at its barricades. "This was all sort of public information," he's said. "It was nothing we invented." Everything that's happened since was always going to happen, sooner or later; the book and the movie merely accelerated an inevitable process.

Whether it was the spark or the fuel, *Moneyball* has dramatically and undeniably altered the world of sports and however many other worlds with it. The MIT Sloan Sports Analytics Conference gathers more than 3,000 industry leaders and students in Boston every March to discuss the latest in sports science and information. (In year one, in 2007, there were only 140 attendees.[5]) Those energized thousands return to the front offices of virtually every franchise of every major sport, where analytics departments are now the norm, redoubling their efforts to discover and exploit statistical innovations. By 2013, the New York Yankees alone had more than a dozen full-time quants on the payroll. Their collective work has changed the way entire games are played, far beyond the confines of ballparks.

For better or worse, modern basketball no longer resembles the sport that once hinged on the fine art of the mid-range

4 Josh Lewin and Jon Heyman, interview with Billy Beane, *Big Time Baseball*, Podcast audio. July 22, 2019.

5 Michael Silverman, "How the Sloan Sports Analytics Conference Grew from a Defunct MIT Class to a Really Big Deal," *Boston Globe*, March 5, 2020.

jumper; an emphasis on shooting efficiency has led to endless exchanges of three-point shots and below-the-basket stuffs. The Houston Rockets, under former general manager and Sloan co-founder Daryl Morey, became the epitome of the NBA's new style of cool-eyed play, soon dubbed *Moreyball*. (Michael Lewis has described Morey as "a person who was happier counting than feeling his way through life.") In the 2012–13 season, an incredible 73.6 percent of Houston's shot attempts came from inside the restricted zone or behind the arc. For all their innovation, the Rockets didn't win a ring, but other teams followed their lead, including the Golden State Warriors. They won three NBA Finals and narrowly lost two others between 2015 and 2019, mostly on the strength of Stephen Curry's long-range proficiency.[6] Like the Boston Red Sox and Chicago Cubs, who each broke long World Series curses with Beane acolyte Theo Epstein at the helm, the Warriors were copyists who learned to outgun the originators.

Across the ocean in Liverpool, the Reds came to dominate the English Premier League in part because of *Merseyball*, their data-fueled approach to the ancient game of football. A slight, bespectacled Welshman named Ian Graham—who holds a doctorate in theoretical physics from Cambridge—built and maintained a database of 100,000 players, making recommendations to the club's ebullient manager, Jurgen Klopp, on acquisitions and deployment. In 2015, Graham had suggested that Liverpool hire Klopp in the first place, believing that his tenure at the German club Dortmund had been better than their on-pitch results indicated. (Graham never once bothered to watch Dortmund play; "I don't like video," he's said. "It

---

6   Jared Dubin, "Nearly Every Team Is Playing Like the Rockets. And That's Hurting the Rockets," FiveThirtyEight.com, December 20, 2018.

biases you."[7]) Because football is low-scoring, luck plays a larger role than it does in other sports, and Dortmund had been unlucky. Liverpool hired Klopp, who combined Graham's analysis with his own intuitive sense of a slashing, fluid game, and went on to win their first domestic title in thirty years.

Even individual sports have begun bearing the uneasy weight of quantification and its sometimes distorting effects. Golf looked on the cusp of upheaval after the early 2020 success of Bryson DeChambeau, the game's so-called Mad Scientist.[8] (DeChambeau first gained notoriety as an amateur for using irons of equal shaft length, which allowed him to have the same swing no matter the club; instead he changed their head weights to differentiate them.) DeChambeau made driving distance his highest priority, as though he were abiding basketball's infatuation with long-range makes. Over two seasons, he added forty pounds of bulk and won the 2020 Rocket Mortgage Classic in Detroit by averaging a PGA record 350.6 yards per drive. "I changed my body, changed my mindset in the game, and I was able to accomplish a win while playing a completely different style of golf," he said after. "I hope it's an inspiration to a lot of people." That September he won the U.S. Open by six strokes at fearsome Winged Foot. He was the only player in the field to finish below par, essentially by swinging at his ball as though it had wronged him.

There is no obvious *Moneyball* wordplay for DeChambeau's approach; *Massiveball* sounds too much like an unfortunate medical condition. But whatever you want to call it, he's done

7 Bruce Schoenfeld, "How Data (and Some Breathtaking Soccer) Brought Liverpool to the Cusp of Glory," *New York Times Magazine*, May 22, 2019.
8 Jim Gorant, "Bryson DeChambeau, the Mad Scientist of Golf," *Popular Mechanics*, April 23, 2019.

the math. Everyone in sports has done the math, and the principal result is that sports will never be the same. In a strange way, *Moneyball* was the derailing instrument that Lewis had begged those Princeton graduates to remember. It was the intruder who changes everything, the chance encounter that alters life's course—including the lives of Michael Lewis and Billy Beane.

———

If Lewis's book received a criticism, it was for its selective allocation of credit: Only Billy Beane saw an unlikely value in Scott Hatteberg's destroyed elbow, and Hatteberg's home run capped the twenty-game winning streak that proved Beane's model worked, even absent playoff success.[9] The film, unlike the book, also turned manager Art Howe into Beane's grumpy foil, because, as Robert McKee will tell you, every movie needs an antagonist, the metaphorical opposition our hero must overcome. In reality, Howe is a lovely guy, so comically lean that I never understood why Philip Seymour Hoffman sported such an impressive paunch to play him. More crucially, the book and the movie, despite each being a quantitative talisman, contain the same spectacular narrative sin. They ignore the trio of dominant young pitchers Oakland possessed at the time: Tim Hudson, Mark Mulder, and, most conspicuously to me, Barry Zito.

In the 2002 season, Hudson, twenty-six, delivered a Wins Above Replacement (WAR) of 6.9 in exchange for his $875,000 salary; Mulder, only twenty-four, posted a WAR of 4.7 for

---

9 In the film, Hatteberg was played by Chris Pratt before he was famous; he's the former catcher who has to learn to play first base because he can't throw from home to second anymore.

$800,000; and twenty-four-year-old Zito, in only his second full season, won twenty-three games, had an ERA of 2.75, a WAR of 7.2, and took home the American League Cy Young Award, all while earning just $295,000.[10] The talented threesome delivered a collective WAR of 18.8 for less than $2 million. Hatteberg's offensive WAR that season was 2.7, and he provided almost perfectly average defense for $900,000 — a solid return, and a fine signing by Beane, but nothing like the value of those three starting pitchers. Barry Zito was the greatest value of them all.

Why do I love Barry Zito? Like Teller's love of magic, my love for him is hard to explain. His performance that season really had nothing to do with it. We were both rookies in our respective professions around the same time, and he definitely gave my career a boost. He was the first athlete who took me up on my invitation to talk somewhere other than the clubhouse. (We went for brunch.) I liked that he carried stuffed animals with him on the road, and scented candles, and special pillows. I liked that his teammates didn't know what to make of him, and I liked that he didn't feel especially obliged to explain himself. I liked that his father, Joe Zito, conducted Nat King Cole's orchestra and wrote songs for Frankie Avalon and Bobby Rydell, and that Joe believed that athletic greatness ran through Barry like music. ("I thought playing baseball was like playing the piano," Joe told me. "To get better, you practiced and practiced and practiced some more.") I liked that Barry threw left-handed, not very hard, and that his signature pitch was a curveball that dropped so precipitously, it reminded me of a broken heart.

---

10 All baseball statistics and salary figures, here and elsewhere, are from baseball-reference.com.

Mostly, I liked that asking Barry Zito, a baseball player, how he did what he did yielded the following answer: "When it comes to creative people—musicians, artists, writers—to be good at what they do, they can't do it all themselves. They have to be a tool for something else. When I'm standing on the mound, I want to let my body be played like an instrument. It's really hard to be consciously unconscious, but that's what you have to be. And you need to believe. Because what you think in here"—he pointed to the side of his head—"is going to happen out there. I might throw a pitch down the middle of the plate, but if I believe the hitter's going to swing through it, he's going to swing through it. If you think something is meant to be, it's meant to be. You can make it happen."[11]

Are those good enough reasons to justify my love for a stranger who played baseball? I don't know. And if they are, why was I a child who became a man who grew to admire those particular traits in a person? I don't know that, either. One invisible thing led to another. All I know is that I followed Barry for his entire career, revisiting him like an old song that serves as its own confirmation bias when you hear it, reassuring you that you are right to feel what you feel.

The last time I saw Barry Zito playing baseball was in 2015. He was close to the end of his career. He was playing catch, long toss, with another pitcher in Nashville, home of the Triple-A Sounds. It was one of those rare occasions when Barry wasn't the most interesting person in the frame. The other player was Pat Venditte: a right-handed pitcher who had trained himself through sheer force of will to throw as well with his left. Venditte was working his way up the

---

11 "He Came from Outer Space," by me. *Esquire*, June 2002.

minor-league system, trying to become the first switch pitcher in decades to earn his major-league shot. Zito was thirty-seven years old, hoping to work his way back into the game after he'd left the A's for the San Francisco Giants in 2007, having signed the richest contract for a pitcher in baseball history, and then delivered seven mostly mediocre seasons, never posting an ERA below 4.00, and only once winning more games than he lost. Now the A's had taken him back, and put him on the farm, to see if he could find whatever had left him.

He could not. He returned to Oakland for just three more appearances, seven combined innings, during which he gave up twelve hits, six walks, and eight runs.

I loved him all the more.

––––––––

When Barry Zito signed with the Giants, his agent was Scott Boras, the most powerful agent in baseball. (Zito had begun his career with Boras, spent his six years at Oakland represented by the more winsome Arn Tellem, and then switched back to Boras when free agency came around. Business is business, even for believers.) Boras works out of his own building, a gleaming cube he built in Newport Beach, California. He employs a small army of lawyers, scouts, researchers, and quants, dedicated to negotiating contracts for current players and finding new players to represent. He is baseball's Ryan Kavanaugh, only with actual success.

Boras, too, has a climate-controlled room in his building's basement, in which a massive computer mainframe hums away. Its database contains every pitch thrown to every batter in the major leagues since 1971. Boras grants his clients access to that database, because a player who performs well mid-contract will sign a bigger contract when it's time to renew. "We try to get our players to understand who they are," he said. Boras also uses that data to construct evidence-based cases for his clients, statistical arguments why they are worth what he thinks they are worth. He tries to get teams to see what he sees.

In Barry's case, Boras collected that argument in a big blue binder stamped with silver foil: BARRY ZITO, FREE AGENT PRESENTATION. It was divided into sections. In one, Boras assembled the statistics of Zito's first six seasons in Oakland. It made for an impressive résumé. Zito had never missed a day's work for injury, presumably because he didn't throw hard; when Oakland scored three or more runs for him, his record was 93–11; he was one of only two starting pitchers in the preceding quarter century with both 100 career wins and 200 innings pitched in each of his first six seasons. The other was Frank Viola. In those first six seasons, Barry also logged more starts, victories, strikeouts, and All-Star appearances than Greg Maddux, another durable finesse pitcher who ended up in the Hall of Fame.

Boras then used that collection of actual statistics to project the remainder of Barry's career. That is the essence of data mining, of course: Let's quantify what *has* happened in order to see patterns and trends that will help us predict what *will* happen. By Boras's perhaps biased calculus, Barry's first six seasons suggested that he would have more starts than Eppa Rixey, more innings pitched than Lefty Grove, more strikeouts than Warren Spahn, more everything than Sandy Koufax, and as many Hall-of-Fame plaques as Greg Maddux.

Boras handed out his binders, and during a busy winter, he fielded significant offers from four suitably impressed clubs: the San Francisco Giants, Texas Rangers, Seattle Mariners, and New York Mets. The Giants had lost Jason Schmidt, their ace, to free agency and were the most desperate of the four. Barry also connected personally with Brian Sabean, San Francisco's general manager. A long dinner together had left them both with deep feelings.

Boras likes when love enters the equation, because it means his client has a talent that is difficult to quantify, and even as a dedicated quant, he's learned that numbers will carry a heart only so far. "You're always looking for a player who has that special something," he said. "In baseball, your value as a player is based not on what you can't do but what you can do. There are a lot of players in the major leagues with only one strength." Those singular, particular talents become effective negotiating tools, both because of their scarcity—a supply of one and a demand of infinity—and because they have a limitless cognitive value. Barry Zito's curveball was the perfect example. If you can't put a number on something, its value becomes whatever the biggest imagination believes it might be. Brian Sabean saw something sacred in that curveball, and paid Barry $126 million over seven years.

It would prove one of the worst signings in modern baseball history. Barry finished his career with 133 fewer starts than Eppa Rixey, 1,364 fewer innings pitched than Lefty Grove, and 698 fewer strikeouts than Warren Spahn. It seems unkind to compare him meaningfully with Sandy Koufax in any way, and in 2021, his first year of eligibility for the Hall of Fame, he received a single vote and fell off the ballot.[12] Oddly, one of the best comps for Barry Zito's career is...Frank Viola. They came within one start of each other: 421 for Barry, against 420 for Viola. Barry's winning percentage was .536; Viola's was .540.

---

12 It wasn't me.

Viola was more effective later in his career than Barry—Viola had a great season with the Mets in 1990, when he was thirty years old—and finished with a career WAR of 47.0 against Barry's 31.9. Taken on the whole, Viola was the better pitcher, which is no great slight against Barry Zito. Frank Viola was pretty awesome. But Boras's blue binder would have proved more accurate in its forecasts if he'd pasted Viola's career statistics into it rather than visions of the Hall of Fame. Of course, then his client wouldn't have become the richest pitcher in baseball history.

It's also possible that everything foretold in that binder *might* have proved true if *only* Barry hadn't signed that contract. He was eating sashimi with a friend when Boras texted him the terms—*7/126*—and he choked on his fish. I believe with all my heart that he never quite recovered from the shock, or the pressure that followed. Baseball's more dispassionate observers would never brook such a neat explanation for Barry's near-immediate collapse, but I think it's equally asinine to ignore such a calamitous event in a young man's life. That contract, and all the attention it commanded, can't be removed from consideration just because its effects are impossible to quantify. Maybe signing Barry Zito wasn't a bad move by the Giants; maybe it was a terrible move *for Barry Zito*. Maybe the contract itself changed his trajectory, the "luck" that Michael Lewis cautioned those students to remember. Maybe he suddenly felt more object than instrument, and the weight of expectation saw him stop believing he could make things happen.

That is my *sense*, knowing Barry as I do, an argument spun entirely out of feeling. I have no scientific proof to support my theory, the same lack of concrete evidence that weakens every narrative explanation for a course of events.

CHRIS JONES

Did deindustrialization lead to today's patchwork of chaotic, populist governments in formerly stable democracies? Some smart people believe it did. Are they right? It seems like they are. They make a good and convincing case. Do we *know* they are right? No. There remains room for debate.

Bad quants, at least, pretend to hold a greater dominion on certainty. Numbers *are* unbeatable when it comes to accounting for what, who, and where. I grant that without reservation. They are the most unassailable form of fact when it comes to documenting what *has* happened; they make for a more secure vault than any memory. *Moneyball* served as a death sentence for many things, and some of them deserved to die. After its publication, clutch hitters became extinct, as much as some people *seem* to rise to the occasion and as much as we'd like to *believe* some people achieve greatness when it's demanded of them most. (If there is a clutch hitter somewhere out there, he should probably learn to try a little harder when the outcome isn't so obviously on the line.)

But like all revolutions, the analytics revolution also had its share of lamentable collateral damage, the innocent bystanders who were swept up in its more righteous purges. Lately, there have been louder complaints of overreach, a growing sense that the relentless pursuit of rational correction has become its own kind of mistake. The case against analytics perhaps found its closing argument during the 2020 World Series, when the extremely mathematical Tampa Bay Rays lost to the Los Angeles Dodgers after manager Kevin Cash pulled lights-out pitcher Blake Snell, because that's what the numbers told him to do. Qualitative fans went *nuts*. That single decision *felt* like a turning point; only time will tell whether it actually was. But Major League Baseball, fearing a wider revolt, soon hired none other than Theo Epstein as a consultant to fix the obvious aesthetic ruin—four-hour games; endless pitching changes; soaring strikeout rates—that quants like him have inflicted on the game. Epstein's new role seemed a little like an admission of his regret. It also felt as though the apology was incomplete, given the scale of the vandalism that's been done.

If there's a scene in *Moneyball*, the movie, I kind of hate, it's when Billy Beane meets with Oakland's venerable scouting department to discuss the holes in their lineup. The scouts are pure archetype, played old and befuddled; they're all silver-haired and slouch-shouldered, with reading glasses and hearing aids, a collection of scratches and sniffs. They spout hilarious-sounding old-baseball speak like, "I like guys like that, that got a little hair on their ass," and "Ugly girlfriend means no confidence," and "Clean cut, good face."

"He passes the eye candy test," one scout says, continuing the prospect evaluations. "He's got the looks, he's ready to play the part, he just needs to get some playing time."

"I'm just saying," another scout counters. "His girlfriend is a six, at best."

It's undeniable that some of baseball's more conventional beliefs amounted to hokum, and the game was ripe for a smart, clear-minded overhaul. The eye test as it used to mean, as an exam that a subject of possible affection must pass, is an outdated way to measure almost anyone. Evaluating a player based on his appearance, on the strength of his jawline, represents a special kind of idiocy. *Of course.* More people look like Joe DiMaggio than will ever hit a baseball like him. Unless we're judging beauty, beauty isn't worth incorporating into many of our judgments.

That doesn't mean all of baseball's collective self-knowledge was specious, or that narrative arguments made by seasoned observers are worthless. There are people who have devoted their lifetimes to the game, and their bones can reveal its truths better than any spreadsheet. I'd submit that they deserve our emulation, not our scorn. Hard-core proponents of analytics might argue that Brian Sabean's mistake was his falling in love with Barry Zito's curveball; he had never seen anything like it, and he was biased by something transitory. Weren't Barry's numbers their own kind of apparition? Aren't the objects of analytical affections equally likely to ghost them? Under laboratory conditions, statistics might prove useful predictors of what *will* happen. But their forecasting record is far from unblemished, and the blind allegiance of the mathematically inclined has sometimes proved badly misplaced. One of my favorite quotes about the limits of analytics comes from Paul Maurice, the long-time hockey coach: "God, they do a horse-shit job of telling you what five guys do."[13] Modeling a simple system is one thing. How do we account for life's more complicated turns? How do we answer our most difficult questions?

I believe there is a new kind of Eye Test that we should seek to pass, and people who do pass it are perhaps more valuable today than ever: in sports, but also across so many fields of work and play. The margin between success and failure has become so impossibly fine, a good beholder can be all the difference between them. Should I make this movie? What makes good art? Who should play third base? How hard will it rain? Is this person lying? Why did that plane fall out of the sky? Numbers alone won't tell us. People will. Human

---

13 Maurice, coaching the Winnipeg Jets at the time, made this statement on February 3, 2021, in defense of his captain, Blake Wheeler, who was being blamed for a costly on-ice mistake. Statistically, it was Wheeler's error. Watching the full play led Maurice to place the blame elsewhere: "He got put in a real tough spot by a horseshit backcheck by somebody else" is how Maurice saw it.

creativity and imagination will. I don't want to make the case for palmistry. I want to make the case for taste, for curiosity, for open-mindedness, for expertise, for love. If beauty isn't a virtue, a good eye still is.

———

The conflict between baseball's analytical hive mind and its hopeless romantics is best captured in, or by, the Rawlings GG Gamer 11.5-inch glove of one Derek Jeter, the Hall of Fame shortstop for the Yankees. Over the early years of his career especially, Jeter was considered a superlative shortstop. When the Yankees acquired a second outstanding shortstop in Alex Rodriguez, Jeter's position was considered unimpeachable enough for Rodriguez to be moved to third base. In the seven seasons between 2004 and 2010, Jeter won five Gold Gloves, the award given each year to the player deemed the best at his position. During the 2010 season, his fielding percentage—the traditional defensive metric—was .989, better than every other shortstop in baseball. He committed only six errors. By those numbers, at least, he was easily tops.

He also had a knack for making spectacular plays when his team needed him to perform miracles. If clutch hitters no longer existed, Jeter made it seem as though clutch fielders still did. No fan will forget his headlong dive into the stands after he caught Trot Nixon's fly ball in the twelfth inning against the hated Red Sox in 2004. (The Yankees won in the thirteenth.) His flip to home in game three of the 2001 American League Division Series against Billy Beane's Oakland A's, when he somehow teleported to foul territory on the *first-base side* to nab Jeremy Giambi at the plate, is considered one of the greatest defensive plays ever made.

Jeter's gifts seemed both statistically significant and im-measurable. Ah, but then—then a different defensive metric began gaining favor: Ultimate Zone Rating, or UZR. Its value is given in runs, either saved by a good defensive player or yielded by a poor one. A player with an UZR of 0 is a perfectly average fielder; plus or minus 15 runs is about the extent of the expected season-long outcome. The purpose of UZR is to give a more complete picture of a player's defense than fielding percentage. It, too, considers errors, but it also tracks an infielder's ability to turn double plays, and his range relative to other players at the same position.

Fielding is much more difficult to quantify than hitting, and even statistical zealots concede that UZR, for which tracking began in 2002, is imperfect. It requires a huge sample size; it doesn't account for positioning or the widespread use of shifts (one of the ugly unforeseen consequences of analytics); whether a play is considered a hit or an error is up to the individual scorekeeper in each ballpark. Still, UZR is considered—indisputably, it just *is*—a more complete assessment of a player's defense than fielding percentage alone. And when it comes to Derek Jeter, UZR and its proponents wish for us to forget what we think we know about him.

Remember that 2010 Gold Glove season, when he made only six errors and shined like a diamond? According to UZR, you're remembering it wrong. Jeter's UZR was −4.7, third-worst among American League shortstops and fifteen runs behind Alexei Ramirez of the Chicago White Sox. Ramirez committed twenty errors against Jeter's six, and errors are obvious and look bad. But in exchange for each of those additional errors, Ramirez gave the White Sox five more putouts and ten more assists, an easy trade. According to FanGraphs.com, Jeter allowed a combined 66.1 more runs to score than the *average* shortstop over the last twelve years of his career. Compared to the best shortstops in the game? Derek Jeter was a defensive liability.

Supporters of a rigorous analytical approach use Jeter's post-career re-evaluation as proof of the limits of human observation. We didn't see a shortstop with grossly limited range; we saw balls go past him untouched and assumed no player would have reached them. That wasn't true: Dozens of times over the course of the season, Alexei Ramirez would have made a play on the same ball. It took UZR to correct that record. If we could be so profoundly wrong about someone as closely watched as Derek Jeter — if the divide between what we swear we witnessed and the dispassionate statistical reality could be so wide — then imagine how often our eyes deceive us.

The entire analytics industry has been built upon the notion that *everything you know is wrong*, which is admittedly sexier advice than mine: *You're doing just fine but could do a little better.* We tend to glorify analytics even when they tell us something we already know, every small finding treated as an intellectual breakthrough. When Doug Pederson led the Philadelphia Eagles over the New England Patriots in Super Bowl LII, much was made of the fact that the Eagles were a team steeped in rational decision-making. The *New York Times* published a glowing story about EdjSports, an analytics firm that advises clients, including the Eagles, with a predictive model founded upon a new statistic called GWC, for Game-Winning Chance.[14] Their great revelation? *Be aggressive.* Teams should go for it, particularly on fourth down. There are high school

---

14 Ben Shpigel, "How the Eagles Followed the Numbers to the Super Bowl," *New York Times*, February 2, 2018.

coaches who have enjoyed years of success by never punting, but now we're expected to believe that Doug Pederson needed the permission of quants to take the same approach?[15] Or that following basic football calculus made the Eagles, in the eyes of the *Times*, "an organization that not only accepts counter-intuitive thinking but encourages it"?[16] Give a new statistic the right acronym, and you're on your way to sainthood.

The Jeter Gulf (TJG), so widely used to illustrate the gap between perception and reality, is in fact an outlier and not just a moderate one: It's an extreme deviation. In 2018, Joe Posnanski, the metrics-minded baseball journalist and author (and also a friend of mine), compared actual defensive statistics against the surveyed opinions of the readers of Fangraphs.com.[17] They—not professional scouts, remember, but regular fans— were asked to rate players based on seven fielding categories: reaction, acceleration, sprint speed, hands, footwork, throwing strength, and throwing accuracy. Those rankings were converted into runs, so they could be compared against the painstakingly quantified likes of UZR. Joe, normally a proponent of advanced statistics, found that "the eye test and the defensive numbers almost always are very close."[18]

---

15 Kevin Kelley, the head coach at Pulaski Academy in Arkansas, began receiving national coverage for never punting as far back as 2015.

16 The Eagles began thinking more conventionally after they went 4–11–1 in 2020 and fired Doug Pederson on January 11, 2021. Pederson's record in five seasons with the team was 46–39–1, and he ended his tenure overseeing one of the worst offenses in the league. There had been no miraculous code-breaking in Philadelphia: The Super Bowl win was an outlier, not some new successful norm.

17 Joe Posnanski, "Hosmer, Trout and Defensive-Metric Dilemmas," MLB.com, February 22, 2018.

18 For instance, fans guessed that shortstop Andrelton Simmons saved 96 runs between 2011 and 2017; by UZR's measure, he saved 99. Infielder Manny Machado saved 81 runs according to advanced defensive metrics; fans thought he'd probably saved 80.

In rare instances, graceless but otherwise effective fielders are underrated by observers. Human fire hydrants like Mike Napoli can be solid fielders even absent a more lithesome grace. As with Jeter, the opposite can also prove true: Fans might overrate a player because he appears more athletic than he performs, better in imagination than practice. (First baseman Eric Hosmer, newly acquired by the San Diego Padres at the time of Joe's writing, was the most significant current aberration; Hosmer looks like a ballplayer and, at the time, had won four Gold Gloves, but his UZR was the worst in the game.)

Far more often, however, there is little or no measurable difference between our perception of a player and statistical fact. "We've been led to believe because of a few examples that the numbers and the eyes see defense in entirely different ways," Joe wrote. "It just isn't true." When it comes to evaluating baseball defense, our eyes, in fact, are nearly perfect instruments.

Dr. Sara Seager has a unique set of eyes: They are an unusual shade of hazel; she doesn't blink as often as most people; and she has spent nearly her entire life using them to look through telescopes.[19] Today she's an astrophysicist and planetary scientist at MIT. Her office isn't far from the site of the Sloan Sports Analytics Conference; she will never be asked to speak there, although she would teach the attendees a great deal. She is the

---

19 I wrote about Dr. Seager for the *New York Times Magazine*. "The Woman Who Might Find Us Another Earth" appeared in the December 7, 2016, edition.

recipient of numerous awards in the physical sciences and a "genius grant" from the MacArthur Foundation. She believes she will be the first human to discover proof of other life in the universe; that means she also believes she will be the first to fix a seemingly intractable flaw in our sight.

Dr. Seager and her fellow astronomers have dedicated themselves to an especially elusive subject of study: light. Other life will live on other planets, or perhaps on their moons—among the smallest lights in the universe. But bright lights always outshine dim ones, and sources of light always outshine their reflectors. Earth is 10 billion times less bright than the sun, and there are stars that are 100 times as big. Nobody can spot a firefly next to the glare from a lighthouse.

That means astronomers have never "seen" another planet outside our solar system—not in the way that most of us think of "seeing," at least. Luckily, Dr. Seager has trained her brain to think more expansively than most. She has to think big to contemplate the scale of the universe. Our galaxy, the Milky Way, is one of perhaps 100 billion galaxies, and each galaxy is home to hundreds of billions of stars, and thousands of billions of planets. "There is a star for every grain of sand on Earth," Dr. Seager said. For her, the answer to the question "Are we alone?" is largely mathematical: The odds that our planet is the only one with life are about as long as we can imagine. "It would be arrogant to think that we're the only ones," she said. The number of grains of sand in a single bucket—never mind a dune, beach, or desert—is a hard number for most of us to contemplate. But Dr. Seager isn't like most of us. She's a certified genius. She also has autism.

My older son, Charley, has autism. Today he's fifteen years old. Raising him has been a beautiful gift and a maddening challenge. He views the world differently than I do. He views the world differently than most people, even most other people with autism. It's hard for me to imagine that Charley might one day be independent, because he's very hard to teach, particularly when it comes to the rules that govern polite society. Charley doesn't respond to people or events *typically*. He doesn't possess any body shame, for instance. Charley could be naked in front of the world, and it wouldn't bother him in the slightest. He wouldn't know why it should begin to bother him. By his reckoning, everybody's body, more or less, is some version of the same. I admire that in a way, but I don't expect Charley will receive admiration if he drops his pants on the school bus. He doesn't know that it's impolite to ask someone about their crooked front tooth or why they're four feet tall. He doesn't understand how money works, that twenty dollars is worth more than five dollars, because he doesn't understand how numbers work. He can't put historical events in a sequence. He will never understand that 1985 happened *before* 1994.

Charley also can't spell, even though he has always loved to read. Everywhere Charley goes, he brings a giant bag of books with him, lest he run out of things to read, and so risk reaching the end of his known universe. Still, the spelling of even basic words defies him. When he was young, I couldn't understand how a child who is such a voracious reader cannot spell. I couldn't grasp how one didn't relate to the other: Reading demands that you know how to spell.

After years of his counseling and therapy, we now know that's not always the case. It's not the case with Charley, because he doesn't read in the usual way. He's never sounded out a word; his eyes don't forge the usual links in the linguistic chain. Instead, he's asked "What word is that?" many, many thousands of times. And I'll say, "poised" or "Atlantis" or "dragonfly," and then Charley will return to his book and never again ask about that word. Charley, we've realized—or we think we realize, because it's impossible to know for sure—has memorized the *shapes* of words. English to him is like Mandarin or hieroglyphics: Words aren't assemblies of letters and syllables; they're shapes with meanings. Each word is imprinted on his brain somehow, like any other memory, like a tattoo made of invisible ink. He can't spell them the way you probably can't draw a realistic portrait of someone whose face you know. For Charley, every word is like your memory of a face; every book is a collection of people he recognizes.

That same hard-to-describe skill—a specific kind of photographic memory, combined with off-the-charts pattern recognition—makes Charley incredibly good at some unusual tasks. One of Charley's teachers once pointed at a field and asked him to find her a four-leaf clover. Within a few minutes, he had found five. Charley has repeated that trick on numerous occasions. For some reason, four-leaf clovers stand out to him the way the brightest star in the sky does to you or me. It's as though they are lit up somehow, or call out to him. My younger son, Sam, is one of those kids who's naturally good at most things. Life is easy for Sam, as hard as it sometimes can be for Charley. If we feel the need to balance the ledgers between our boys, we tell them to go outside and find as many four-leaf clovers as they can. Charley will come back with handfuls and Sam with none.

I don't know why Charley can see four-leaf clovers so easily; I don't really know *how* he sees anything. What I do know: Charley sees differently than I do. We can look together at the same object, the same person, the same moment in time, and even though we are father and son, we each see something totally different. Our separate ways of looking at the world reveal divergent truths. When we're both looking at a busy street, the fact that Charley sees *escape* when I see *danger* fills me with terror. But when we look at the same green field, and Charley sees only the four-leaf clovers, it fills me with wonder.

Dr. Sara Seager is a similarly unlikely source of revelations. She and other astronomers have identified thousands of planets outside of our solar system, because they have learned to look at the stars differently—or, in Dr. Seager's case, because she's always seen them differently, like Charley and his clovers.

Sometimes, astronomers identify something because of the absence of something else. Black holes exist, because otherwise in their place would be light. Other times, they've found planets because they've detected their *effects* on something else. Planets possess enough gravitational pull to make their host stars "wobble." Nothing else could make a star wobble, so that wobbling star must have a planet orbiting nearby. And sometimes, they know something is there because something else is there, and one couldn't exist without the other. Dr. Seager told me to imagine you've found a table with chairs around it. It's not a massive reach to think that sometimes people must sit there.

New planets have been discovered through data, in transit, and the infrared. Astronomers often have favorite methods— Dr. Seager is one of the inventors of the transit technique: a planet passing in front of its star will make a tiny eclipse, revealing its silhouette—but colleagues often use different techniques to confirm one another's work. In the search for other life in the universe, there is no such thing as too much proof.

On our own planet, statistics sometimes reveal things that we might not otherwise see. They can confirm suspicions with harder evidence and occasionally furnish corrections to the record, as they have with Derek Jeter's defensive reputation.

But when an answer is hard to find, why would we choose to search for it with a single method? That so often seems to be the argument for analytics: It is the one best way. Why shouldn't we be more like astronomers and search for solutions in every conceivable way, to make sure we're seeing what we believe we're seeing? What's the advantage of having everyone looking through the same set of lenses? Young statisticians and old scouts both love baseball, and 95 percent of the time, their eyes reach the same conclusions. When it comes to those blurry margins, why wouldn't I still want multiple looks? Why would I ever refuse another perspective? Maybe there is something you can divine more clearly than anyone else—whether a movie is good, or whether a dish needs more or less salt, or whether a cancer is the killing sort. Isn't it better, for you and for us, if you champion your differences in perspective, and seek opportunities where your gifts might be best applied, and try to use your methods more creatively? I'm not sure there's *one* best way to do anything. Charley has shown me there isn't even one best way to read.

———

At the time of this writing, Justin Jirschele is the youngest manager in professional baseball. He was the youngest in 2017, when he was twenty-seven years old and the Chicago White Sox made him the manager of their Low-A Kannapolis Intimidators. (They're now called the Cannon Ballers.) He remained the youngest in 2020, when he had turned thirty and was picked to lead the Double-A Birmingham Barons before

COVID-19 canceled the season. When minor-league baseball resumed in 2021, he won nine of his first twelve games in Birmingham, including five of six against an opposing manager twenty-two years his senior.

Justin began his baseball life in Clintonville, Wisconsin, the second son of Sheri and Mike Jirschele, who spent thirty-six years in the minors as a player and manager before finally becoming the third-base coach for the Kansas City Royals in 2014 and winning a World Series ring in 2015.[20] As a toddler, Justin strode naked through clubhouses with a towel over his shoulder, emulating the men he wished to be. He visited his father on the road mostly in Omaha, where Mike managed the Triple-A Storm Chasers for twelve seasons, grooming a generation of Royals prospects. When Mike finally reached Kansas City, he had already coached twenty-four of the forty men on their roster.

Justin himself grew up to become a middle infielder, less gifted than driven. In four minor-league seasons with the White Sox organization, he fought to make up for his relative lack of physical tools with his baseball acumen, the wisdom-by-osmosis that he had inherited during all those years around his father and the game. "He was probably the best player on the field with the least amount of talent," Nick Capra, Chicago's director of player development, told me. By then, Justin's coaches had already tabbed him as more of a managerial

---

20 I first met the Jirscheles when I wrote about Mike's arrival in Kansas City for *ESPN The Magazine* ("A Long Journey into Spring," in the March 19, 2014, issue). They are the sort of people who meet you once and send you Christmas cards forever. I next wrote about Justin's managerial journey for the *New York Times Magazine*. ("Can Baseball Turn a 27-Year-Old into the Perfect Manager?" in the September 14, 2017, issue.) We tell each other "I love you" whenever we catch up, which is fairly often. My account of him is entirely truthful but contains no objectivity.

prospect than a playing one. "Great baseball blood," Tommy Thompson, one of his former minor-league skippers, answered when I'd asked him what he saw in Justin. "There's something about managing that you grow to. I think he's that guy." The White Sox turned Justin into a minor-league hitting coach when he was only twenty-four, and three years later gave him his first club to run.

Justin really is a baseball savant, and I was surprised less by his ascendancy than by how old-fashioned a lot of the assessments of him were. The White Sox are one of the most analytically inclined organizations in baseball; combined with the Cubs, Chicago is one of the capitals of *Moneyball* Nation. Rick Hahn, the White Sox general manager (at the moment, at least), is a former agent, with degrees from Harvard Law and the Kellogg School of Management. He never played the game. Yet when it came to what Hahn and others saw in Justin Jirschele, I heard so many references to his blood and pedigree, it was though his admirers were talking about a prized horse.

Despite our determination to rid the world of intangibles, intangibles remain. In sports, they're perhaps most seen— *exposed* is probably a better word—in football quarterbacks. The NFL, generally speaking, has proved more institutionally resistant to analytics than other leagues; for many, film still reigns supreme. "I call them ana-*lie*-tics," ESPN analyst Mel Kiper has said. "To me, you have to look deeper."[21] Most

---

21 Kiper said this to ESPN's Kevin Van Valkenburg when discussing the 2020–21 arrival of Buffalo Bills quarterback Josh Allen. Most observers thought Allen wouldn't amount to much in the NFL, mostly because his statistics were ordinary, especially when it came to his throwing accuracy. Kiper saw something else in Allen and always ranked him highly. "How Buffalo Bills QB Josh Allen Went from Mediocrity to NFL MVP Contender," appeared on ESPN.com on January 6, 2021.

teams seek to quantify talent within an eighth of an inch of their lives. The sum of a potential draft pick's college career is dissected with traditional statistics: yards passing, completion percentage, touchdowns, interceptions. At the NFL Scouting Combine, their speed, jumping ability, height, weight, and hand size are measured. (Bigger hands theoretically mean they're less likely to fumble the football.) They complete the Wonderlic, a controversial written exam that supposedly takes stock of their intellectual capacities, important because modern NFL offenses are as complicated as surgeries. At last, prospects sit down with interested teams during all-important interviews. And after all of that analysis, whether a young man with a strong arm will lead his franchise to the Super Bowl or become the latest first-round quarterback to achieve absolutely nothing can still seem to come down to chance. Top picks like Ryan Leaf flame out; Tom Brady falls to the sixth round and wins seven rings. According to veteran coach Bruce Arians, about 30 percent of any selection remains a pesky function of hunch and guess. "And that's if you've really done all the work *and* you get lucky," he's said. "The hardest thing to evaluate is the heart and the head."[22]

Hence the challenge in evaluating baseball managers: *All that matters is their heart and their head.* Those are the instruments of their profession. There is nothing in them to quantify. The only statistic available to measure their performance, winning percentage, isn't particularly useful in the minor leagues, when player development is far more important than winning or losing. In fact, when success is seeing your best players get better and leave you, losing might be the stronger signal of

---

managerial ability. "We don't even look at winning percentage," Hahn said. "It's more about their ability to communicate across the entire dugout, to teach and evaluate their own players. It's much harder because it's not quantifiable. You're dealing with a softer science."

Managers are expected to turn the projections of their front offices into on-field reality, but they are themselves immune to statistical analysis, the way a tool can't be used on itself. Even Hahn, who behaves as purely and dispassionately as a man who cares deeply about something possibly can, has trouble imagining his manager acting as clinically. "Too much of the managerial job is beyond playing the right percentages," he said. Managers are baseball's aristocrats, powerless next to the Ivy League quants who have become the masters of their franchises but comparatively divine. When I spoke to Hahn, Rick Renteria was his manager, a defiant occupant of some middle ground between science and art.[23] "I love numbers," Renteria said. "I use numbers. They're important indicators for me. But you have to give that information a life of its own. The human element."

Justin Jirschele's trajectory is a uniquely human one. After he became a manager, he'd call his dad every night and have hours-long conversations about each of their games, about the choices each of them had to make, or saw others make, and why they made them, and whether they were right.[24] Justin's

---

23 Renteria and the White Sox "agreed to part ways" on October 12, 2020, after the organization entered the expanded playoffs as the top American League seed and then stumbled against Billy Beane's Oakland A's. Renteria was lauded for his clubhouse culture but criticized for his more granular in-game decision-making, particularly his bullpen management.
24 At the time of this writing, Mike Jirschele has returned to mentoring young players for the Royals: He's the bench coach for their High-A Quad Cities River Bandits.

very first managerial decision, other than who played where when his Intimidators took the field, was whether to send a runner home or hold him at third base. (In the low minors, managers also coach third.) In the Jirschele family, that is a loaded question.

At the end of Mike Jirschele's first season in Kansas City, he stood beside the bag in the bottom of the ninth inning of game seven of the World Series. The Royals were hosting the San Francisco Giants and losing 3–2 with two out and nobody on. (Just by reaching the World Series, Brian Sabean had done something Billy Beane hadn't done, despite his less analytical approach.) Alex Gordon lifted a ball that fell inches beyond the reach of Gregor Blanco, San Francisco's center fielder. Left fielder Juan Perez thought Blanco was going to make the catch and found himself out of position; Perez chased down the ball on the warning track and kicked it around. Gordon rounded second and churned his way toward third. Perez finally corralled the ball and threw it to strong-armed shortstop Brandon Crawford, who had migrated onto the grass in shallow left. Crawford turned just as Gordon rounded third, and Mike Jirschele held him up. The next hitter, Salvador Perez, popped out, and the Royals lost the series with the tying run stranded on third.

I was at that game, and afterward the extended Jirschele family retreated to a nearby Holiday Inn for commiseration drinks and the usual post-game debriefing. Justin's baseball education was ceaseless. Mike had been asked about his call several times already, and he was incredulous that anyone might have thought to send Gordon. It was retroactive wisdom, applied after everyone knew Perez popped up. Mike told Justin about everything he had considered in the thirteen seconds it had taken for Gordon to reach him. He saw exactly where

Crawford had caught the throw from Perez, right in the pocket of his glove, and he saw how well positioned his feet were—by Mike's expert eyes, they were perfectly positioned—to make an accurate throw home. Future independent analysis proved that Mike had been right, and Gordon would have been out by several feet, and Mike would have likely been looking for a job. But he'd made that decision almost instantaneously.

In other ways, thirty-six years went into Mike's fateful stop sign. Baseball might seem like a slow game, but it requires its decision makers to reach their conclusions quickly. That, I realized, was the essence of the Jirschele family's particular skill set: Over years of shared experience, they had built a kind of intellectual muscle memory, an ability to distill their previously won knowledge without conscious thought, which they combined with their knack for predicting what's about to happen. Justin also held his first runner, because he didn't want to make the first out at home, reducing the chances his team would have the big inning he had begun to envision. Every call for him was another chance to apply the lessons of the past to a future only he could see. That's how he made his present, no matter how chaotic, manageable.

The Jirschele family also plumbed a far deeper emotional well every day they went to work. Justin's grandparents, Don and Mary, had eight children. (Don managed amateurs for long enough in Clintonville that the local ballpark is named after him; for the Jirscheles, baseball blood is multi-generational.) Four of them were boys, including Mike; four were girls. When the eldest son, Doug, was eleven years old, he began walking on the balls of his feet. Tests revealed muscular dystrophy, which had first surfaced in an attack on Doug's Achilles tendon. The girls were all carriers but free from symptoms, but doctors told Don and Mary that all of their sons were destined for wheelchairs and early deaths. Mike, the second-born, mystified them by somehow escaping the disease, but his younger brothers, Pete and Jim, did not. Justin's three uncles each made it to forty, but not by much. Justin can remember the entire family—his grandparents, his uncles, his mother, and his siblings—piling into vans in the summertime, wheelchairs folded into the back, and driving to Omaha to see his father and the game they all loved. "I wouldn't trade those trips for the world," Justin told me, barely getting out the words.

Watching Justin manage baseball is an ongoing lesson in the powers of mindfulness. He still talks about baseball with wonder. He's captivated by its infinitude, at the range of possibility that exists in the space between its expected and actual outcomes. In his nightly conversations with his father, they pulled apart entire contests as though each was a kind of symphony. First they found its movements, and then they examined each of its notes. The discordant ones stood out to them the most. Good ears are doomed to disappointment. The Jirscheles also believe that being careless with blessings is a sin.

In 2020, when COVID-19 saw Justin at home in Wisconsin for the first summer in years, with his wife, Liz, and their new baby girl, his grandfather died. In Don's garage, there was the hitting tee and net that Justin had spent countless hours using, hoping to turn his stroke into one of major-league quality. He became better at different facets of the game instead. Justin's education was particular, and unconventional, and precise, and all of it combined to make him one of one, the perfect man to do a job that no machine in the world could do, or even judge. There were signs of triumph and struggle everywhere in Grandpa Don's house—family photographs that got bigger and then smaller; wheelchair ramps; shelves of trophies and pulley systems capable of lifting adult children into bathtubs and onto changing tables. Over one in the upstairs bathroom, a small, framed print was hanging on the wall. "Love never fails," it read.

———

In January 2020, shortly after Derek Jeter was elected to the Hall of Fame with 99.7 percent of the vote, he broke down "The Flip" on *MLB Tonight* with Harold Reynolds. "My job is to watch the runner," Jeter said by way of introduction. The runner that night was poor Jeremy Giambi, standing with his hands on his hips on first, blissfully unaware of the fate that awaited him.

Oakland's Terrence Long hit the ball down the right-field line. Jeter watched its trajectory and did some quick, private calculations. *Automatic double*, Jeter knew. The Yankees had prepared for such a scenario; Jeter had practiced being the third cutoff man on the first-base side, in the event that Giambi couldn't be caught at home but Long somehow could be nabbed stretching for third. Jeter had two potential targets, which necessitated additional internal calculus. "The Giambi family is not very fast," Jeter said, "respectfully." Never mind how the Yankees had practiced. Jeter decided that Giambi was the more likely of the two to be caught, and his focus was no longer divided.

When Jeter began crossing the infield toward the first-base side, he saw that outfielder Shane Spencer's throw was preordained to fly over the heads of the first two cutoff men. Watching the replay, Reynolds mentioned Spencer's arm angle, which Jeter dismissed with significant prejudice. "This is the new analytics here. You talking about arm angle? I didn't look at arm angle! I looked at the ball." The way he knew the ball off Long's bat was destined to be a double, he knew Spencer had overcooked his throw the instant the ball left his hand.

My favorite articulation of that almost hard-wired understanding—it can seem like a strain of clairvoyance, except that it's earned rather than bestowed—comes from an expert carpenter, Mark Ellison. His skills are such that a wonderful writer for the *New Yorker* named Burkhard Bilger followed him around on his job sites for months.[25] At some point, Bilger watched Ellison do something remarkable with a table saw, a saw expressly designed to make straight cuts. Ellison used the side of the saw's blade rather than its teeth to make a *curved* cut, and all the while he chatted with an apprentice, as though he weren't paying attention to any of the many things that were going on around him, including the blade spinning perilously close to his fingertips. Bilger said something to Ellison about it, and Ellison remembered a ballplayer, Roberto Clemente, and how he seemed to *know* where a batted ball was going to drop to Earth. Clemente would turn his back to the play, run to the spot, and turn and wait for the ball to meet him. "Your body just knows how to do it," Ellison told Bilger. "It understands weight and leverage and space in a way that your brain would take forever to figure out." Ellison could hold a conversation while demonstrating insanity with a table saw because he wasn't using his mind to make the cut. "I figure something out and then I'm done thinking. I don't bother with my brain anymore." His ability wasn't a superpower; it was a reward. Bilger considered and discarded the "muscle memory" analogy I used to describe the Jirschele family training, their

---

25 Burkhard Bilger, "The Art of Building the Impossible," *New Yorker*, November 23, 2020. I implore you to read this story. It's a beautifully crafted piece about beautiful craft.

ability to catalog the past in order to predict the future. Instead he called that seamless, transcendent drive toward perfect action—the elusive flow state—"embodied analysis."

That night against Oakland, Jeter's embodied analysis saw him sprint toward the first-base line, snag the errant ball on the hop, and toss it home, where Giambi was tagged out standing up. The Yankees went on to win the game, 1–0, and eventually the series, three games to two.

Was Derek Jeter an all-time great fielder? No, he was not. The analytics are indisputable. Did that play also contain an element of good fortune? Sure. If Giambi doesn't try for home, Jeter fields the ball, tosses it back to the pitcher, and the inning continues with men on second and third.

Did he possess a Hall-of-Fame understanding of the game that still allowed him to change the course of it? Absolutely, he did. That play isn't lessened by what we now know about Jeter's fielding abilities. It's all the more remarkable, as well as proof of the heights to which devotion will lift you. Maybe he had limited range, but the special way he saw the game made him capable of greatness all the same. Michael Lewis, relying on his own particular gift for story, looked at Billy Beane and saw the same set of unusual eyes, eyes that discovered something surprising in a game that people had played for more than a hundred years. The same sort of singular understanding told Mike Jirschele to hold Alex Gordon at third, and Mike, in turn, passed on that same unparalleled vision to Justin. Together, the Jirscheles unearthed hidden truths about baseball because they saw *beyond* the game—the way Mark Ellison could feel out the best possible shape for a shapeless piece of wood, the way Dr. Sara Seager looked at the stars and saw life instead of light, the way my boy Charley's eyes turned four-leaf clovers into beanstalks.

WEATHER

A 100 Percent Chance of Uncertainty.

*Computer modeling works best when inputs
are typical and outcomes are within expected
ranges. But we live in an age of extremes—
climate is a glaring example—which makes
our talent for adaptability worth practicing.
We can imagine possibilities, both positive
and negative, that models can't fathom.
That means we can also see more opportunities, and dream of better remedies. In fact,
the more abnormal the situation, the more
likely a skilled human will outperform a
machine. The best time for people to shine is
during life's storms.*

On September 22, 2008, in the Bob Barker Studio at CBS's
Television City in Los Angeles, a former weatherman and his
wife took seats 004 and 005 for the morning taping of *The Price
Is Right.*[1] Approaching sixty, Terry Kniess had climbed the

---

1 I first wrote about Terry for *Esquire* in August 2010. The story was called
"TV's Crowning Moment of Awesome." Terry also wrote a book about
his experience called *Cause and Effects*. We've kept in touch over the
years; I enjoyed getting to know him. His story was optioned for film
but has not yet been made, because getting stuff made in Hollywood, as
we've discussed, is very difficult.

75

TV meteorology ladder from then-minor-league Las Vegas to Waco, Texas, to Springfield, Missouri—local billboards touted his "Terrybly Accurate" forecasts for KSPR—and finally to the big time in Atlanta, where he won two Southeast Regional Emmy Awards. When he was done with the weather, he and his wife, Linda, moved back to the desert, where they had always felt most at home. They were happiest in low humidity.

Terry was a very good weatherman. He was strong on TV, precise and authoritative, with a deep, powerful voice. More important, his predictive capacities were as robust as his delivery. Today, many TV meteorologists are not trained meteorologists; they are presenters, passing along computer-generated forecasts delivered by the National Weather Service and other central forecasting offices. But when Terry began his career, he had to divine the weather before he went on TV to explain it.

In Las Vegas, friends would joke about his job and its seeming ease—"Today it's going to be hot and sunny"—but Las Vegas has always been a challenging place to be right, including about the weather. It doesn't rain on many days, but it's sudden and violent when it does come. Terry became expert in desert storms. He was excellent at pattern recognition, the essence of weather forecasting: knowing that a particular barometric pressure coupled with a certain wind lift will result in flooded streets some significant percentage of the time. Terry could see rain coming when others couldn't.

Retired from his meteorology career, Terry found a new venue for his skill set: casinos. At first he worked in surveillance, copping the night shift at Circus Circus, a fading casino toward the downmarket end of the Strip. In a windowless room filled with monitors, Terry learned to read the mannerisms of chiselers as clearly as he once read fronts. He knew they came out on holiday weekends, when the floors were busier and they found concealment in crowds; they walked the floor longer than tourists before sitting down, hunting for weak dealers; they invariably selected some new transplant who used a pinch tuck rather than a palm tuck when he dealt his cards, all the edge a professional needed;[2] they nursed their drinks and bet in unnatural ways. Even the best of them fell into routines, the rhythms of being human.

The casino called them cheaters, but Terry saw them as opportunists, searching for imperfections in a system that had been otherwise rigged against them. It wasn't their fault the system had holes. Terry being Terry, he soon found himself sitting at his kitchen table, staring at decks of cards. Blackjack was the most vulnerable game to people like him. If you can remember how many face cards have been pulled, or how many aces remain in the deck, you can turn the casino's slight edge into your own advantage. Even if the casino wins a game only 51 percent of the time, you will lose all of your money so long as you keep playing. If *you* win 51 percent of the time, you can make a living.

Terry sat at his table and flipped through deck after deck until he could keep perfect count of the cards. Then he took everything he'd learned in TV studios and Circus Circus and walked into a casino. He sat at the one seat—the seat to which a weak, right-handed dealer will inadvertently reveal the most

---

2 Blackjack dealers give themselves two cards, the first one face up, the second one face down. If a dealer lifts the down card off the top of the deck with his fingertips—if he pinches the card—there's a better chance that he will expose it to the player to his immediate right, the one seat, than if he palms the card off the deck and uses his hand as a shield. Even the most simple-seeming arts present room for subtle improvement—or exploitation.

information—and crushed enough blackjack that the casinos wouldn't let him play anymore.

In the summer of 2008, the hits kept coming: Terry and Linda had to put down Krystal, their beloved Maltese. They were consumed by grief. "Such a special little dog," Terry said. "She could walk backward, you know." Krystal had also helped with his forecasts; she hid from advancing storms before humans could sense their arrival.

A friend had recently appeared on *The Price Is Right*, and she suggested to Terry and Linda that the show might provide an unlikely boost. It's the longest running game show in history in part because it's unchanging, as though purposefully devoid of surprise, and millions of people had found a comfort in its routines over the years. *The Price Is Right* premiered in 1956; its "modern" version debuted in 1972. Since then it had been hosted by only two men, Bob Barker and Drew Carey. They both rocked the same skinny microphone, and they both reminded you to have your pet spayed or neutered.

Like so many of our entertainments, *The Price Is Right* follows a hero's journey, progressive in its risks and rewards. First, four apparently random people are called out of the frenetic audience to begin play.[3] From Contestants Row, they are asked to guess the price of some smallish item. If they make the best guess out of all the players, they are brought up on stage to play a pricing game—Plinko, Any Number, Cliff Hangers, Secret "X"—the same roster of souped-up carnival

---

3 There is nothing random about being called to "come on down." Producers talk to every member of the audience, in small groups, on their way into the studio. Because contestants never know when they're on camera, the producers want them to be the sort of people who are always smiling, and they pick people whose faces are naturally positive. Resting angry mouth is a surefire eliminator.

games that have always been wheeled out to leaping house-wives and college students skipping school. Their old slot on Contestants Row is filled by someone else from the audience, and over the course of an episode, six players will appear on stage. After they win or lose their pricing game, they spin something called the Big Wheel, which really is random. The pair who spin the closest to $1.00 without going over meet in a final showdown, the Showcase. There they each bid for a collection of big-ticket items, cars and trips and whatever else, worth tens of thousands of dollars. Again, the person who comes closest to the actual retail price of the prizes without going over wins. If a player somehow gets within $250 of the total value, he or she wins both sets of prizes. That hardly ever happens, and nobody had ever guessed the value of a Showcase exactly.

Terry and Linda Kniess followed their friend's advice a little more diligently than she might have anticipated. They started recording the show every morning and watching it in bed every night. Linda's brain worked something like her husband's, but her gift was figures; she was in charge of staff scheduling at the Las Vegas Convention and Visitors Authority, and she kept mental track of 260 part-time staffers and their hours. Given Linda's command of numbers and Terry's sense for patterns, they watched the show differently than most people, even from their first fateful viewing. Almost by instinct, they started looking for angles, applying their own particular skills to a new opportunity. They were subconscious practitioners of the Eye Test, on the hunt for possibilities that no one else could see.

Terry soon found the game's most glaring weakness, which also happened to be its greatest strength: *The Price Is Right* never changed. He first noticed one prize, a distinctive backyard smoker called the Big Green Egg, when it appeared a second time, and then a third. Its price was always $1,175. He saw more prizes repeating. Almost every prize, in fact, made multiple appearances. There were a lot of them, maybe a thousand, but they were part of a rotating pool that had its outer limits.

Terry and Linda looked at each other from opposite sides of their bed; they knew opportunity when they saw it. When you can forecast the most complex weather and breach the defenses of blackjack tables, committing a thousand numbers to heart isn't an especially nervy proposition. Terry and Linda began memorizing prize values the way Terry had counted cards and Linda kept track of staffing hours. They got a strange, shared charge from the process—the thrill of possibility that bank robbers must feel, planning a heist.

After four months of preparation—"Good TV is rehearsed TV," Terry liked to say—they decided they were ready. They packed the car for Los Angeles. They were the fourth and fifth people in line that morning when the gates at CBS swung open. They talked to the producers on their way in, and the producers took note that Terry Kniess had a great voice and a face that belonged on TV. Terry was among the first several contestants chosen to play. He took his place and waited to see the first prize for which he might bid. He hoped he would know it.

Out came the Big Green Egg. Terry bid $1,175. A special bell sounded, indicating that someone had made a perfect guess—or "guess." Three of the contestants hoped they were right. One of them knew he was.

Oddly, Terry then lost his pricing game, called Switch? It's deceptively simple: Two prizes are displayed, and two prices. Put the right price with each prize, and you win both. Terry was shown an Apple computer and a pair of exercise bikes. He told Drew Carey the computer was worth more. It was not. "I didn't see that there were two bikes," Terry told me after, "and I thought a terabyte sounded like a lot of memory." Terry then spun the Big Wheel, where his master plan might have been derailed; there was nothing he could do but hope. He spun 90 cents, proving himself lucky as well as good, and advanced to the Showcase.

He was pitted against a woman named Sharon. She had won her pricing game, which gave her an advantage over Terry: She could bid on the first collection of prizes or pass them to Terry and bid on whatever package came next. The first Showcase began with a karaoke machine; then came a pool table; then came a seventeen-foot camper. Sharon passed. Terry was forced to bid. He looked at the prizes, looked at the audience, and then leaned into the microphone in front of him. He said his bid as though he were reading it off a teleprompter: "$23,743."

"Wow," Drew Carey said. "That's a very exact bid."

Sharon then saw her Showcase: trips to Chicago; Banff, Alberta; Edinburgh, Scotland; and Cape Town, South Africa. She bid $30,525.

"We'll be right back, folks," Carey said. "Don't go away."

And then the show stopped.

Even before Terry Kniess showed up, it had been a wobbly stretch in the long and storied history of *The Price Is Right*. Not only had Carey replaced Bob Barker, a beloved institution who referred to the show's most faithful followers as Loyal Friends and True, but a long-time producer named Roger Dobkowitz had also been let go to make way for fresh blood. Fans had complained, and there had been rumors of revenge plots. A woman named Kathy Greco, who protected the book that contained all the winning prize values, felt a sickness rising in her throughout that morning's taping. Apart from Terry's misfire at Switch?, every contestant had won his or her game. The show, which pays for the prizes it gives away out of its production budget, had already surrendered, among other things, two cars, an entertainment center, $2,000 in cash, and a Big Green Egg. *The Price Is Right* was getting rolled.

Now Greco looked at her book. Sharon had made an impossibly good guess. Trips are notoriously difficult to get right because they contain so many variables. She had missed by just $494, a bid that would have seen her in Chicago and Banff and Edinburgh and Cape Town almost all of the time.

But Terry—Terry was exactly right.

Carey watched as Greco fled behind some curtains. He followed her and knew instantly that something was amiss. "She was white as a sheet," he said.

"He got it right on the nose," Greco said to him.

"Has that ever happened?" Carey asked.

"No."

"Holy shit."

Greco decided the fix was in. Carey couldn't argue with the evidence. How else could Terry have been perfect? $23,743? That really was a very exact bid.

"Everybody thought someone had cheated," Carey told me. "I thought, *Fuck, they just fucking fucked us over.* Somebody fucked us over. I remember asking, 'Are we ever going to air this?' And nobody could see how we could. So I thought the show was never going to air. I thought somebody had cheated us, and I thought the whole show was over. I thought they were going to shut us down, and I thought I was going to be out of a job. I was like, Fuck this guy. When it came time to announce the winner, I thought, *It's not airing anyway. So fuck him.*"

Carey returned to the other side of the curtain. He announced Sharon's bid first. She must have allowed herself to think she had won.

Then Carey turned to Terry. "You bid $23,743," he said through clenched teeth. "Actual retail price: $23,743. You got it right on the nose. You win both Showcases." That was it. Terry and Linda drove back to Las Vegas with more than $50,000 in prizes.

After that calamitous taping, a calm returned to the Bob Barker Studio. Further investigation revealed no grand fix; there was only a particularly determined weatherman, who had spent more time on something than anyone else might reasonably expect. CBS aired Terry's episode after all, but not until December, consigning it to the ratings doldrums. Carey was torched for his lack of enthusiasm when he announced the perfect bid; Loyal Friends and True sneered that he was either too new or too cynical to recognize game-show history. ("Oh, I would have run with that, you bet," Bob Barker told me.)

By then, Terry and Linda had sold the karaoke machine, pool table, and camper to pay the taxes on the rest of their winnings. They enjoyed the trips. "First class," Terry said. "Just wonderful." They kept the Big Green Egg, which sat shining in the sun by their pool out back. I stood out there with Terry in the heat, the light bouncing off the metal frames of his glasses.

"It's crazy how random life is," he said.

Using satellite imagery and computer modeling, we're more adept at forecasting "typical" weather than ever. When you look at your phone's weather app on a Monday, its prediction of Saturday's weather is as accurate as the next-day forecast was in 1980.[4] Algorithms are better and quicker than human meteorologists at processing high volumes of inputs, such as atmospheric pressure and brightness temperature. Machines don't have off days.

But more and more, weather isn't typical. Storms follow their own rhythms, escalating in frequency and pitch. Since 1980, there have been more than 200 weather and climate events in the United States that have each caused more than $1 billion in damage.[5] The U.S. government has three central bodies charged with forecasting those disasters and trying to lessen their devastating effects on lives and property: The Storm Prediction Center in Norman, Oklahoma, keeps watch for tornadoes; the Weather Prediction Center in College Park, Maryland, monitors rains and floods; the National Hurricane Center in Miami looks out for storms with eyes. A number of recent storms have been severe and complicated enough to command all three national bodies to attention—not just their computers, but the skilled human beings who monitor them.

Among extreme weather phenomena, the tornado presents the greatest challenge to American forecasters. According to the National Climate Data Center, 40 percent of all severe weather events in America are spawned by thunderstorms. For something so common, meteorologists still struggle to predict exactly when and where funnel clouds will touch down. The

---

4   Eric Berger, "Modern Meteorology Was Born 60 Years Ago Today," Ars Technica, April 1, 2020.

5   In 2020, my Canadian home insurer sent the following note to explain rising premiums: "Since 2013, insurance claims for damage due to natural disasters such as fires, flooding, and storms have doubled compared to the previous six years." The town of Fort McMurray, Alberta, for instance, was devastated by wildfire in 2016, when 2,579 homes were burned to the ground.

same data-fueled models that let us more reliably plan our golf outings are responsible for some advances: Over the last four decades, the average tornado warning time has lengthened from three minutes to fourteen. "Researchers have made huge improvements in tornado lead times," David Stensrud, the head of Penn State's Department of Meteorology and Atmospheric Science, has said. "But for many people, fourteen minutes isn't enough."[6]

Like audiences and their fickle desires, the weather is a moving target.[7] That's particularly true in the American Southeast, an increasing hotspot for funnel clouds. Meteorologists refer to the burgeoning stretch between eastern Texas and Georgia, and the Gulf of Mexico and Tennessee, as Dixie Alley, a nod to the traditional Tornado Alley of the Great Plains.[8]

Tornado Alley still leads the country in tornado frequency. Between 1984 and 2014, Texas saw by far the most tornadoes of any state, with about 140 each year. (Total area is a factor, obviously: more acreage, more tornadoes.) Kansas was visited by about eighty. But Dixie Alley has seen both a growing number of storms and a rise in storm intensity. Between those same years, Alabama had the highest average number of annual deaths in tornadoes, with fourteen. Missouri, Tennessee, and Arkansas have also fared worse on the fatality front than Texas, the first of the Tornado Alley states on the list, which averages four deaths each year.

Those facts are unassailable. Now comes the hard part: Why

---

6 Penn State, "New Weather Model Could Increase Tornado-Warning Times," *ScienceDaily*, October 1, 2018.
7 We're not going to argue about this here. See: a mountain of numbers-based evidence and scientific consensus.
8 Madison Park and Emily Smith, "Tornadoes in the Southeast Are Getting Worse—and They're Often the Deadliest," CNN.com, March 4, 2020.

are Dixie Alley storms on average more deadly? Here, the data gives us the frame of a picture. Southeastern tornadoes move faster and stay on the ground longer. They are also more likely to happen at night. More than 40 percent of tornadoes in Arkansas, Kentucky, and Tennessee come after dark. There are fifteen states, mostly in the west, in which fewer than 16 percent of storms are nocturnal. (The Southeastern storm season extends into winter, when there is less daylight.) That darkness makes them harder to see, and more likely to catch their victims asleep in their beds, oblivious to the warnings that often come only minutes or seconds ahead of touchdown.

There might be other explanations for the deadliness of Dixie Alley, but now we enter the realm of narrative—using our *sense* of things to come up with the *why*. Perhaps Tornado Alley's wide-open vistas make tracking storms easier, compared to the mountainous sockets of the Southeast; Southeastern tornadoes tend to be "rain-wrapped" relative to their prairie cousins, also making them harder to see; homes in states like Alabama are less likely to have basements for shelter; population density is higher; there are more trees to topple and turn into projectiles. Take a strong, fast-moving tornado, slip it into a valley at night, wrap it in rain, and fill it with downed trees, and you've built what seems, intuitively at least, a weapon of mass destruction.

But the most dangerous aspect of Dixie Alley might be its newness. Perhaps its population hasn't had enough experience with tornadoes: Unlike the more storm-proofed people of Kansas or Oklahoma, they don't know as well what's coming, or how to deal with it when it does come. Local meteorologists are also dealing with phenomena that are unfamiliar to them. In March 2020, a tornado cluster ripped through the Nashville area, killing twenty-five people and doing more than a billion dollars in damage; at least fourteen tornadoes touched down multiple times over thirty-four hours, presenting an impossible forecasting challenge. Those murderous tornadoes arrived with almost zero warning—in terms of sounding the alarm to seek shelter, but also in terms of climate's grander scheme.

History doesn't always build on itself. Not every gain is incremental. The arc of Barry Zito's career is a good example; everything changed when he signed with San Francisco. The mortgage crisis of 2008 is another, more significant cataclysm: with smallish, periodic exceptions, the value of real estate had almost always gone up. Forces of human creation, namely the sub-prime mortgage market, made a lie out of that historical truth. Or consider the job losses in 2020, caused by a pandemic which no model could have predicted. The bottom dropped out of what had been a tight market for labor.

In his 2007 book *The Black Swan*, statistician Nassim Nicholas Taleb wrote about such low-probability, high-impact events; he also pointed out our tendency to make their arrival seem inevitable in hindsight.[9] That leads to a difficult question: If something terrible was about to happen, and its consequences were obvious in advance, then why didn't we do anything about it? Either way, there must have been a failure of imagination: The debate is only whether it occurred before or after catastrophe. But by Taleb's reckoning, at least, climate change is not a true black swan. We're not pretending to understand something that we don't understand. We *know* it's happening, and none of us should be surprised when our future does not operate like our past.

Let's pause to return to *The Price Is Right* for a moment;

---

9 Nassim Nicholas Taleb, *The Black Swan: The Impact of the Highly Improbable* (New York: Random House, 2007).

it's more fun to think about than environmental collapse. After Terry Kniess blew through the Bob Barker Studio, the producers of the show realized they had to change the game. Anyone single-minded enough could do what he did. Terry had exposed their vulnerability in a very public fashion— even the *National Enquirer* documented his feat—which gave them the justification to ramp up what had been a fairly modest makeover. They embarked on the game-show version of building a better mousetrap.

The Price Is Right always had its invisible fortifications. Some pricing games are harder to win than others, like Range Game or That's Too Much. Both involve stopping the game when you've reached what you think is the right range of price. Most players submit to a natural tendency to guess somewhere around the middle, which is usually too early in the case of Range Game and too late for That's Too Much. If the producers want to save money that week, they push the prize values to either extreme, and it's highly likely that players will guess wrong.

With Terry's perfect bid as cover, the show's producers employed their use of extremes to wider advantage. They factored more chance into the games, and they also changed up the prizes. They added more luxury items, which increased the stakes for the viewers at home and added a bit of glamour to the proceedings, but also made their values less intuitive for their coupon-clipping contestants. Nobody who shows up for a taping of *The Price Is Right* will just happen to know the price of a Burberry coat. If prizes do repeat, particularly big-ticket items like cars, they'll add or subtract options, including floor mats or the stereo system, to keep the prices changing. They've taken away the game's history, essentially. That makes it impossible for its players to predict the future. Remove the usual inputs, and all most contestants can do is guess. If they guess right, it's a function of luck more than a matter of skill.

Predicting the weather in Dixie Alley is a much higher-stakes version of *The Price Is Right*. Never mind Burberry coats, or even that fourteen-tornado cluster that tore through Nashville in 2020. Meteorologists are being asked to anticipate storms they haven't seen in their lifetimes. Imagine the EF5 monster that flattened Joplin, Missouri, in May 2011, the deadliest tornado in the United States since 1947. Or the Super Outbreak only a month before. There were 360 tornadoes between Texas and Canada during that stretch, a record for a single calamity, including four EF5 tornadoes that touched down in Mississippi, Alabama, Georgia, and Tennessee on April 27— killing more people in a single day than any tornado cluster since 1925.

Massive tornadoes aren't the only modern outliers. The National Weather Service in San Francisco issued a Twitter bulletin on September 9, 2020, that smoke from surrounding wildfires was going to affect local weather and air quality, but admitted that the smoke levels were "beyond the scope of our models."[10] The smoke levels were also dismissed as incorrect by Washington state's air-quality measuring instruments, which needed to be tweaked. "We've convinced the algorithm to come to terms with the bitter truth," a post on the Washington Smoke Information blog confessed. Wildfires aren't just consuming more acres each season than ever before (2018 was the worst one by measure of land devoured until 2020's horrific late summer); they're expressing different appetites, and

---

10 Sarah Kaplan, the climate reporter for the *Washington Post*, wrote on Twitter (@sarahkaplan48): " 'This is beyond the scope of our models' is 2020 encapsulated." Seriously.

the former equations used to predict fire spread are proving inadequate. Today's fires run big and hot enough to create their own weather, and the closest proxies that modelers can find are World War II's bomb-fueled firestorms.[11] It's difficult for people to forecast something that's never happened, but it's impossible for computers, which can do only what they're told. Models that rely on ordinary inputs don't work in extraordinary circumstances. The blank space that exists beyond the ends of "typical" can be filled by only a certain strain of human imagination. Extremes in climate, but also in countless other facets of our existence, are a kind of bad behavior. Luckily, we're a species that has demonstrated an equal talent for disobedience. We just have to be brave and smart enough to know when to practice it.

———

On January 28, 2014, snow began falling out of a low sky in central and northern Alabama. James Spann watched its dance through his window in Birmingham. He was nearly as unusual as snow in the south. The most trusted voice in weather in the region, he'd been a presence on local televisions since 1978; the following year, when he was just twenty-three years old, he was named chief weatherman at WAPI-TV. At the time, he was one of the youngest chief weathermen in the country. He also had no formal meteorological training. But he went on to win several awards for his work, including an Emmy.

Later in his long and mostly accurate career, Spann twice received national notice. In 2004, he hosted a special about severe

---

11   Daniel Duane, "The West's Infernos Are Melting Our Sense of How Fire Works," *WIRED*, September 30, 2020.

weather safety, concerned especially with surviving tornadoes. Spann had witnessed firsthand the aftermath of the growing number of deadly twisters in his home state—in 1989, on Palm Sunday in 1994,[12] in 1998, and late-fall outbreaks in 2000, 2001, and 2002—and he wanted to prepare an unprepared population for more.

Perhaps paradoxically, after Alabama sustained three hurricane strikes in two years in addition to its spate of twisters, Spann next gained attention in 2007 for his public skepticism that climate change was caused by humans. Temperatures had risen and fallen before, Spann argued; today's indisputable uptick was a temporary function of Earth's ever-evolving ecosystems. By his measures, the growing belief that carbon-dioxide emissions were changing the weather was unfounded and pseudo-scientific: "For many, global warming is a big cash grab," he said. He felt that climate was another one of God's instruments, and that God alone wielded it. Humans could do nothing but try to shelter themselves from His increasing wrath.[13]

Spann's outspokenness made him something of a rogue agent in his profession. A devout Southern Baptist, he had indisputably sought to save the lives of his fellow Alabamans from Dixie Alley's new storms. He also denied what most climate scientists believed fueled them. But in the state of Alabama,

---

12 That storm killed twenty worshippers at the Goshen United Methodist Church in Cherokee County; Spann interviewed its devastated former pastor and her husband as part of his special.

13 Spann is one of the more prominent signatories of "An Evangelical Declaration on Global Warming," which reads in part: "We believe Earth and its ecosystems—created by God's intelligent design and infinite power and sustained by His faithful providence—are robust, resilient, self-regulating, and self-correcting, admirably suited for human flourishing, and displaying His glory. Earth's climate is no exception."

Spann's contradictory-seeming blend of fealty and faith made him an object of almost universal devotion. His viewers didn't confuse his word with God's, exactly, but he was seen as His most reliable messenger.

Spann's forecast for that January day had been typically definitive: "There will be a light dusting of snow and no travel complications for Birmingham." Absent a competing narrative, the citizens of the northern half of Alabama went to school and work. God's chosen weatherman had given them no reason to do otherwise. Snow-moving equipment was sent south, where higher accumulations were expected. The north went about its business.

Then the snow got heavier and began to stick. Spann's supposed dusting turned into a couple of inches of snow instead—well within the accepted margin of error during a blizzard in upstate New York, perhaps, but the difference between making it home and not for thousands of Alabamans. The snow-moving equipment wasn't where it needed to be, and Interstate 65 and other thoroughfares became long sheets of ice, clogged with paralyzed cars and trucks. Five people died, dozens were injured, and untold numbers slept in their offices, schools, and cars. The Federal Emergency Management Agency uses the so-called Waffle House Index as an informal measure of storm severity.[14] When the local Waffle House closes, something very bad has happened. Two of Birmingham's Waffle House locations closed. Something very bad had happened that day in Alabama.

James Spann suffered for it. He had been confident in his

---

14 Annie Blanks, " 'Waffle House Index' Is a Real Thing during Disasters. How Does the Restaurant Chain Do It?" *Pensacola News Journal*, September 1, 2019.

forecast. He had slept soundly. That January morning, he was on his way to speak to students at a middle school when pictures of traffic bedlam began popping up on his Twitter feed. He pulled over and registered his horror. "None of it made sense to me," he said. "I never processed anything like that in all these years of doing weather."[15] He decided to head to work and soon was among those stranded motorists, forced to abandon his Toyota 4Runner and walk a mile to the station. He filmed himself on his trek, his trademark suspenders hidden by his winter coat. "Wow," he said in his familiar baritone. "I guess this is the price you pay for one of the worst forecast busts in a thirty-five-year career."

He had already begun his self-analysis, walking past the rows of lost cars. The weather that day had defied existing patterns, the way our weather increasingly has. Formerly simple math has been made more complicated by the lack of precedent. Normally, when the temperature doesn't climb out of the twenties in Birmingham, which it didn't that day, the air is too dry for much snow to accumulate. Bigger falls come around the freezing mark. That day, the temperatures were as forecast; the precipitation was not.

"You will probably never hear me say the word 'dusting' ever again," Spann said. "That's going to haunt me for the rest of my life." He wrote an apology to his viewers and received national attention once again, written up as a key figure in a cautionary tale in the *New York Times*: the weatherman who blew it.[16] (He was not the only one. Atlanta forecasters had missed the mark as well, with equally disastrous repercussions.) Spann

---

15 Bob Carlton, "Watch James Spann Walk a Mile in the Snow and Apologize for His Snowpocalypse 2014 Forecast 'Bust,'" al.com, January 28, 2015.
16 Kim Severson, "Atlanta Officials Gamble on Storm and Lose, and Others Pay the Price," *New York Times*, January 29, 2014.

resolved to continue his work, and he was largely forgiven by his public.[17] He has saved many lives since his blunder, finding redemption during a tornado outbreak that happened three months later, and again during the Easter storms of 2020, when twenty-one separate tornadoes touched down across his home state. But Spann remained a cautionary tale on the dangers of overconfidence, in both his own past performance and the weather's. In an age of perpetual adjustment, he had demonstrated the dangers of being set in your ways.

———————

On the surface at least, meteorologists and astronauts don't seem to have much in common beyond their shared under-standing of atmospheric pressure and air currents. But the National Weather Service's local offices in Houston and the Johnson Space Center are each home to a collection of surpris-ingly similar human specimens. You'll see a lot of tucked-in golf shirts. And the modern incarnations of both jobs demand a seemingly contradictory set of personality traits: adaptability and resilience.[18]

An astronaut's feet are good physical markers for his or her adaptive abilities—their fortitude when it comes to the constant, low-level stress of living somewhere they're not designed to live. On Earth, to which we are beautifully suited, we develop calluses on the bottoms of our feet to protect them from the rigors of walking. Without gravity, astronauts never

---

17 As of this writing, he has 430,000 followers on Twitter.
18 I've written about space for years, including the book *Too Far from Home: A Story of Life and Death in Space* (New York: Doubleday, 2007), numerous *Esquire* articles, and the Netflix series *Away*. It was canceled by an algorithm after one season. This book is basically my revenge.

walk. The International Space Station does not have what we'd consider a "floor." A vague sense of up and down is maintained inside its cylindrical hull, but it's an artificial remnant of life on Earth, manufactured for psychological reasons. The bottoms of an astronaut's feet rarely feel contact for months on end, with the exception of prescribed stints on the zero-gravity treadmill, mounted perpendicular to the toilet. In space, every surface is a wall.

The human body is, by nature, a ruthlessly efficient machine when it comes to getting rid of things it doesn't need. An astronaut's feet will spontaneously shed their now-unnecessary calluses as though they were sweaters on a summer day; one astronaut feared he'd acquired an orbital strain of trench foot when thick wedges of his heels began falling off. ("Should I be worried?" he asked Houston.) In the best astronauts, the calluses don't just disappear but migrate to the *tops* of their feet, because they've become used to slipping them under footholds. They've learned to move like monkeys through trees; they've become acrobats in weightlessness, trapeze swingers without need for a net.

NASA employs a bevy of psychiatrists and psychologists to help select and monitor its astronaut corps. They *want* to see evolution in their long-duration crews. Trying to live in space as you live on Earth will, in time, break even the most determined mind. Those flipped calluses are hard-won symbols of acceptance, of submission in a fight that cannot otherwise be won. The way swimmers caught in rip tides are told to yield to the currents until they are released, astronauts are meant to surrender to their strange environment until it's not so strange anymore. They need to learn to sleep while strapped to a wall; they need to accept drinking their coffee through a straw; they need to remember that their bowels no longer receive an assist from gravity. They have to become a new version of us to survive in their new home.

But those same psychiatrists and psychologists also need astronauts who refuse to submit to other demands, the sorts of changes that manifest themselves in ways less benign than soft feet. That's where resilience comes in: the ability to endure *acute* stress, usually related to some unfortunate turn of events. Living in space is hard. NASA needs to find people who will be able to endure prolonged separation from their families and friends, even when something bad happens on Earth; who can withstand the considerable mental and physical burdens of rocket launches and spacewalks; who will fight for their lives and the lives of their crewmates when the odds aren't in their favor.

Simply put, great astronauts will bend, because they're adaptable, but not break, because they're resilient. They really are opposite virtues, and even in the exceptional collection of men and women we send into space, it's rare for somebody to possess both in abundance and equal measure. In 2014, when NASA bosses began searching for the first of their astronauts to spend an entire year in space, they looked for candidates within their existing ranks who scored well in both categories. They did not find many.

They set their focus on a fifty-year-old man named Scott Kelly. Outwardly, he was ordinary—neither short nor tall, neither fat nor thin. He had no hair and needed glasses. But inside, Scott was different from almost everyone else on Earth. He was famous within NASA for his response to the infamous "box test," when astronauts are locked inside a coffin-like crate to see how long they can stand the confinement; Scott fell asleep. He had completed a six-month mission previously, and when he needed help from the ground, he had asked for it—a sign of strength, not weakness: *This is really starting to hurt me,* he wrote his girlfriend at the three-quarters mark of his mission, the stretch when despair is most likely to set in. His twin brother, Mark—also an astronaut, now a member of the U.S. Senate for Arizona—had married a congresswoman named Gabby Giffords. Scott was in orbit on his six-month mission when Giffords was shot in a Tucson supermarket parking lot, and while the ensuing hours and days weren't easy, he survived them. He had developed calluses where he didn't have them before.

A NASA psychologist named Al Holland had tested Scott extensively before making his recommendation to NASA: "Highly adaptable and highly resilient," Holland wrote in his final report. Scott Kelly should be the first American to spend a year in space.

Scott wasn't sure whether he wanted to complete another long-duration assignment. "A year is a long time," he said, referring to the lives of his two teenage daughters. But he felt obligated to try. "If someone asks you to do something, especially if it's hard, you shouldn't say no," he told me. His mission was an analog for a crewed journey to Mars; we don't need to make a Mars-capable ship if there aren't members of our species who can also survive the years-long trip.

In a strange way, life on Earth is changing so rapidly, becoming so chaotic and random and extreme, that all of us risk knowing the uncertainty of space travelers, and it is up to us to choose what of our former selves to keep and what to discard. We, unlike computers, can decide to evolve; we're naturally capable of enormous self-adjustment. That's a distinctly human advantage. Californians lived through a fire season in 2020 that turned the sky redder than it is on Mars. The lockdowns that followed COVID-19 gave us perhaps the closest proxy possible to life in orbit. When Scott Kelly went to space in 2015, he tried night after night to find the lights of Houston. Like many of the weather forecasters below, he was surprised how often his home was lost under storms.

———

On Thursday, August 24, 2017, a year after Scott Kelly returned home, a well-organized hurricane inched toward the Texas Gulf Coast, approaching Galveston like a ship easing its way to shore. In contrast to Dixie Alley's relative unfamiliarity with tornadoes, the region had been given more than a century of terrible practice with storms. Galveston had suffered the deadliest hurricane in history in 1900; as many as 12,000 died after American meteorologists ignored the warnings of their more seasoned Cuban colleagues.[19] Hurricanes Carla (1961), Alicia (1983), and Ike (2008) took their own share of Galveston's remains. Now came Harvey.

The National Hurricane Center consulted with both the Storm and Weather Prediction Centers—Harvey was enormous and capable of many bad things—and issued its essential conclusions, reached through its usual computer modeling. Harvey would land somewhere between Corpus Christi and Port O'Connor. The Center's meteorologists believed Harvey would carry fairly strong winds into Houston that weekend, with gusts topping forty miles per hour. Their forecast also predicted heavy but not catastrophic rains, about fifteen inches in parts of the city. Harvey's likely outcome was certainly inconvenience for the country's fourth-biggest city, and possibly

19 Erik Larson, *Isaac's Storm: A Man, a Time, and the Deadliest Hurricane in History* (New York: Vintage Books, 1999). This is a really good book.

considerable flood damage; Houston was built, unwisely in hindsight, in a swamp. No flooding event in Houston could be considered a black swan, exactly, but not many people would have looked at the numbers and thought they added up to disaster.

But at those local offices of the National Weather Service, teams of meteorologists scanned the incoming forecasts and felt their first prickles of unease. The NWS has 122 offices throughout the country, tasked with fine-tuning national forecasts into local ones. The Houston office is the only one that shares its building with its home county's Office of Emergency Management, and there are several nearby reminders of Houston's vulnerability to water. The building is on top of a mound of earth, and the offices are purposely located on the upper floor.

When Harvey made its approach, the local warning coordination meteorologist was fifty-two-year-old Dan Reilly. He had been on the job for twenty-four years. "When something bad is coming, that's really when we need to be at the top of our game," he said. That's also when humans can most employ their particularly human gifts. He didn't dispute the national forecasts, but he wasn't going to accept them blindly, either. Harvey would present challenges because of its size, which mirrored the exponential growth of modern Houston; it's a huge city by area, and different pockets of it might experience radically different amounts of rain. But the forecast was only half of Reilly's concern. It didn't matter how accurate his forecasts were, or his warnings, if nobody heard them.

A few miles away in League City, a shy, usually quiet man named Eric Berger, then forty-four years old, sat in his home office. He was sipping from a glass of Cabernet, toggling between tabs on his computer. The only decoration was the Galileo thermometer on his windowsill. Eric, his wife, Amanda, and their two daughters were living in a rented apartment while they built their dream home in nearby Clear Creek, and he hadn't bothered to unpack. Stacks of boxes rose around him like the walls of a fort.[20]

Eric writes professionally about space, with a particular interest in human spaceflight, but he's also a trained meteorologist. He became fascinated by the weather after Tropical Storm Allison came to town in 2001; he shared his obsession with a modest but devoted audience on his Houston-centric blog, Space City Weather, which he founded in 2015. The night before Harvey arrived, he put the finishing touches on a post titled, "Harvey Late Night: Some Final Thursday Thoughts." He took one more look at the National Hurricane Center's official forecast. Like his peers at the local NWS office, Eric wanted to agree with it. He departed only when it came to the rain.

The unanswered question is what happens to Harvey once it reaches the coast, Eric wrote. *Where will it go, and will it go fast enough? Houston's rainfall totals over the next five days depend on this, and we just don't know.*

As a leisure-time meteorologist, Eric held two advantages over his professional counterparts. The first was that he could express doubt and often did; TV meteorologists, with their bigger audiences, feel greater pressure to express certainty. No one wants to hear them say: "I don't know." Second, Eric wasn't compelled to use any specific model. U.S. government

---

20 Eric is a friend of mine; we met while covering the same rocket launch in Kazakhstan. I later wrote about Eric's weather forecasting for *WIRED*'s January 2018 issue. The story was titled "Meet the Unlikely Hero Who Predicted Hurricane Harvey's Floods." We keep in regular touch. He was embarrassed by the story, a little, but I was glad to celebrate him. Eric's voice is exactly the kind we need to hear—the expert's expert.

forecasters generally use American models, but dozens of quality models are produced around the world, and like the humans who design them, no two make precisely the same predictions. Some models are more reliable than others, and some are more successful at forecasting certain weather phenomena. Their differences explain the "spaghetti plots" that accompany hurricane bulletins, the divergent paths that are weighted and averaged into the dreaded "cone of uncertainty."

Eric's preferred model for hurricanes was not an American one. He liked the European Centre for Medium-Range Weather Forecasts' Integrated Forecasting System, more popularly known as the European model for obvious reasons. Based in Reading, England, and funded by twenty-two members of the European Union and twelve cooperating states, it was better financed than most other models and, at the time, had unrivaled computing power.[21] It was Eric's sense that the European model proved more accurate than even the National Hurricane Center, as though its trans-Atlantic distance gave it a better perspective.

That Thursday night, the European model differed significantly from the U.S. government forecast on the matter of rain, predicting twenty-five inches rather than fifteen. Such a substantial difference gave Eric pause. He returned to the basics of forecasting and did his own calculations, based on the prevailing weather patterns of the upper atmosphere. Eric was worried by the seeming lack of steering currents, which push a

---

21 In February 2020, the National Oceanic and Atmospheric Administration announced a major upgrade in its supercomputing powers, tripling its capacity and doubling its storage and processing speed. According to a news release, the hardware, which will allow NOAA "to unlock possibilities for better forecast model guidance through higher-resolution and more comprehensive Earth-system models," comes online in early 2022.

storm from wherever it is to wherever it's going. The absence of any obvious engine suggested that Harvey might stall over Houston, which meant the European model's graver precipitation forecast made stomach-sense to him. Harvey carried a lot of the gulf's warm waters with it. Houston would be in trouble if the storm stuck around.

Eric took another sip of wine and settled on delivering a prediction he didn't want to believe but did: *Big-time floods are coming to Texas*, he wrote. He gave Houston two options: *pretty bad*, or *really really bad*.

Normally, Eric's individual posts saw between 5,000 and 10,000 visitors. In the next twenty-four hours, that particular entry received 207,334. Overnight, Eric had become a locus of trust, at the center of two storms. He wasn't sure how word about him had spread, but it had spread nonetheless, and now he was a voice of considerable authority. People began coming to him with specific questions about the weather and how it might affect *them*. They weren't coming to Dan Reilly at the National Weather Service for advice. Nor were they asking their search engines. They were coming to Eric Berger, a husband and father who was sitting next to his Galileo thermometer, in his temporary accommodations, sipping from another glass of red wine.

Of course, Eric wasn't depending on his trick knee for his forecasts. He was using the best information available to him, much of it in the form of data; he was then using his experience and knowledge to interpret that data in his particular way. His new readers seemed to understand that about him. Almost immediately, they saw him as more than a simple messenger. He was their appointed guide, charged with leading them through fearsome, unfamiliar territory. One reader asked him to predict the rainfall in San Antonio, 200 miles west. Someone asked about Colorado County, and someone else about the neighborhoods near Ellington Field. One woman wanted to know Eric's opinion about possible flight cancellations on Saturday; her husband was supposed to leave for a business trip. A man named Petey James noted that the big fight between Conor McGregor and Floyd Mayweather was taking place Saturday night, and he wanted to know whether he should scrap his plans to watch it at a local bar. A woman named Deb Walters asked whether she should still host a planned party near Dacus on Saturday afternoon.

It's alarming, in hindsight, how many people saw Eric as a kind of oracle, many of them strangers to him until their arrival at his blog. His regular followers knew that he could be trusted, but hundreds of thousands of people in danger had decided without much supporting evidence to follow his lead—exactly the sort of irrational decision-making that spooks data scientists.

"These are dangerous times," Tom Nichols, an academic and professor at the U.S. Naval War College wrote. "Never have so many people had access to so much knowledge, and yet been so resistant to learning anything."[22] A dangerous strain of anti-expertise has infected our post-Internet lives. Some potent combination of media illiteracy—any nut job with a Facebook page can become a limitless source of misinformation—a growing distrust of "elites" and traditional messengers, and the Dunning-Kruger effect[23] has led a significant percentage

---

22 Tom Nichols, *The Death of Expertise: The Campaign Against Established Knowledge and Why It Matters* (New York: Oxford University Press, 2017).

23 Social psychologists David Dunning and Justin Kruger scientifically validated something most of us already suspect: The most incompetent people often see themselves as highly competent, and people who are actually capable tend to underestimate themselves—because they're "smart enough to know what I don't know."

of the population to believe they are smarter than actual smart people. All opinions are given equal weight, whether they come from someone who has spent a few hours in the Internet's darkest corners or someone who has dedicated his or her life to arrive at the opposite understanding. As in much of the American response to COVID-19, the line between information and misinformation has never seemed so blurred, and the value of actual intelligence has never been so high.

Unfortunately, the *Moneyball* revolution has also contributed to the problem, the unintended collateral damage that accompanied its real contributions to many aspects of our lives. If a guy working at a pork-and-beans factory could prove baseball's so-called experts wrong about so many things, then why should we trust anyone in authority? We can all fashion ourselves as experts.

Fortunately, Eric Berger was someone who deserved Houston's collective faith. In those anxious days before Harvey made landfall, he found a sweet spot of our time, the dream scenario for any of us who wish to do or make something important and lasting. He was someone who years ago couldn't have commanded an audience, but given modern tools and sensibilities, now he had found one. He was *adaptable*. He also had the talent and expertise to have earned it. If he was forced to rely partially on instinct by the wildness of the circumstances, he knew that his was an informed instinct. He felt needed, and he felt ready to meet that need. He was *resilient*.

When Eric woke up that Friday to find his legion of new visitors, he also found that the models had been updated. Dan Reilly had seen them, too. Now the computers forecast far heavier rains than they had only the night before, and the models had started to align in their fearsome predictions, spitting out projected totals that nobody in Houston could imagine: twenty-five inches, then thirty, and finally fifty. More than four feet of rain. Models that usually expressed precipitation amounts in shades of blue had turned pitch black.

For someone as careful as Eric, a reputation for overstatement would be nearly as bad as a history of underestimation. You can see the appeal of hysteria: If a meteorologist wishes never to repeat James Spann's "dusting" disaster, he or she need only predict calamity every time out. Sooner or later, he or she will be proved right: Bad weather will come. But Eric had determined that he would never engage in "storm porn," the frenzies that make people deaf to warnings that actually need to be heard.

That's because he had been wrong before. Back in 2005, when he wrote occasionally about the weather for the local paper, he had misfired, along with many others, about the dangers of Hurricane Rita: *I am not going to sugar-coat this, my friends*, he'd written. *As a Houston resident and property owner, I am truly mortified right now.* People suffered for the needless evacuation, and his own error had made an impression on him. His site's motto was "Hype-free forecasts for greater Houston." He had learned that there is one way to be right about the weather, and two ways to be wrong.

On that Friday before the worst of Harvey hit, he looked at the models again, and he looked at the comments piling up under his posts—he saw the names of his neighbors, and he saw that they were still making plans. The storm's leading edge had arrived, and rain had started falling against his window. Eric looked at the rain, and then he looked at his hands on his keyboard.

A very serious flooding situation is coming, he wrote.

He wrote it two more times for emphasis.

A very serious flooding situation is coming.
A very serious flooding situation is coming.
He looked at the clock. It was 3:15 p.m. He remembered Deb Walters in Dacus, and he hoped she had canceled her party.

———

There was nothing Eric Berger, Dan Reilly, the National Weather Service, or the National Hurricane Center could do to stop Harvey, or lessen its rains. In some ways, James Spann was right that the weather occupies a place outside of our reach. It's not entirely within our understanding anymore, if it ever was. But it is not outside our imagination, or our empathy. Over the coming terrible hours and days, meteorologists saved untold lives in Houston, because their readers and listeners believed them when the weather was beyond belief. They formed a rescue chain joined together by faith rather than hands.

In the middle was Eric Berger. He was a human being, and somehow the warnings sounded different coming from him. He told his readers that he was emptying his garage in advance of the storm, ferrying his own precious belongings up to his apartment, including light fixtures, a microwave, and a tub destined for his new house. He shared that Amanda and his daughters were leaving their apartment for her sister's house, built on pilings and less exposed to the wind. Eric chose to stay with his readers, behind his growing wall of boxes. He watched the rain falling hard enough for it to seem more like a solid than a liquid, and he felt an almost spiritual need to ensure his neighbors followed his family's lead to higher ground. On Saturday night, when Harvey stalled, and its bands backed up like traffic, and parts of Houston saw five inches of rain fall in an hour, he began using language that was available only to someone like him: *This created what meteorologists properly call a seething nexus of hate*, he wrote.

By that Sunday, a million people were reading Space City Weather, including the guidance-seeking leadership of the Houston Methodist Hospital and Baylor College of Medicine. That's how desperate the city was for a human voice. *I wish we could tell you when the rains will end*, Eric wrote, *but we can't. Here's one thing we are sure of, however. The rains will end. After that the sun will come out.*

It was Tuesday before he could write: *It's over.* Nearly seventy people were dead, many of them drowned in their cars, and $75 billion in property had been lost. Eric had been right to be worried, and his readers had been right to put their faith in him. It would be a mistake to think of him as some kind of meteorological oracle, a human barometer. That's not who or what he is. The machines and models could have proved more correct in their forecasts, as they so often do. They are remarkable instruments. But after Eric had made his forecast, he had done something that no machine or model could ever do: He made people feel less alone in the middle of the worst storm of their lives. He shared his own fears and losses. He wrote Petey James and told him not to go to the bar, and he was relieved to learn that Deb Walters had, in fact, canceled her party.

Sometimes we're trying to crack simple and unchanging systems, the way Terry Kniess saw opportunity in *The Price Is Right*. But especially these days they're more likely to be complex and in motion, like the weather, or the baseball season, or the strangeness of life in space or during a pandemic, and that's when our searching, experienced eyes and knack for metamorphosis can shine brightest. The advantage returns to us—our opportunities are their greatest—when we're asked to find within ourselves the hearts of astronauts: when there is no history upon which to rely, when our future doesn't look anything like our past. Chaos demands the best from us. And sometimes, as it did with shy, careful Eric Berger, chaos finds the best of us, too.

POLITICS

Lies, Damned Lies, and Statistics.

Numbers are often portrayed as indisputable, as though statistics never lie. When we get complacent about data, we can reach wrong, even dangerous conclusions, including about our fellow human beings. The algorithmic tools that are meant to improve our understanding of one another have, in fact, blinded and divided us. True clarity won't return until our former, more rigorous methods do. When there are no good shortcuts, you need to return to intimate, analog work.

Conor McGregor is the greatest politician I've ever met. I hung out with the Irish MMA fighter in New York City in early 2015, not long after he'd left a German rival named Dennis Siver with enough gashes in his face to look as though he'd been glassed.[1] I'd watched that fight and been taken with Conor immediately. I liked the way he fought—he stood straight up, his fists cocked almost foppishly, like the gentlemen pugilists

---

1   I wrote about Conor McGregor for *Esquire* multiple times. The New York story was titled "Conor McGregor Doesn't Believe in Death" and appeared in the April 2015 issue.

from the time of monocles—but there was something magnetic about *him*, a dangerous charisma, a wild charm. I caught him during that strange transition from obscurity (he had been a plumber in his native Dublin) to global celebrity, long before Petey James had asked Eric Berger to help him decide whether to brave a hurricane to watch Conor fight.[2] His next scheduled bout, against Brazilian champion José Aldo, would make him whatever he wanted to be. He had a tattoo of a gorilla eating a human heart on his chest, but he didn't yet have a tiger's face on his stomach. On that freezing day in New York, he was twenty-six years old and on the move, a bullet train between stations.

It's challenging to be in the company of someone like Conor McGregor. It's *spiritually* challenging. During our unsettling time together, he walked down the middle of Manhattan streets rather than on sidewalks, because he had not personally agreed to our systems of road sharing. He ate the way storms consume coastlines. He saw fashion as another means for him to apply pressure to other men, and we went into the Christian Louboutin store in the Meatpacking District, where he tried on a pair of clownish sneakers, glare-white with chunks of jagged plastic all over them. They cost $1,700. Conor put them on and looked at himself in the mirror. Dee Devlin, his then girlfriend, now wife, was with us. "If you like them, get them," she said. Conor looked at them again. "If someone says something—

---

2 The seed of the Floyd Mayweather fight was actually planted that day in New York. I asked Conor, innocently enough, who would win a fight between them. "If I fought Floyd, I would kill him in less than thirty seconds," he said. "It would take me less than thirty seconds to wrap around him like a boa constrictor and strangle him." That made such good sense to me, I buried the quote fairly deep in the story. But that quote went viral, Mayweather saw it, and things happened the way they happen. I did not receive a cut of the nine-figure purse.

whap," he said, and those ridiculous sneakers were suddenly slicing through the air. Conor was firing roundhouse kicks in the middle of the store. I was thinking, *This is not something we normally do here, Conor*. The salesman sported a different look, which was: *Please don't kick me in the face*.

When I say that Conor was a great politician, I mean I've never seen someone so good at campaigning. He was the champion of so many causes, and the foe of so many others, and he had the power to make you subscribe or unsubscribe to them instantly, even if they ran contrary to tenets you've held sacred your entire life. He was so unlike me, I marveled. I follow rules. Conor bought the shoes and wore them out, splashing through slushy puddles, because why worry about the state of $1,700 sneakers? I care about the condition of expensive objects! But when you're in the company of someone who questions everything, *you* start to question everything, including everything about yourself. "He makes you believe everything he believes," Dana White, the UFC's president, told me later. Conor sensed that I was wobbled by his company. "You tell someone the truth about themselves and they crumble," he said obliquely. Dee was more direct, leaning into my ear: "He wants you to be better than you are."

At some point, we began talking about time. I'm extremely punctual. I spend a lot of time worrying about being late, even though I have never been late for anything in my extremely punctual life. Conor doesn't obey clocks. He sleeps when he's tired. He eats when he's hungry. Hours, minutes, seconds are human inventions. Why accept the limits imposed by artificial structures? Why feel the need to follow their relentless dictates? Is that any way to live a life? I didn't have a very good answer. All I could think was, *Because*.

Again and again, Conor challenged my allegiance to

convention. Sometimes, he cast *belief* as a negative, constraining force, a governor. "*Ritual* is another word for fear, manifested in a different way," he said. Sometimes, belief for him was a powerful, positive agent. He believed he could be something other than a plumber. He believed he would beat the hell out of Dennis Siver. He believed he would soon conquer José Aldo. (He did, with one punch, in thirteen seconds.) Belief could either limit us or make us limitless, depending on whether we saw it as a master or a tool. Conor told me flat out, as though he were telling me his lunch order, that he didn't think he would die, because he doesn't believe in death. "Even in death, they say your vision, you can see everything," he said.

That's when I did something very stupid.

I can't really explain today what I was thinking, except I got caught up in Conor's belief that he could walk on ceilings if he wanted badly enough to be upside down. We had been talking about submissions like chokes and arm bars, and I thought perhaps I could resist a rear naked choke. Not that I could claw my way out of it, but I could simply decide not to go to sleep, like a kid determined to stay up past his bedtime. I stated my belief out loud. Conor nodded at my suggestion— *all righty then*—and stripped down to his underwear, because of course he did. He climbed on my back and put his left heel on the point of my hip and dug his right heel into my groin. That gorilla on his chest burrowed its face between my shoulder blades. Then Conor slipped his right arm in front of my neck and crossed his left arm over the top of my spine, as though his arms were the blades of giant scissors. I couldn't see his face, but he was smiling with his mouth, and he was crazy with his eyes. He squeezed.

Conor was right. We should question authority. We should seek to defy expectation. But belief will take you only so far.

Reality—the fundamental truth, the laws of gravity and every-thing else—can't be overlooked, however much we might wish to ignore it. Cars will win every fight with pedestrians. Clocks will tick. And the reality is that if a skilled MMA professional puts enough pressure on your carotid artery to cut off the blood flow between your heart and your brain, you will pass the fuck out.

The idea that numbers never lie is obscene. Numbers are routinely used to deceive. (Raw numbers are especially prob-lematic, but percentages and probabilities can also be used to misrepresent reality.) Worse, because statistical lies employ numbers, they are more likely to be accepted as gospel—and so are more insidious than regular, prosaic lies. Humans, despite much evidence to the contrary, are fairly skilled at sniffing out even the most lyrical nonsense. But who can argue with math? Numbers are binary. Numbers are fact. *Numbers never lie.*

Malcolm Gladwell, the patron saint of books like this one, fell into such a trap in his book *Talking to Strangers.* Perhaps because his previous works had been criticized for their re-liance on anecdotal evidence[3]—any argument can be proved if you're selective enough—Gladwell cited an unimpeachable-seeming statistic in a section on the poet Sylvia Plath. "Poets die young," Gladwell wrote. "And of every occupational cat-egory, [poets] have far and away the highest suicide rates—as much as fives times higher than the general population."

Five times higher. That is a fairly exact multiplier. It also

---

3 I imagine this book will receive similar criticisms. I reject them. True stories are the original evidence.

seems, on the surface at least, like something that's probably right. That number *feels* like it's true. Poets are weirdos. They're introspective. They wear black. They're probably vegetarians. Of course they kill themselves more often than the rest of us do.

A dedicated reader named Andrew Ferguson was nevertheless dissatisfied by the claim. Unfortunately for Gladwell, Ferguson was also reviewing his book for the *Atlantic*.[4] Ferguson's immediate concern was the "occupational category" part of the poet-suicide equation. Was Gladwell referring to professional poets? Anyone who wrote poetry? How many poets realistically could list "poet" as their occupation? Surely most of them, even the most successful of them, have other jobs with which to finance their ennui, and those other jobs might be part of their problem.

Ferguson checked with the Bureau of Labor Statistics, curator of the Standard Occupational Classification System and its 867 ways to make a living. He did not find "poet" among them. The closest he found was "Writers and Authors," a category so broad—"baggy" is the superior adjective that Ferguson chose—as to be useless when it comes to mining any specific truths about poets and their predilections.

Gladwell, however, had provided a citation for his supposed mathematical fact. Superscript is oddly authoritative; you might not enjoy footnotes, but subconsciously you respect them. Ferguson wondered whether there was a statistical method he was missing. He dutifully followed a trail of citations. Gladwell had mined his statistic from a 1998 edition of the ominous-sounding journal *Death Studies*; a college professor

---

4 Andrew Ferguson, "Malcolm Gladwell Reaches His Tipping Point," *Atlantic*, September 10, 2019.

named Mark Runco had included it in a paper titled "Suicide and Creativity." Runco, in turn, cited his own source, a clinical psychologist named Kay Redfield Jamison. She had produced the "five times" statistic in her book *Touched with Fire*.

Ferguson, a special kind of obsessive, now wondered: How did Jamison come up with that number in the first place? She didn't make it up, he discovered, although she might have, and a lot of people would have believed her. She studied the lives of "all major British and Irish poets born between 1705 and 1805," a rather specific time and place that perhaps isn't relevant to modern suicidal math. Never mind. How did she determine whether a poet was "major" or not? She consulted old poetry anthologies to see how often he or she was mentioned. She determined that thirty-six major poets were born in that century-long span, making major poets the rarest birds. Apparently a major poet is born, on average, only every two years and nine months.

Two of the major poets born in the British Isles between 1705 and 1805 had gone on to kill themselves. In his review, Ferguson pointed out that one was a doctor, and so might have killed himself for physician-related causes; the other was seventeen, and so perhaps a victim of more routine teenage angst. Still, two of Jamison's sample population had died by suicide. Two of thirty-six is a little more than 5 percent. About 1 percent of non-major poets die by suicide. Major poets, therefore, are five times more likely to kill themselves, including, alas, the doomed but indisputably major Sylvia Plath. So said Kay Redfield Jamison, and next said Mark Runco, and next said Malcolm Gladwell.

Not so fast, said Andrew Ferguson. "This is thin soup," he wrote. "But for Gladwell, as for so many consumers of social science, the intuition becomes real only if it's quantified, even when any kind of useful quantification is implausible on its face." Gladwell's desire to answer his critics had made him vulnerable to a different, more modern error of belief: that we can measure the immeasurable. With a vigor that made his review go viral, Ferguson denounced such "sketchy statistical manipulations" and "pseudo-science." An argument isn't more or less valid because of the *kind* of evidence used in its support. Whether a case is empirical or observational is neither here nor there; it's the *quality* of the evidence that matters. The five times statistic was replete with quantitative sins, from a minuscule sample size to selection bias. It was worthless.

John Pfaff, a professor at Fordham Law and a self-described criminal justice quant, held up Ferguson's thorough debunking as though he'd revealed the bogeyman who lives under the bed of every writer of fact: "[O]ften secondary sources launder really bad counting," Pfaff warned.[5] You need to go to the original source. Ferguson had gone to the original source, and he had discovered a spring of statistical bullshit.

There are countless examples of numbers being used to deceive rather than clarify. Perhaps not surprisingly, politicians and government bureaucracies have proved both good at, and given to, statistical mythmaking. On the spectrum of sin, an earnest but failed attempt to quantify something that can't be quantified is fairly minor. Political lies, particularly when they serve to change something fundamental about how we're governed, can lead to disastrous real-world results.[6]

Under the Donald Trump administration, for instance, the U.S. Consumer Financial Protection Bureau was accused by

---

5 John Pfaff wrote this on his Twitter account, @JohnFPfaff, on September 10, 2019.
6 I am not some weird anti-government person. But because I believe in government, I want government to be good.

a former employee of using "statistical gimmicks" to roll back proposed Obama-era regulations designed to curb the problematic payday loan industry. Providing short-term, high-interest loans to people who can't live paycheck-to-paycheck has become both highly lucrative (despite its being effectively illegal in twenty states, there are more payday-loan storefronts in the rest of America than McDonald's restaurants) and parasitic to the working poor (half of all payday loans become toxic, accruing interest payments larger than the amount of the original loan). The new regulations would have limited how much people could borrow and how often, hopefully preventing their becoming entangled in unpayable debt. According to the former employee, who left a scathing fourteen-page memo in his out-box as a parting gift, Trump's incoming appointees arrived determined to gut the rules and set about making a supposedly data-driven case to nix them.[7] In so doing, they demonstrated "fundamental misunderstandings" about the agency's role and research, and pressured the bureau's rank-and-file to use "inaccurate and inappropriate" data to build the counterargument to the argument those same employees had spent five years making.[8]

U.S. Customs and Border Protection was also found to have padded certain statistics, trying to justify the Mexican border wall. According to the agency, assaults on its officers increased in 2016 and again in 2017, reversing a trend of more peaceful interactions with illegal immigrants. In the fiscal year 2017, the

---

7   Rules can't be changed arbitrarily or for political reasons; to escape risk of legal challenge, new rules must be justified by research that calls the effectiveness of old rules into question.

8   Nicholas Confessore and Stacy Cowley, "Trump Appointees Manipulated Agency's Payday Lending Research, Ex-Staffer Claims," *New York Times*, April 29, 2020.

numbers were shocking: There were apparently 786 assaults, an increase of 73 percent, despite a significant decrease in apprehensions. A more violent border demanded greater security, did it not? Except that the numbers were inaccurate by most rational measures. In one case, a single incident somehow accounted for 126 assaults. How? Because it involved seven officers and six detainees using three different projectiles: rocks, bottles, and tree branches. Seven times six times three equals 126.[9]

Such statistical quackery is not just a Trumpist phenomenon, of course. The relatively benign government of British Columbia, Canada, has claimed that 23 percent of its forests qualify as "old growth," or forests that have been left untouched for centuries. ("True" old growth takes about 250 years to develop.) That's 13 million hectares, which, in a province that derives significant revenue from logging, seems like a considerable buffer between today's landscape and a barren one. But three ecologists who previously worked for the government did a deeper dive on those numbers and found that, in fact, an alarmingly small amount of old growth remains. The scientists believe there are only 35,000 hectares of productive old-growth forest within provincial boundaries; those millions of other classified hectares include low-productivity forest—untouched, perhaps, but only because they consist of small trees high in the mountains. Rachel Holt, one of the authors of the study, argued that even within those 35,000 sacred hectares, only 2.7 percent of the trees are actually old. "We're talking a tiny fraction of a fraction," she said. "We've basically logged it all."[10]

9 Debbie Nathan, "How the Border Patrol Faked Statistics Showing a 73 Percent Rise in Assaults Against Agents," Intercept, April 23, 2018.
10 Stephanie Wood, "B.C. Old-Growth Data 'Misleading' Public on Remaining Ancient Forest: Independent Report," Narwhal, June 4, 2020.

Such "bad stats" aren't a case against good analytics; they are an all too human failure. But in the rush to quantify our existence, too many of us have become too accepting of supposed statistical fact, including when they're relayed to us by our governments. Maybe we're too scared to admit that we don't understand the math. Maybe we don't want to seem like Luddites. Maybe the analytics movement has been a little too effective in its self-promotion and occasional bullying. Bullshit is still bullshit, and sometimes numbers, like narrative, are used to help spread it, and about subjects far more serious than the suicidal tendencies of major poets. Besides, everybody knows that it's dentists who kill themselves. Four out of five, or something like that.

———

Fermi estimation is a quick-and-dirty method of bullshit detection when lies are expressed as numbers. It's a curious, practiced way of thinking—extremely on brand for the Eye Test—as well as a way to make reasonable guesses about unknowable figures. Enrico Fermi was a gifted Italian-American physicist who built the world's first nuclear reactor in Chicago; he was also a beloved teacher who mentored eight future Nobel Prize winners. Today, companies such as Google include "Fermi problems" in their recruitment process, and certain professors like to put them in their exams. Good answers are proof that someone can think logically, making them more likely to be right when they make guesses, and, more valuably for our purposes, harder to deceive. Doing Fermi estimations makes your brain both more and less pliable.

Here is a classic Fermi problem: "How many piano tuners are in New York City?" No one happens to know such an arcane fact. But it's a knowable answer, and it's also one that most people, at first blush, tend to get hugely wrong.

Be honest—what answer popped into your head when you first read that question? Unless you're familiar with Fermi and his work, your answer was probably in the low thousands. (I asked my parents, both professors, the same question: My dad guessed 5,000, and my mum guessed 500.) If I, or someone with the requisite authority like my father, were to tell you that 5,000 piano tuners ply their trade in New York City, you would probably believe me. You have no reason not to believe me. You have no concept of what the actual answer might be.

Except that by using Fermi's methods, you could come up with a *plausible* answer, through a series of estimations that you probably *can* make. How would you begin to figure out how many piano tuners are in New York City? (Google uses Fermi's adopted home of Chicago in their quiz, if you want to prep.) You'd start with the population of New York City—eight million or so? Now, how many individual households are in New York City? Some families, some single people, some in between—eight million, divided by maybe three per household, something like that? That gives us a rough estimate of 2.6 million households. How many of those households have a piano? Now our estimates start getting harder—confirmation bias and other subjectivities creep into the mix. I don't know many people who own pianos, and all I hear about New York accommodations is that they are small. I'm going to say that one household in twenty owns a piano. That leaves us with a now quite rough estimate that there are 130,000 pianos in New York City.

How often are pianos tuned? I haven't the slightest idea. I'll assume that some people tune their pianos obsessively, and

120

other people haven't heard their pianos played since grandma died. Let's guess that the average piano is tuned every two years, which seems reasonable to me, a man who neither plays nor tunes pianos. That means 65,000 pianos are tuned in New York City every year.

Now we know our demand. Which brings us to our supply: How many piano tuners would be required to tune 65,000 pianos a year? Well, how long does it take to tune a piano? An hour? Two? Let's posit that in a solid day, a semi-industrious piano tuner can knock out four pianos, what with traffic and a break for a nice lunch. (Professional piano tuners strike me as more careful than driven.) And let's assume that piano tuners work like nearly everyone else—five days a week, a couple of weeks off for vacation. Four pianos a day, that's twenty pianos a week, that's 1,000 pianos a year. Return to our original suspicion that 65,000 pianos are tuned in New York every year, and divide that number by our estimated annual workload of 1,000 pianos, and we might guess that 65 or so piano tuners realize their perfectly tuned dreams in New York City.

Do we know that for a fact? Dear readers, we do not. (The correct answer to Google's Chicago question is about sixty, which means I've underestimated the answer for New York City by a considerable margin: Three times the city suggests three times the piano tuners, or about 180.) But we do know that if, for whatever reason, someone tried to tell us that 5,000 piano tuners work in New York City, we could guess that he or she was either misinformed or lying.

Fermi estimation is neither for or against the use of numbers; it's a defense against the misuse of them. It can as readily employ numbers to counter false narratives. David Epstein, a deep thinker and author (and another friend of mine, because every writer apparently knows every other writer), puts out an excellent newsletter.[11] On August 11, 2020, he wrote about Fermi estimations and their uses, including calculating the number of piano tuners working in major metropolitan centers. After the devastating explosion in Beirut on August 4, David watched his Twitter feed fill up with its usual conspiracy theories and crank assertions—that the explosion was caused by a missile, or a cache of Hezbollah weaponry stockpiled by the port. Then he saw a tweet from a user named @quantian1 who used an unexpected series of Fermi estimations to make a different case.

Explosions of disparate causes have widely varying "detonation velocities," or the rates at which their shock waves expand. Watching video of the blast, assuming it was taken by a smartphone at the usual rate of thirty frames per second, and using Google maps to estimate the distance from the epicenter of the blast to a nearby stack of grain elevators, @quantian1 calculated a detonation velocity of about 3,000 meters per second. "Consistent with ammonium nitrate, not black powder," he or she wrote in conclusion. (Ammonium nitrate has an actual detonation velocity of about 2,700 meters per second.) The cause of the explosion in fact turned out to be a pile of warehoused ammonium nitrate. A Fermi estimation, in this case using hard data, proved remarkably accurate, and also, in more hair-trigger circumstances, might have prevented a retaliatory strike or the scapegoating of some politically expedient target. Fertilizer, not gunpowder, is a crucial distinction. It was also one that could be made without stepping foot inside the resulting crater.

---

11 David is the author of two excellent and popular books: *The Sports Gene: Inside the Science of Extraordinary Athletic Performance* (New York: Penguin Group, 2013) and *Range: Why Generalists Triumph in a Specialized World* (New York: Riverhead Books, 2019). I highly recommend both.

———

Indian Springs, Nevada, seems an unlikely place to go to war. It's a desert town of 1,000 or so residents, about forty-five minutes northwest of Las Vegas, near the appropriately named settlement of Mercury. It gets unreasonably hot in the summer. It has a small public library. But it's home to Creech Air Force Base, which means it's home to the 15th Reconnaissance Squadron and 3rd Special Operations Squadron, which means it's home to a battery of young men and women who pilot lethal military drones over war zones from the relative comfort of their air-conditioned bunkers. Using joysticks, they can drop Hellfire missiles on distant targets half the world away. Despite their separation from the consequences of their actions, the people who do the job can become seriously damaged by it. Technology has made humans killing other humans, whatever the cause, both easier to do and difficult to digest. Modern war necessitates a lot of self-deception.

Four former servicemen went to the *Guardian* to tell their awful story. One of them, a ginger-haired twenty-nine-year-old named Michael Haas who showed up to his interview in a Chicago Blackhawks jersey, said of his experience: "Ever step on ants and never give it another thought? That's what you are made to think of the targets—as just black blobs on a screen. You start to do those psychological gymnastics to make it easier to do what you have to do—they deserved it, they chose their side. You had to kill part of your conscience to keep doing your job every day—and ignore those voices telling you this wasn't right."[12]

---

12   Ed Pilkington, "Life as a Drone Operator: 'Ever Step on Ants and Never Give It Another Thought?'" *Guardian*, November 19, 2015.

Most technology is neither good nor bad innately. What matters is how we use it. Rockets can take us into space and ferry us to the moon; they can also be used to deliver warheads into the bedrooms of faraway families. This is true of analytics. Technology, including technology that seeks to model and codify our behavior, can sometimes help us make better decisions. It can also reduce our fellow humans to data points—especially when we're already inclined to think of particular humans as *others*—making the truth of their lives more unknowable to us than it already is. "Deep memetic frames" compound the ways we already simplify and try to make sense of the world's chaos; rendering people faceless is a loaded first step toward hateful belief.[13] The same instruments that can help us understand ourselves better can also make us blind to the daily reality of our fellow humans or, worse, cast them as the enemy—as *black blobs on a screen.* Math, particularly exponential math, can be a terrible agent of remove.

It doesn't, then, take much of a turn to make modern technology sinister, and we've proved alarmingly capable of being both the screwdriver and the screw. Lies are one problem; our modern means to *amplify* those lies, and the malignant real-world actions they inspire, are another. The use of bots on social media is an obvious example. Game recognizes the automation game, and suddenly hostile foreign governments can interfere in domestic elections by making the fringe seem larger than it is, sowing mistrust and division. One recent study of Twitter found 167,000 apps fueling an army of automated accounts, churning out tens of millions of tweets

---

13 Whitney Phillips, "We Need to Talk about Talking about QAnon," *WIRED*, September 24, 2020.

that violated Twitter's rules against abuse.[14] In the European Union, work is underway on a "swarm" of AI-powered drones designed to patrol borders for illegal immigrants, reducing desperate asylum seekers to their heat signatures; there are fears the drones will be equipped with Tasers and rubber bullets. "It's only a matter of time before a drone will be able to take action to stop people," Noel Sharkey, emeritus professor of robotics and artificial intelligence at Sheffield University, has warned.[15] In North Carolina, politicians used data to write laws to disenfranchise African-American voters, a methodical approach to voter suppression that saw TV host John Oliver aghast that someone had finally "Moneyballed racism."

British prime minister Boris Johnson's already tumultuous tenure nearly devolved into total anarchy when his government's use of algorithms struck many Britons as anti-human. After COVID-19 ended the 2019–2020 school year early, secondary-school teachers were asked to predict the grades of their students in their comprehensive exams, known as A-levels. Like the American SATs, A-level results determine university placement. Teachers thought the best of their kids, and final grades ended up higher than usual: a kindness inflation. That qualified too many students for too few places, and Ofqual, the United Kingdom's public overseer of exam results, used an algorithm to flatten the scores. That meant 40 percent of students opened their results and found them lower than they had expected, and their chosen universities sometimes revoked their placements. At the bottom end, students

---

14 Andy Greenberg, "Twitter Still Can't Keep Up with Its Flood of Junk Accounts, Study Finds," *WIRED*, February 8, 2019.
15 Zach Campbell, "Swarms of Drones, Piloted by Artificial Intelligence, May Soon Patrol Europe's Borders," Intercept, May 11, 2019.

who had been given passing marks received failing grades for exams they did not take. The courses of their lives had been changed by machines.[16]

Worse, the algorithm—touted by the government the way all artificial intelligence is sold to us: fair, unbiased, objective—was in fact particularly ruthless when it came to students of disadvantage. One of its bedrock considerations was the past performance of a student's school as well as the student him- or herself. Students at schools that traditionally had good results—elite, expensive colleges—saw their grades go up by nearly 5 percent; students at city schools in poor areas, largely immigrants and people of color, saw theirs go down, sometimes as much as two grade levels. Johnson's Conservative government appeared to be using the missed exams as a reassertion of *place*, resurrecting the classism that still haunts British life.

Leyston Sixth Form College, a school in London's still-gritty East End, saw 47 percent of its students receive a grade cut. Gill Burbridge, the school's principal, called it a scandal, and she was far from alone in her disgust. "Young people and parents right across the country, in every town and city, feel let down and betrayed," Keir Starmer, leader of the opposition Labour Party, said in a statement. Legal challenges were mounted, and there were widespread calls for the head of Gavin Williamson, Britain's beset education minister. Eventually, the machine-adjusted results were scrapped, and students were awarded the grades that their teachers had given them.[17] Williamson said he was "incredibly sorry for all those students

16 Megan Specia, "Parents, Students and Teachers Give Britain a Failing Grade Over Exam Results," *New York Times*, August 14, 2020.
17 Aubrey Allegretti, "Exams U-turn: Teacher Estimates to Be Used for GCSE and A-level Grades as Controversial Algorithm Ditched," news.sky.com, August 18, 2020.

who have been through this," leaving the word "this" to do an awful lot of work.

Roger Taylor, the silver-haired head of Ofqual, also apologized for his role in the debacle. (He naturally posted his *mea culpa* online.) "We realized that we had taken the wrong road here, and needed to change course," he said. "It became very clear to us that this was not commanding public support." It didn't take a genius to figure that out. On August 16, there had been student protests across the country, with some burning their A-level results for the cameras. At an angry demonstration in London's Parliament Square, one student told the crowd how she'd lost her place in medical school because of her deflated results. After chants of "Fuck the system" and "Fuck Eton," the elite of the elite, a new chant rang out: "Fuck the algorithm."[18]

———

During 2020's apocalyptic fire season along the American Pacific coast, smartphone cameras weren't capturing how red the sky looked to the people standing under it.[19] Some users cried conspiracy—tech giants didn't want the world to know how fearsome the situation had become—but in truth the problem was an algorithm that was struggling to make sense of things it wasn't designed to understand. Sony builds nearly half of all smartphone cameras and trains them to see by feeding them hundreds of millions of images; the machine then uses that knowledge to reproduce accurate images of similar

---

18 I watched video of the protests on the Twitter feed of @HUCKmagazine, posted on August 16, 2020.
19 Ian Bogost, "Your Phone Wasn't Built for the Apocalypse," *Atlantic*, September 11, 2020.

things. But the algorithm wasn't fed pictures of fire skies, leaving it confused by the amount of red it was registering in otherwise ordinary-seeming scenes of houses, cars, and trees. These weren't volcanoes, after all. Some people's smartphones corrected what they decided must have been an error, making light conditions seem more typical than they were and washing out a horribly vibrant reality—because that reality was so extreme, their cameras doubted their own lenses. They didn't believe they were seeing what they were seeing.

After decades of dominating our political conversations, polls, too, appear increasingly unable to capture the truth about us. In 2020, when President Joe Biden beat Donald Trump, national polls missed the mark by even larger margins than they had in 2016, when they had overwhelmingly predicted that Hillary Clinton would win. Certain state polls were also catastrophically wrong. The day before the 2020 presidential election, Biden was expected to win Wisconsin by more than eight points; he won by a whisper, 0.7 percent. Ohio, Florida, and even Texas were thought to be statistical dead heats and maybe even in play for the Democrats; Trump won all three by comfortable margins.

The misfires extended beyond Trump's weirdly inelastic popularity, influencing down-ticket races: Polls overestimated the potential of Democratic candidates by an average of four points—a margin of error that made those polls effectively useless in close races. Republican senator Susan Collins of Maine didn't lead in a single pre-election poll over Sara Gideon, her Democratic opponent. Collins won the actual race by more than eight points. Democrat Jaime Harrison seemed in the running in South Carolina, where he faced off against Senator Lindsey Graham, the Republican stalwart. Outside money started pouring into the apparently competitive state, and Harrison raised more cash in the final quarter than any Senate candidate in U.S. political history. He lost by more than ten points.

Fairly or not, Nate Silver's vaunted FiveThirtyEight.com took much of the post-election heat. Silver's models, which weigh and aggregate a number of outside polls, had become famous in 2012, when he had correctly forecast every state's preference for either President Barack Obama or Mitt Romney, including nine notoriously difficult-to-predict swing states. Analytics had once again proved unbeatable. In 2016, however, Silver had fared less well. He was *less wrong* than most; three days before the election, the Princeton Election Consortium gave Clinton a 99 percent chance of victory, while Silver gave her a 71.4 percent chance. Wrong is still wrong, and Trump was one of the few presidential candidates in history who woke up *surprised* he was going to be president.

Like every good scientist, including data scientists, Silver sought to learn from his mistakes. One of the problems with models is that they aren't always open to correction: They are built to run in a particular way, and, without human intervention, they will run that way forever. The problem in 2016, Silver later explained, had not been with his model, exactly.[20] He was loath to blame the machine. In most circumstances, FiveThirtyEight's system was fully automated. Poll numbers, adjusted in his proprietary model by factors like the state of the economy and projected voter turnout, among other things, went in, and probabilities came out. It was only as good as the polls and other data that fed it. (Silver himself doesn't poll.) And sometimes, human subjectivity—which Silver regards as

---

20 Nate Silver, "How I Acted Like a Pundit and Screwed Up on Donald Trump," FiveThirtyEight.com, May 18, 2016.

a kind of analytical cancer—still entered the mix. In his narrative posts about Trump, especially in 2016, he disparaged Trump's chances in part because Nate Silver, the man, had found Trump's ascent "unthinkable." For him, 2016 wasn't a warning sign that polls had their limits. He saw it as a reminder to redouble his commitment to doing better math.

On Election Night in 2020, Silver's tweaked model and approach led to a prediction that Biden would win 89 percent of the time, possibly in a landslide, by more than 300 Electoral College votes. Silver tried to ward off 2016's recriminations by cautioning that Trump's 10 percent chance was not a zero percent chance; something that happens one time in ten is something that happens fairly often.[21] He was concerned particularly about Pennsylvania, which Biden probably needed to win and where his lead seemed tenuous. In fact, the darker horse very nearly came through. Biden won by more than four points nationally, but his Electoral College margin, 306-to-232, was far narrower than it appeared: Trump would have won if about 40,000 votes had shifted sides in key states, including poll-challenging Pennsylvania.

The polling industry's 2016 reckoning was obviously incomplete; whatever corrections were made weren't corrective enough. The analytical fever of 2012 has truly broken. There remains disagreement over only the cause. Polling participation has declined for decades, particularly among certain demographic groups. Whites without college degrees, for instance, are "resistant" to polling; they also voted overwhelmingly for Trump. Others argued that certain voters were "shy" about their preference for Trump and unlikely

---

21 Nate Silver, "I'm Here to Remind You That Trump Can Still Win," FiveThirtyEight.com, November 1, 2020.

to admit their allegiance outside the polling booth. Pollsters also seemed to have trouble calibrating their turnout expectations, which underestimated the huge voter turnout in 2020, especially among Republicans. Relatedly, pollsters struggled with accounting for mail-in voting and pandemic fears, which influenced Republican and Democratic voters in different and pivotal ways.[22]

But here's the real problem: The difference in American political allegiance has become so fine, U.S. elections have become almost impossible to predict with math alone. A 2 percent margin of error in national polls would account for the difference in believed and actual outcome in both 2016 and 2020, especially given the vagaries of the Electoral College and Democratic dominance in certain high-population states, such as New York and California. We tend to think of 2 percent as not very much, when it can mean everything. An error can be both modest and massive at the same time.

Believing that 2024 will be any different is foolish. Trump's surprise win in 2016 meant that by 2020, more poll respondents *believed* he would win against Biden than *wanted* him to win, evidence of a growing lack of faith in polls.[23] *After* 2020's surprisingly razor-thin results across the ballot, that credibility gap will have only widened. It's probably a good thing: When poll numbers are seen as sacrosanct, they can alter the results they are meant to predict. Perhaps Democratic votes were depressed in places like Wisconsin, where Biden supporters might have felt less compelled to vote because of his seemingly

---

22 Scott Keeter, Courtney Kennedy, and Claudia Deane, "Understanding How 2020 Election Polls Performed and What It Might Mean for Other Kinds of Survey Work," Pew Research Center, November 13, 2020.
23 Harry Enten, "How Trump Has Broken the Polls," CNN.com, May 3, 2020.

insurmountable margin. And the $57 million that went to Jaime Harrison's campaign in its final months—think about that sum for a moment—could have been better spent in races that were actually competitive, or on just about anything else. Remembering how Fermi cautioned against treating numbers as truth, or maintaining the same skepticism about polls that some people have learned to feel about algorithms, would have prevented people from setting millions of dollars on fire.

"To all the pollsters out there, you have no idea what you're doing," Lindsey Graham crowed at his victory party. "And all the liberals in California and New York, you wasted a lot of money. This is the worst return on investment in the history of American politics."

Unlike the polls in South Carolina, Graham wasn't wrong.

———

Polls aren't the only one of our supposedly objective mathematical instruments with a distorting effect on our politics. Facebook has been accused of fiddling with its algorithm to favor conservative voices, the most strident conservative voices in particular—to the point that the social media giant potentially swung the 2016 U.S. election in favor of Trump. (POLITICO called it "a pivotal theater in the electoral war."[24]) In the lead-up to the 2020 election, Facebook seemed an increasingly right-wing echo chamber. The posts with the most engagement came largely from Trump and his allies outside the mainstream media: Ben Shapiro, Dan Bongino, David Harris Jr., Franklin Graham. If you're not on Facebook

---

24 Alex Thompson, "Why the Right Wing Has a Massive Advantage on Facebook," POLITICO, September 26, 2020.

or engaged in conservative politics, those names (other than Trump's, of course) might be only a rumor to you. But they are influential figures on the right, largely because of their enormous Facebook followings. (Shapiro routinely sees more engagement than the *New York Times* page.) While Trump and Biden combined to spend nearly $200 million on ads on the platform, "organic content" masquerading as political coverage is far more widely seen and more likely to be trusted. It's the real currency, and if the algorithm favors one side over the other, that's an obvious built-in advantage.

An anonymous Facebook executive insisted to POLITICO that the algorithm is neutral; right-wing voices simply possess a certain *quality* that makes them more engaging on social media. Setting aside for a moment the fact that "neutral" algo-rithms don't exist—humans make them, and so they contain everything that humans contain, including bias—the executive made a logical if unsettling case: "Right-wing populism is always more engaging," he or she said, because the content speaks to "an incredibly strong, primitive emotion" by cater-ing to people's anger and fear. "That was there in the [19]30s. That's not invented by social media—you just see those re-flexes mirrored in social media."

POLITICO found several counters to that argument, among them Adam Conner, who worked for Facebook for years and now finds himself at the liberal Center for American Progress Action. "It's absurd for Facebook to say this is just something that's playing out in a neutral way," he said. "Facebook is not a mirror—the newsfeed algorithm is an accelerant." Trump's refusal to concede the 2020 race wasn't granted much merit in America's courts, for instance, but it gained plenty of traction on social media. "Stop the Steal," a viral right-wing group that contested Biden's victory, gained 350,000 members in a single day before Facebook shut it down for spreading misinformation and rallying supporters to take dangerous real-world action. "The group was organized around the delegitimization of the election process," a Facebook spokesperson said in a statement, "and we saw worrying calls for violence from some members of the group."[25] It was too late. Those calls for violence turned into actual violence on January 6, 2021, when Trump supporters stormed the U.S. Capitol.

Biden spokesperson Bill Russo also questioned the mirror analogy before wondering out loud about the wider damage that social media has done to us: "This is not a feature of our society that we must simply accept," Russo said. "It is a choice to create an algorithm that feeds the distrust and polarization that are tearing us apart."

Liberals pointed to evidence that Facebook substantially tweaked its algorithm to mollify conservatives, who harbored their own suspicions about the engine's supposed neutrality. While Twitter slapped warnings on many of Trump's inflammatory tweets before the 2020 election—and continued the practice after, when the soon-to-be-former president posted hundreds of times that Biden had cheated until he was finally banned—Facebook had scaled back its own attempts at limiting the spread of conspiracy theories and false news. When an internal investigation highlighted several right-leaning pages that traded in lies, senior executives, including Joel Kaplan, Facebook's vice president of global public policy and a noted Republican voice within the company, opposed shutting them

---

25 Julia Carrie Wong, "Facebook Removes Pro-Trump Stop the Steal Group over 'Calls for Violence,'" *Guardian*, November 5, 2020.

down, fearing complaints from Trump and his allies.[26] When you're selling traffic, and both sides are giving you hundreds of millions of dollars, it's important to try to keep that traffic flowing in a way that makes the most people happy. Or, even more profitably, angry and scared.

Technology has allowed each of us to build our own universes, and that same technology has made us more likely never to leave them. Facebook has more than 2.7 billion monthly users, giving it enough power for some observers to liken it to a Doomsday Machine. Its megascale makes it impossible for humans to control anymore; Facebook employs thousands of moderators to delete its most damaging and inflammatory content, but they don't stand a chance. "[T]here aren't enough moderators speaking enough languages, working enough hours, to stop the biblical flood of shit that Facebook unleashes on the world, because 10 times out of 10, the algorithm is faster and more powerful than a person," is how Adrienne LaFrance memorably put it.[27] We've feared *the rise of the machines* for decades, but we imagined killer robots—we saw *The Terminator*—not some insidious, invisible parasite. We thought the enemy would be something outside of ourselves. Instead, in the search for a truly captive audience, it's proved far more efficient to turn us on one another.

Similarly, our instruments of self-measurement have become instruments of consignment. Consciously or not, we are all pollsters. Lately we've taken smaller, narrower samples, which leads to a failure in each of our internal analytics: The smaller

---

26 Elizabeth Dwoskin, Craig Timberg, and Tony Romm, "Zuckerberg Once Wanted to Sanction Trump. Then Facebook Wrote Rules that Accommodated Him," *Washington Post*, June 28, 2020.
27 Adrienne LaFrance, "Facebook Is a Doomsday Machine," *Atlantic*, December 15, 2020.

the sample, the less likely it is to be representative of the larger population. Algorithms feed us more of what we're already consuming. Follow one political voice, and you won't receive recommendations for the counterargument. You'll find yourself consuming more of the same, giving us the false impression that everyone is thinking what we're thinking. We spend so much time looking in mirrors, we start to believe they're windows. *Our* Truth becomes *the* Truth. And then we're surprised when reality proves us liars.

———

So how do we fix things? If algorithms, polling, and social media have conspired to turn our politics into a harmful, inhumane, combustible mess, how do we begin to repair the damage? First, yes, of course, we have to become better at discerning lies from the truth, including when it comes to data-driven fables. But I believe we have to do more. We have to do what we do whenever any machine is broken. We have to turn the machine off.

A motorcycle mechanic and philosopher named Matthew B. Crawford wrote a *New York Times* bestseller, *Shop Class as Soulcraft*, that made a more complete argument in favor of human rather than technological excellence than I can muster here: "Back to basics, then," he wrote, and then he made a compelling case for old-fashioned manual labor, as both meaningful work for society's greater good and nourishing work for the practitioner.[28] That might seem like a simplistic answer to our problems of modern remove, but that's because

---

28 Matthew B. Crawford, *Shop Class as Soulcraft: An Inquiry into the Value of Work* (New York: Penguin Books, 2009).

we've been conditioned to accept our current way of operating as the only way of operating.

I would invite you to consider the superior, purely analog performance of a man named Tom Konchalski.[29] He died on February 8, 2021, at seventy-four, after a long fight with cancer, and a campaign immediately began to see him inducted into the Basketball Hall of Fame. ESPN's Pablo Torre called him "the most important evaluator of teenage basketball players in America." There was little opposition.

Konchalski worked in the gyms of New York City. He was tall, six-foot-six, but not a skilled player despite his height. His gift was in seeing the truth about others. He was an all-league beholder. His tools were simple: his prodigious memory, his love of the game, a yellow legal pad, a typewriter, and his kind, trained eyes. He did not own a computer or a mobile phone, and he never once drove a car. His basketball analysis did not incorporate spreadsheets or even stopwatches. He sat down, and he watched the game, and then he went home and typed out his honest evaluations of its players. He photocopied his newsletter and hand-packaged and mailed it to generations of college coaches across America. Bobby Knight, Rick Pitino, John Calipari, and Mike Krzyzweski were among his subscribers. They trusted Konchalski's starred ratings of prospects and his whimsical little observations. "Scores like we breathe!" meant that a kid was definitely worth more than one look. Konchalski was almost never wrong about the future prospects of a young player. He remembered enough of the past to see into their future.

Is there any reason to think the political arena is different

---

29 Corey Kilgannon, "Basketball Prospector," *New York Times*, February 1, 2013.

than a basketball gym, an election any different than a game? If there is a gap between them today, it's only because we've found profit in complications. That wasn't always the case.

In 1966, when Robert Caro set out to write a biography of Robert Moses, the controversial New York master planner and builder, he faced an order as tall as Moses's monuments: His subject was a hugely secretive man who engineered enormous civil projects in one of the most layered cities on Earth, and Moses refused to speak to him. Moses also told other people that if they wanted to stay in his good graces, they would be wise not to talk to Caro, either. Caro was shut out.

Rather than give up, he took out a large sheet of paper and put a dot in its center. The dot represented Robert Moses. Caro then drew a series of concentric circles around the subject he wished to understand. In the first circle were the people closest to Moses: family. Then came a slightly larger circle of friends. Then came a circle of significant acquaintances. Then came a circle of casual encounters. Then came a circle of people who had met Moses only once. "He wasn't going to be able to get to them all," Caro told me.[30] But Caro could get to them. He just had to be willing to put in the work.

When Caro delivered his massive final manuscript to venerable Knopf—*The Power Broker* is a doorstop, 1,162 pages long; it also won the Pulitzer Prize in 1975 and has never been out of print—his editor, Robert Gottlieb, was immediately absorbed by the amount of detail, of personal insight, that Caro had assembled. (Caro wrote his first draft longhand, by the way.) The editor didn't hit a speed bump until he reached a single paragraph on what would become the 214th page of the book.

---

30 I wrote about Robert Caro for *Esquire*. "The Big Book" was published in the May 2012 issue.

In the scene, Bella and Emanuel Moses, Robert's parents, were depicted spending a summer morning in 1926 at their lodge at Camp Madison, a retreat for poor and immigrant children that Bella had helped found. They were leafing through the *New York Times* and saw an article that explained their son, still learning how to wield power, had lost a $22,000 judgment for illegal appropriations. "Oh, he never earned a dollar in his life and now we'll have to pay for this," Bella said.

Both Bella and Emanuel Moses were long dead, and Gottlieb didn't understand how Caro could have learned of that moment with the necessary assurance. Moses had the resources to sue Knopf into oblivion; *The Power Broker* had to be airtight. Gottlieb asked Caro to walk him through his reporting.

Caro began his work with his outermost circle. Among its population were the campers and staff at Camp Madison, from whom he might glean some glimmer of Moses's relationship with his parents. First, Caro acquired the camp's attendance roll and employment records. Then, he went through the New York Public Library's impressive collection of phone books. He called every now-adult child and now-retired adult he'd managed to cross-reference. One of them, Israel Ben Scheiber, was the camp's former social worker. He also happened to deliver the *New York Times* to Bella and Emanuel Moses each morning. That's how he came to be standing with them in the sun when Bella expressed her frustration with her deadbeat son, and he remembered the moment exactly, which he relayed to Caro, who wrote about it in his book, having devoted a considerable amount of energy to acquire that small but revealing detail about Moses family relations.

"So that's how," Caro told Gottlieb, who resolved never to ask his writer again how he had come to learn something.

"Every step of that story is by all ordinary standards

insane," Gottlieb told me decades later, while he was enjoying a sandwich with an old man's gusto for simple pleasures. "But he didn't say any of it as though it were remarkable." By Caro's reckoning, he had simply performed his version of Teller's kind of magic: the purest sort of reporting practiced to an extremely high standard. Caro treated writing as manual labor. "You feel almost like a cabinetmaker, laying planks," he told me. "There's a real feeling when you know you're getting it right. It's a physical feeling." He used the same rigorous, profoundly human approach for his landmark, multi-volume biography of Lyndon Johnson. When we met in 2012, he'd been working on it for forty years; his planned three books had become four, then five. Caro was into his eighties, and he was making plans to go to Vietnam because he still wasn't done with his reporting. All of it was completely nuts; all of it was completely amazing. "We're dealing with an incredibly productive, wonderful mania," Gottlieb said.

John McCain was also a wonderful maniac. I know these are politically charged times, and I'm going to ask you, please and thank you, to stick with me here. I didn't agree with McCain very much politically, but I liked him, John McCain the man, a great deal. When I started spending time with him, in 2006, those truths could still co-exist.

McCain was sixty-nine years old, a lion of the U.S. Senate, and the presumptive Republican nominee for the 2008 general election. He was the clear favorite, at least. Our first words were exchanged in an SUV in the parking garage at Madison Square Garden, shortly after he'd finished speaking to an unreceptive class of graduates from Manhattan's New School. Some had stood and turned their backs to him when he took the stage; there was concern that someone was going to throw dog shit at him, because that had been the talk. After, he was heading to a fundraiser in Connecticut, and I tagged along for the ride. We shook hands and then he called his wife, Cindy, on his cell phone. "Yeah, it was pretty rough," he told her. "I miss you, honey." I was shocked by how unguarded he was, the anti–Robert Moses. I remember thinking, *I guess we're doing this*. It was the start of two years together, on and off.[31]

Reading Caro's work taught me that to understand power, you have to understand the people who seek it, to learn to read them like a favorite novel. I spent those two years watching John McCain campaign, trying to emulate Caro's insatiable curiosity, his relentless drive toward his subject's soul. Nobody would dispute Caro's knowledge of Lyndon Johnson, even though his epic biography is devoid of analytical dissection. It's spun entirely from narrative, and so, too, was my understanding of John McCain. I still believe in the moral authority of stories. I heard McCain tell the same jokes about Marines coming from broken homes a thousand times to a thousand audiences. I saw one of his aides comb his hair, because McCain's own war wounds left him unable to lift his arms above his shoulders. I watched him hold court in the back of his bus, the Straight Talk Express, where a horseshoe of seats surrounded a massive box of donuts every day, because he couldn't bear the idea of spending one second alone. It was an ongoing lesson in the pursuit of power, but mostly I was steeped in the value of close contact, of human intimacy.

---

31 I wrote about John McCain several times for *Esquire*. The first story was titled "One of Us" and appeared in the August 2006 issue. We spent less time together as the campaign wore on, partly because of the Republican machine that rose up around him, partly because he and his staff knew I thought some of his choices were wrong, most notably his selection of Sarah Palin as his running mate. He had let a monster out of the box. I was surprised by how sad I was when he died. I learned a great deal from him, and enjoyed his company. John was one of one.

The moment I truly understood McCain came when he nearly dropped out of the race. By September 2007, he didn't look like he was going to be the Republican nominee, let alone the American president. Everything had fallen apart. McCain's record on the Iraq war was hurting him, his finances were cratering, his team was splintering. Polls, *wrong again*, wrote him off. We spent thirteen hours crisscrossing Iowa, because McCain had reverted to his basest political instincts, boiling down his campaign to the places he felt were the most familiar, with the company around whom he felt the most comfortable: He spoke to small groups of veterans, mostly in VFWs and Legion halls, and made sure to shake every one of their hands. That was it. People forget now, after everything else that happened, but in the fall of 2007, that was the sum of his entire campaign. He was speaking to rooms with fewer people than he had fingers.

That night we flew from Waterloo, Iowa, where the bus got lost trying to find the airport, to Portsmouth, New Hampshire. That plane had ten seats, but only four were occupied. People fall away from a candidate in descent like ice calving off a glacier's face. There was McCain; an old war buddy of his named Orson Swindle; Brooke Buchanan, a twenty-something-year-old press secretary, one of five survivors of an office that once employed twenty-five; and me. Campaigns don't get much more intimate than that. We took off into the night. McCain was in a foul temper. He picked up a sheaf of papers that represented the next day's plans. They didn't exactly include arenas. "Here's the twenty-seventh version of the schedule," McCain said. "They must chop down a whole fucking forest every time they make a change. I don't know why they can't just print out one page." Then he fell asleep.

Small planes fly higher than big ones. We were at 41,000

feet. The horizon curved. There were the orange lights of cities ahead of us; the setting sun was glorious behind us. The sky seemed enormous.

McCain stirred. Buchanan told him that she was worried he wasn't eating enough. He'd campaigned all day fueled by an apple fritter, a coffee, a handful of chips, and a can of Red Bull. There was some chilled Chinese food stashed up front, plastic boxes on plastic trays. McCain choked back a cold egg roll and then a fortune cookie. He read the fortune and passed it back to me without a word.

The game isn't over until it's over.

He asked for it back, and he tucked it away. McCain was superstitious, and that fortune was something he needed in his pocket. The next day, he woke up in a better place than I'd seen him in weeks. He practically bounded onto the bus. It was beat-up and low-rent, a stripped-down version of the luxurious coach he had once ridden, but it still had a horseshoe of seats with pinhole burns rather than donuts in the back, and he told stories there, on the rides between more VFWs, more Legion halls. We covered a lot of ground; he had to win New Hampshire or else. Somewhere along the way, he remembered Bob Dole's campaign for president, when Dole got dismantled by Bill Clinton in 1996.

"I was with him the last two weeks of his campaign, constantly," McCain said, looking out the window at the passing colors. "One of the things that was very moving—and admittedly, he didn't give great speeches and I understand that—but you'd see in the crowd these older men with the crossed skis, the 10th Mountain Division hats on. And after the speech you'd kind of see Bob go over and they'd come over, and it was fascinating to see that. It was very touching to see that. It makes me emotional even now when I think about it."

McCain had tears in his eyes, remembering. And then we went into some smoke-filled dungeon, and he leaned into the veterans gathered there, gripping their yellow-fingered hands, and he did that again and again and again, until something remarkable happened: He won New Hampshire, and then eight more primaries. John McCain once more became the favorite, and he went on to win the Republican nomination. One of the next times I flew with him, it was on a JetBlue charter, and every seat was occupied.

That's when I was taught a second, sadder lesson about politics. When the presidential race gets down to two people, each party builds a massive scaffolding around them. They become statues under constant repair. Everything becomes programmed and planned. Anything that resembles edge, any minor personality quirk that might be portrayed by the other side as a defect, gets sanded down. There is too much at stake for a candidate to be driven by instinct anymore. The influence of focus groups and surveys and consultants carrying reams of "opposition research" becomes suffocating. The man or woman in the middle of it all barely has room to breathe.

McCain knew more about politics than almost any living person. He had won his first election, to the House of Representatives, in 1982; he'd been re-elected to his Senate seat five times; he'd negotiated bipartisan legislation on incredibly complex issues, like healthcare and campaign finance; he'd sought and lost the Republican nomination in 2000; he'd single-handedly engineered his comeback in 2008. And now a fearsome, and fearful, apparatus surrounded him, and he was told by a bunch of scheming dorks waving poll numbers that *everything he knew was wrong.*

It didn't matter how he wanted to do things, or what had worked before. His plane had the same horseshoe of seats as the back of his bus, but I don't remember anyone ever sitting there. A presidential candidate shooting the shit with the press? No one would ever authorize it. McCain was surrounded by people and yet was forced to spend time quiet and alone, his literal nightmare scenario. He was constantly overruled about important things. He wanted Joe Lieberman to be his running mate. His advisers determined that forty-two-year-old Sarah Palin, who'd been elected the governor of Alaska only two years before, would have wider appeal to key voting demographics. The pick was obviously a train-wreck-in-the-making. Never mind some seasoned practitioner of the Eye Test—any functioning human could have spent five minutes in the same room with them and realized how bad was the match. But like Ryan Kavanaugh's moviemaking mainframe, the machine thought it knew better. It tried to make the pieces fit.

It was a disaster. Maybe McCain never stood a chance against then-Senator Barack Obama. He had dedicated his life to public service for the chance to hurl himself into a political buzz saw. But I have no doubt that he would have fared better had he been himself—had a man with decades of political experience and success been trusted to know more about politics than another shitty wonk. Maybe the pressure had made him doubt even himself. All that mattered, McCain should have known, was that ordinary people felt close to him. They liked him when they knew him. After reading these last few pages, do you feel as though you know a little more about John McCain? What gave you that new knowledge? Words or numbers? Proximity or distance? Do you like him more or less than you did? That's how he might have won. Instead, he became someone else, and he lost.

On Election Day afternoon, I watched Mark Salter, McCain's confidant and speechwriter, drag a desk from his hotel room into the parking lot, so that he could chain-smoke while writing his candidate's concession speech. His loss was that inevitable. I'm not sure how much McCain blamed himself for his self-abandonment, and how much he blamed his advisers, but he and Salter made a clear choice in those waning hours that McCain would finish the race as himself. Finally extricated from the Republican Party's political machinists, free from having to indulge reactionary people whom he didn't like very much, McCain in defeat gave his best speech of the entire campaign. (Palin also asked to speak; McCain told her, not all that politely, that her voice was no longer needed.) I couldn't help watching and wondering how different his campaign might have been had *that* John McCain been the man that Americans got to know. His message was his and his alone, and it was warm, kind, brave, noble. With time it might prove one of the last, rattling gasps of bipartisanship, the death throes of a once-shared American ideal.

"Tonight," he said, his pale skin almost translucent under the light, "tonight, more than any night, I hold in my heart nothing but love for this country and for all its citizens, whether they supported me or Senator Obama. I wish Godspeed to the man who was my former opponent and will be my president." John McCain was not a perfect man, but his imperfections were what made him human. And his humanity, like the rest of his reality, like every single truth about him and his political fate, became obvious only with a lot of time and not very much distance. When we reduce our politicians and our politics to glib, partisan math, the supposed clarity we receive in exchange is an illusion. It's an exercise in the worst kind of faithlessness. We need to trust our eyes over the poisoned visions of cynical machines. Analog work, manual work, is honest work in the truest sense. Not every job lends itself to handwork, of course, but those jobs that do are better performed by people who are measured and careful and who use the tools that allow them to be those things. The best editing is done with pencil to paper. That's how Robert Caro still works. Spending weeks and months with McCain taught me that we should never forget that politics is about people—and their motivations, and their hopes, and their fears—and they are worth getting to know, for better and for worse, in ways that models will never allow us. Each one of them, every one of us, is the smallest circle in a series of concentric circles.

CRIME

Murder with Numbers.

*I dont know that law enforcement benefits
all that much from new technology. Tools
that comes into our hands comes into theirs
too. Not that you can go back. Or that you'd
even want to.*
                    — Sheriff Ed Tom Bell,
                    No Country for Old Men[1]

When Drew Carey told me in his colorful way that he didn't
wish to recognize Terry Kniess's perfect bid on *The Price Is
Right*, I couldn't understand the animus. Long after it became
clear that there had been no big fix—only that a man with a
particular set of skills had picked a lock that had been waiting
for decades to be picked—Carey remained a little too purple

---

1 This quote is from Cormac McCarthy's novel *No Country for Old Men*
(hence the missing apostrophe in "don't," which was hard for me not
to insert). Sheriff Ed Tom Bell was played in the film with a weary
uncertainty by Tommy Lee Jones. *No Country* is one of the rare instances
when the book and the movie it inspired are equally good, and in this
case, equally great. They both speak deeply to our time—including, to
my mind, our modern approach to crime and punishment. Some of
our scientific advances have been helpful. Some have been incredibly
harmful. We need to get better at seeing which is which, and never forget
that criminals and their victims, despite the labels we attach to them,
are each human beings, exhibiting particular strains of human behavior.
And sometimes human police, although also imperfect, are still the best
instruments to decide who did what to whom.

about everything. He's an unrepentant gambler, with a known affinity for blackjack and its opportunities for exploitation. When we spoke, he had just finished taping an episode; during a commercial break, he had bantered with an obsessive fan in the audience named Michael, who rattled off the historical values of Range Game prizes with incredible precision. "I'm taking you to Vegas," Carey told him.

Wasn't Terry just a hyper-realized version of Michael? Hadn't *The Price Is Right* simply made the mistake of giving a very good card counter the one seat with a weak dealer?

"Yeah, but that's not what happened," Carey said.

What? What happened?

"There was that guy, in the audience," he said. "Ted."

———

When I found Ted Slauson, he was forty-four years old, living in San Antonio, Texas, and writing math problems for standardized tests. He had grown up in northern California and began watching *The Price Is Right* when he was six or seven years old. Ted was already precocious at math. Numbers were his four-leaf clovers. By the time he was in high school, he told me, he began noticing that prizes repeated. Unlike Terry and his telltale Big Green Egg, Ted was first tipped off by the reappearances of mundane grocery items: Turtle Wax, Rice-A-Roni, and Campbell's Cream of Mushroom soup.[2]

Right about that time, in 1984, a part-time ice cream salesman named Michael Larson appeared on a new game show

———

2 It was always Campbell's Cream of Mushroom because Bob Barker, a devoted animal activist, insisted that the show be free of animal products: no fur, no meat. So, lots of mushrooms.

called *Press Your Luck*.[3] The heart of that game was the Big Board, which had eighteen squares on it. Each would flash with lights for a microsecond. When a contestant pressed a button, the lights stopped, and the player had "landed" on that square. Behind it might be a prize, usually cash. Occasionally, the square hid a Whammy, a diabolical cartoon character who erased the contestant's earnings to that point, yielding the somewhat famous plea, "No Whammy, no Whammy." Each successive spin risked setting you back to zero. Hence, contestants were constantly forced to choose whether to walk away with their winnings or "press their luck."

That was before Larson came along. He had bought a new-fangled appliance called a VCR, and he had taped episodes of *Press Your Luck*, watching them in slow motion and hunting for patterns in the lights. Larson knew that creating true randomness was close to impossible for humans, whose built-in sense of rhythm makes randomness seem uncomfortably discordant. He gave each square a number. Sure enough, a pattern emerged. And for whatever technological or cosmic reason, a Whammy never appeared behind the squares that Larson had labeled number four and number eight. So long as he timed the lights and landed only on those two squares, he wouldn't be pressing his luck at all. He'd be bulletproof. The average winning contestant on *Press Your Luck* took home a few thousand dollars. After a record forty-five consecutive spins without finding a Whammy, Michael Larson had collected $104,950 in cash as well as a sailboat and trips to Kauai and the Bahamas before he collapsed in exhaustion.

Ted Slauson also bought a VCR—every invention carries

---

3   Like *The Price Is Right*, *Press Your Luck* also appeared daytimes on CBS, from 1983 to 1986.

with it unforeseen uses, and so unforeseen opportunities—and recorded *The Price Is Right.* He collected freeze frames of prizes and prices; he found that having the numbers attached to a visual cue helped him remember them. Between 1989 and 1992, Ted traveled to Los Angeles for more than twenty tapings but was never chosen to be a contestant. On July 15, 1992, he was finally told to come on down. His nametag read THEODORE. Bob Barker greeted him warmly. "Theodore!" he said. "You made it! You made it! Theodore has been a Loyal Friend and True. How many times have you been here?"

"Twenty-four," Ted said, because of course he knew exactly how many times he'd been there. It wasn't long before one of *The Price Is Right's* standby prizes—the Berkline Contemporary Rock-a-Lounger, an absolute beast of a chair—was wheeled onto the stage. Ted leaned down toward his microphone. He had prepared for years for this moment. "$599," he said. The bell that announced a perfect bid rang.

Ted won his pricing game, too. His winning streak came to an end only when luck entered the equation: Unlike Terry, he was out-spun at the Big Wheel. His quest was over.

Luckily for Ted, *The Price Is Right* loosened its eligibility requirements in 2002. After ten years away from the stage, contestants could appear again. Ted began returning to Television City. By then, he had traded his VCR for a video-capture device on his computer. He made digital flashcards for about 1,300 prizes, which he could run through in training sessions in about an hour.

In May 2002, outside the Bob Barker Studio, Ted met a young man named Brandon in the line; Ted told Brandon that if he was lucky enough to have his name called, he should check with him before he gave his answers. (*The Price Is Right* has always encouraged audience participation—a chorus of suggested bids greets every new prize.) Brandon heard his name called. I found a recording of the episode, and when a Ducane gas grill was displayed in front of him, he clearly looked to Ted, who signaled the bid with his hands: $1,554.

The perfect bid bell rang. "Have you seen that prize on the show before?" Bob Barker asked Brandon. No—that guy, in the audience, had given him the answer. The studio cameras found Ted, who gave the thumbs up. "Well, that explains it," Barker said. Four minutes later, Brandon had won a car.

Brandon didn't give Ted a cut of his assisted winnings, but Ted didn't really need the money. What Ted liked was recognition. He craved *acknowledgment*. He reveled in the feeling that he was the best at something, even if that something was his mastery of *The Price Is Right*. In that studio in Television City, he was the oracle on top of the mountain. Although he never heard his name called again, he kept making his pilgrimages, even after Drew Carey replaced Bob Barker. He stood in line again and again, waiting to go into the studio, and if he found himself in conversation with someone he liked, someone he felt deserved his help, he'd tell them: *Look to me*.

On the morning of September 22, 2008, Ted waited in the early-morning darkness for the gates to open. He was the third person in line. The two people ahead of him were an older couple, Norbert and Frances. The fourth and fifth people in line were a friendly couple, a man with a kind face and a deep voice and a woman who told Ted about the loss of their dog, Krystal. Ted liked them instantly. Their names were Terry and Linda Kniess.

"Look to me," Ted told them.

Terry heard his name called. Out came the Big Green Egg. Ted told me that according to his database, that was the grill's third appearance on the show, making it a relative rarity. Its price had also changed between episodes, rising from $900 to $1,175. (I checked: These are both true facts.) Ted told Terry to go with $1,175, he said, and Terry was exactly right. Everyone else began looking to Ted that day, and everyone had won. Ted said his only mistake came when Terry played Switch?, because he didn't realize there were two bikes, and he thought a terabyte sounded like a lot of memory. Ted knew all the other prize values that day, the way he knew that his Berkline Contemporary Rock-a-Lounger was $599, and Brandon's Ducane gas grill was $1,554. That morning, he had played his equivalent of a perfect game. He had even nailed the value of Terry's Showcase to the dollar, a trick that Ted rarely managed.

Ted returned for that afternoon's second taping, he told me. After receiving a "Sicilian death stare" from Kathy Greco, he was given a seat from which the contestants could neither see nor hear him. Not nearly as many people won. He later heard "through unofficial channels" that he was no longer welcome in the Bob Barker Studio, the way Terry had been banned from Las Vegas casinos. That was the end of Ted's pilgrimages to *The Price Is Right*.

Ted wasn't mad that Terry had won. He didn't want a cut of his winnings, either. But Ted wanted credit for what he'd done. He had worked hard, for nearly his entire life, to earn his expertise. Now someone else had blundered into his first taping and left with a historic triumph, claiming the title that Ted had deserved, and manufacturing the narrative to justify it. When I spoke to Ted, he told me that he had stopped watching the show entirely. "It's just not much fun anymore," he said. "It's just guessing now. The prizes might as well be a million dollars." Terry had broken everything about *The Price Is Right*, including Ted's love for it.

I hung up the phone with Ted and felt sweat start to surface on my forehead. I had committed a cardinal journalistic sin: I had fallen in something like love with my subject. I really liked Terry Kniess—I still like Terry. I loved the arc of his story, the connections between the weather and blackjack and *The Price Is Right*. Look at the world a certain way, and everything can seem predetermined. Fate becomes a physical force rather than a metaphysical idea, which is equally comforting and terrifying depending on how your life is working out in that moment. I also enjoyed my time with him. I *wanted* his story to be true, because I wanted my affection for him to remain unsullied. I had succumbed to his narrative, but also to my own desires, not only for a good story, but for the company of good people. Ted was also a good person—an even better example than Terry for the purposes of the Eye Test, a testament to the power of focus, the potential born of lifelong devotion. But if he was telling the truth, then Terry probably wasn't.

Drew Carey, for one, believed Ted's version of events. Ted was the one who had been banned from *The Price Is Right*, not Terry. I had seen Ted's success and verified his account. Everything he'd told me checked out. His story felt more complete than Terry's. It was less dramatic, but more correct, with fewer holes. Terry countered that he had no idea that Ted was a ringer, had no reason to trust him over his own course of study. That was *possibly* true, but there was no hard evidence, no way to support or deny that claim or any of his others. Terry also suggested that he'd been lucky with his perfect Showcase bid, that he had arrived at the round number given his knowledge—$23,000—but that the last three digits—$743—were a guess based on previous good fortune: It represented the date he'd married Linda, April 7, and her birth month, March. He'd showed me their wedding certificate and

Linda's passport as proof. "I know I would ask to see it," he said to me. If he'd made up his story after the fact, he had made it up with a basis in fact.

I still held some faint hope that Terry and Ted were both telling the truth. It's possible that two obsessive men happened to sit beside each other one morning, sharing the same desire, demonstrating their love the same way. Patterns also sometimes occur randomly. But that requires some magical thinking on my part. What were the odds? When I wrote an earlier version of this story for *Esquire*, I presented Terry's and Ted's cases and left it up to the reader to determine who was telling the truth. I ended with a tale that Terry told of his and Linda's winning trip to Banff. ("Just wonderful.") They had seen a wolf carrying a beaver in its mouth, he told me. He had tried to take a picture but had fumbled with his camera and missed it. They had gone back to their hotel and told people what they had seen, but nobody else had ever seen a wolf carrying a beaver in its mouth, and so nobody thought they were telling the truth.

How else do you decide who to believe?

———

In 1829, the establishment of the Metropolitan Police of London, widely considered the first modern police force in the world, began a long, uneven process of bringing order to the rule of law. England had been governed by the Statute of Westminster for nearly seven centuries, and the Met replaced its disorganized, often ineffective bands of volunteer parish constables and watchmen. People, certainly criminals, weren't quick to embrace what felt like a mean, unwanted presence. The line between street justice and official justice remained blurred.

The new police had two ways to obtain legitimacy in the eyes of a skeptical populace. Not surprisingly, they employed both: fearsome, brute force and increasingly systematic approaches to solving crime. Scotland Yard could become Scotland Yard only if its record was seen as unimpeachable, and there were persistent efforts there and around the globe to improve the science of criminology.

At its root, police work is a series of identifications: Who did what to whom? In the late nineteenth century, police forces began codifying their means of putting the right name to the right face, relying on the particular methods of a French anthropologist named Alphonse Bertillon. The son of a statistician and possibly something of a lunatic—his ghoul-eyed bearing was compared to that of a necromancer—he devised the Bertillon System, a standardized recording of body measurements and distinguishing features to identify repeat offenders. (His anthropometry included everything from measuring arm span to classifying essential nose profiles: hooked, straight, or snub.) When cameras came along, Bertillon standardized the mug shot, too. Police in Birmingham, England, are believed to have been the first to photograph criminals in the 1850s, but their early efforts were inconsistent, often resembling casual portraits. Bertillon's unfussy front-and-profile head shots remain how we photograph criminals today.

His work was far from flawless, despite its long reach: It was useless at codifying children or anyone else whose proportions and features changed dramatically in time. Bertillon also claimed powers he did not possess, sometimes with disastrous results. He was one of the expert witnesses who helped convict Alfred Dreyfus in 1894 and 1899, using specious (and incorrect) handwriting analysis to further an infamous miscarriage of justice. In the end, however, the original Bertillon

System was betrayed mostly by humanity's limited physical range: No matter how carefully a human body is measured, there is another human body out there just like it. Only its soul differs.

In 1887, Major Robert W. McClaughry, then the warden of the Illinois State Penitentiary in Joliet, imported the Bertillon System to the United States, wishing to keep better track of his prisoners. In 1899, he became the warden of the sprawling federal prison at Leavenworth, Kansas; he appointed his son, M. W., his records clerk. In 1901, Leavenworth received the otherwise unremarkable William West as a guest, and M. W. McClaughry had the honor of checking him in, dutifully taking his measurements. Two years later, a man named Will West arrived. The two inmates shared more than a handle. According to the Bertillon System they were the same person, and to this day their mug shots remain close to indistinguishable.[4] But they were indisputably two different men. They were both in the same place at the same time.[5]

M. W. McClaughry attended the World's Fair in St. Louis in 1904, and there he met Sergeant John K. Ferrier of Scotland Yard, a pioneer in the semi-nascent science of fingerprints. Our collective understanding of fingerprints took a long, shared, creative effort. As far back as 1788, a German anatomist named J. C. A. Mayer wrote that the friction ridge patterns on the tips of the fingers appeared unique to each human. In 1853, British-born Sir William James Herschel moved to India to work for

---

4 Their twin mug shots are available online if you wish to compare them yourself. William West has a ridge across the top of his head in profile; otherwise they bear a striking resemblance.

5 Robert D. Olsen Sr., "A Fingerprint Fable: The Will and William West Case," *Identification News* (later the *Journal of Forensic Identification*), Vol. 37, No. 11, November 1987.

the East India Company, where he received a contract for road binding materials "signed" with a palm print. He spent his life-time proving that friction ridge prints are not only unique to each of us, but they are also unchanging. (Think about that for a moment. Virtually everything else about our bodies evolves. Our fingerprints do not.) In 1880, a British medical missionary named Henry Faulds first proposed that fingerprints could be used to identify criminals and, more important, exonerate the innocent. Sir Francis Galton, a cousin of Charles Darwin, interested in the inheritance of physical features, picked up the mantle, codifying what he termed the "minutiae" of finger-prints, including loops, whorls, bifurcations, ending ridges, and enclosures. These became more popularly and delight-fully known as Galton's Details. In 1892, a gruesome child murder in Argentina became the first criminal mystery solved by fingerprint evidence—in that case, it was bloody—and ten years later, our dotty old friend Alphonse Bertillon pinched a Parisian murderer using fingerprints, which he had added to his ever-expanding classification system. After the World's Fair in St. Louis, the McClaughry family soon imported their second scientific method for identification, and among M. W.'s first subjects were William and Will West. Their fingerprints were obviously distinct from each other, and the only practical means to tell them apart.[6]

So began a veritable stampede of progress in the field of forensic science. Never mind the dubious recollections of eye-witnesses who sometimes confused tall for short and fat for thin. Hair and fiber samples, shoe and tire impressions, bite marks, burn patterns, handwriting samples, and bloodstain-

---

6   Alan McRoberts, editor, *The Fingerprint Sourcebook* (Washington, D.C.: National Institute of Justice, 2011).

pattern analysis often superseded more human accounts in criminal trials—a century of increasing rigor that culminated with the first use of DNA evidence to convict a child rapist and murderer named Colin Pitchfork in Leicestershire, England, in 1988.[7] Justice prevailed because science did.

Unfortunately, we now know that in the century between fingerprint and DNA analysis, we fell for a host of pseudo-scientific nonsense, and countless innocent men and women have lost the rest of their natural lives because of it. In fact, another man had been convicted of Pitchfork's crimes before he was—had even confessed to them, the victim of another supposed "science," that of police interrogation.[8] "Junk forensics" are the terrifying equivalent of "bad stats," the trail of spurious bullshit that so often nips at the heels of actual science, and whose failures are obscured—and made more lethal—by its noble counterpart's successes. When you see the world for its lies, it's hard not to go blind to the truth.

More than 360 Americans have been exonerated, after prosecution, by subsequent DNA analysis; nearly half of them were convicted in part because of deeply flawed forensic arguments. (Juries have been conditioned to trust forensic evidence over human testimony by police procedurals such as *CSI: Crime Scene Investigation*.) Among their unfortunate number: An Indiana state trooper named David Camm served thirteen years for murdering his wife and two children, found guilty in part because of testimony from "experts" about eight specks of blood found on his T-shirt. A notorious burglar

---

7 Celia Henry Arnaud, "Thirty Years of DNA Forensics: How DNA Has Revolutionized Criminal Investigations," *Chemical & Engineering News*, Volume 95, Issue 37, September 18, 2017.
8 Douglas Starr, "This Psychologist Explains Why People Confess to Crimes They Didn't Commit," *Science*, June 13, 2019.

was later convicted for the crime, and Camm was released.[9] "People see what they want to see," Richard Kammen, one of Camm's attorneys, has said of bloodstain-pattern analysis. "It's as accurate as a Ouija board."

Keith Harward spent thirty-three years in prison after he was wrongfully convicted of rape and murder, largely because six different analysts supposedly matched his teeth to bite marks on the victim. (One of the analysts, Lowell Levine, had argued that bite marks are as telltale as fingerprints.) Harward, too, was later exonerated by DNA evidence, and began a campaign against the use of junk science in prosecutions. He crashed a panel of forensic dentists at a conference in New Orleans, telling his alarmed audience: "There's no Gods in here."[10]

Cameron Todd Willingham was not saved by his innocence. He was executed for the deaths of his three children, who died in a fire at their home in Corsicana, Texas, in December 1991. Willingham had to be handcuffed by police to keep him from re-entering the burning home; the stricken father, who had a record as a petty criminal and wife beater, struggled hard enough to give a police chaplain on the scene a black eye. He was later charged and convicted of murder by arson, in part because of the testimony of Douglas Fogg, Corsicana's assistant fire chief, and Manuel Vasquez, one of the state's leading arson investigators. "You learn that fire talks to you," Fogg told the author David Grann. Vasquez claimed similar powers. "The fire tells the story," he liked to say. "I am just the interpreter." In the weeks before Willingham was executed, far more expert analysis determined that

9 Pamela Colloff, "Blood Will Tell," ProPublica.org, December 20, 2018.
10 Radley Balko, "Man Wrongly Convicted with Bite Mark Evidence Confronts Bite Mark Analysts," *Washington Post*, February 16, 2017.

the fire was accidental, likely caused by faulty wiring or a balky space heater. It had been cold that winter morning. But the state of Texas was unmoved by actual science, and Willingham was killed by lethal injection in February 2004. Among his last words: "The only statement I want to make is that I am an innocent man convicted of a crime I did not commit."[11]

Good police work, unlike death, offers no shortcuts. In a way, the whole of forensics, its vast collection of gifts and curses, its truths and its lies, was contained in one of its founding fathers: Alphonse Bertillon. His story is the story of analytics. He got some things so right that certain of his accomplishments remain accomplishments today. But those rational corrections gave him an irrational belief in his own infallibility. He looked at his fellow citizens and saw vessels custom-made to hold secrets, and then in his sometimes magnificent madness he looked in the mirror and saw a machine put on this Earth to learn them. What he should have seen was just another man.

The latest attempt to make crime and its prevention more "objective" is the widespread use of algorithms. Data has long been used to determine which areas need more intense policing, the way ambulance services analyze call volumes to help decide how many paramedics should come in for a shift. Now algorithms are used to make more personal decisions on behalf of the governments that employ them. In Philadelphia, AI determines how closely people are monitored during their

----

11 David Grann, "Trial by Fire," *New Yorker*, September 7, 2009.

probations. In the Netherlands, an algorithm suggests which welfare recipients are more likely to cheat the system. In Bristol, England, a predictive algorithm was designed to flag teenagers likely to step up their criminal ambitions.

Proponents defend the use of algorithms in criminal justice the way automation is always defended: It's cheaper, more efficient, and less prone to bias or human lapses in judgment. If you find it alarming that a machine will determine your prison sentence, feel free to put your fate in the hands of a judge who might be having a bad day. "Automatic pilot is an algorithm," Dr. Richard Berk, a professor at the University of Pennsylvania who designed Philadelphia's probation-risk algorithm, has said. "We have learned that automatic pilot is reliable, more reliable than an individual human pilot. The same is going to happen here."[12]

Dr. Berk is probably right. With the exception of the Concorde's grounding, we've rarely chosen as a species to slow down. But there is a growing concern about the influence of machines on how we govern ourselves. Philip Alston, the special rapporteur on extreme poverty and human rights to the United Nations, has warned that governments poorly employing AI risk "stumbling zombie-like into a digital-welfare dystopia." Criminal justice seems like an especially fraught field for data's widespread application. It seems like it, because it is.

In her bestselling book *Weapons of Math Destruction*, Cathy O'Neil, a mathematician and data scientist, gives a thorough accounting of the perils of Big Data.[13] O'Neil was

---

12 Cade Metz and Adam Satariano, "An Algorithm That Grants Freedom, or Takes It Away," *New York Times*, February 6, 2020.

13 Cathy O'Neil, *Weapons of Math Destruction: How Big Data Increases Inequality and Threatens Democracy* (New York: Broadway Books, 2016).

drawn to numbers innately; as a child, she was obsessed with prime numbers, and she spent hours factoring the numbers on passing license plates. "Math provided a neat refuge from the messiness of the world," she remembered. But then she became an adult and saw up close—first as a professor at Barnard, and then as a hedge-fund quant during the 2008 economic collapse, and finally as a reformer and humanist—how math has increasingly *contributed* to the world's messiness.

Damn, she wrote a good book. O'Neil explored the myriad ways algorithms are used and their insidious effects. Sometimes those effects are accidental, and sometimes they are purposeful, but almost universally they target the poor, uneducated, and powerless. By her measure, a model qualifies as a WMD if it has scale, does undeniable damage, and is inscrutable, resistant to fixes even when its flaws are exposed. She found many that met her requirements.

Type the wrong request into Google, and you'll start seeing predatory ads for diploma mills and payday loans. (A search for "PTSD" will find you on some unexpected mailing lists. Scam institutions like the University of Phoenix target combat veterans, because it's easier for them to get government loans to pay their inflated tuitions.) Companies use credit scores and specious algorithmic "personality tests" to weed out job applicants who might have suffered debt or mental illness, furthering their isolation and sense of despair. The same use of credit scores to set car insurance rates—because financial reliability presumably translates to road reliability—might see a person in debt with a clean driving record charged more for his insurance than a solvent person with drunk driving convictions.

Mathematical models, by their nature, sacrifice individual fairness in favor of collective efficiency, and when someone gets caught on the wrong side of the equation, corrections are hard to make. Machines tend to render what O'Neil called "unflinching verdicts." They also aren't nearly as objective as their makers might claim. We have invented countless instruments that can do things that we can't do ourselves. But those instruments are not something *outside* of ourselves, held at some measurable, objective remove; like the robots that have taken our places on the factory floor, they are *extensions* of ourselves. When Microsoft unveiled a Twitter chatbot named Tay in 2016, it took less than twenty-four hours of human interaction for it to become intolerably bigoted. Microsoft gave up trying to delete its more offensive tweets and pulled the plug.[14] Algorithms, too, contain everything we contain. The technologies we use to help us make decisions are themselves the product of decisions we have made, and it's insane to pretend otherwise. It's the same flawed processing that makes a Christian dismiss Scientology as a "made-up religion," or a baseball player deride Whirlyball as an "invented sport." Christianity and baseball weren't found in nature. Nor was any algorithm. "Models are opinions embedded in mathematics," O'Neil wrote.

Racism, she noted, is its own primitive predictive model, hard-wired into the circuitry of people we call racists. Most models sort masses of people into "buckets" of like-seeming individuals. Those individuals can then be expected to behave certain ways, and that predictable behavior warrants certain treatment and attention. A good teacher demonstrates positive attributes and should be rewarded for them; a bad teacher displays negative others and should be fired. What do racists do? They presume that someone's race dictates their behavior

14   James Vincent, "Twitter Taught Microsoft's AI Chatbot to Be a Racist Asshole in Less than a Day," The Verge, March 24, 2016.

(negatively), and so they should be treated differently than other people (also negatively). Racists, like algorithms, pre-emptively sort people based on expected behavior rather than judging them on their actual behavior.

The creators of algorithms might try to argue they are race blind, because race isn't factored explicitly into their models, but many of them use zip or postal codes to predict outcomes, particularly when it comes to risk. Let's return to the example of car insurance. You can be the safest driver in automotive history, but if you live in a neighborhood that's deemed "high risk" by an algorithm, you will be charged more for the same coverage than a less capable driver on the other side of the tracks. Too often, the "wrong" places are also home to higher percentages of minorities. "In our largely segregated cities, geography is a highly effective proxy for race," O'Neil wrote. Because it's hard for algorithms to understand *who* or *why*, they sort the world into default collections of *what*.

Facial recognition represents perhaps the most egregiously subjective example of supposedly objective "sorting." You might be surprised to learn that an estimated 117 million Americans have had their faces downloaded into police identi-fication networks.[15] They have proved accurate when used on white men, which is not surprising when you take a wild guess at who designed them. Research has proved facial recognition is worse at correctly identifying men of color (Google had to issue a famously sweaty apology in 2015 when its photo app identified three smiling African-Americans as gorillas) and woeful when it comes to women of color. In one study,

---

15 Clare Garvie, Alvaro Bedoya, and Jonathan Frankle, "The Perpetual Line-Up: Unregulated Police Face Recognition in America," Georgetown Law Center on Privacy & Technology, October 18, 2016.

facial recognition algorithms examined the photos of 271 dark-skinned women and identified 35 percent of them as *men*, setting aside the somewhat taller order of correctly assigning their names to their faces.[16]

In January 2020, Robert Julian-Borchak Williams, an African-American man in Detroit, earned an unwanted distinction: He is the first known American to have been arrested after having been wrongly tabbed by a facial-recognition algorithm.[17] The American Civil Liberties Union of Michigan has since come to his aid: "We've been active in trying to sound the alarm bells around facial recognition, both as a threat to privacy when it works and a racist threat to everyone when it doesn't," an ACLU attorney said. After Williams came home from work one day, police cornered him in his driveway and handcuffed him in front of his wife and two distraught daughters; he was charged with shoplifting five watches from Shinola. Williams was photographed, fingerprinted, swabbed, and held overnight in a detention center. The next day, he sat across from two detectives in an interrogation room. They showed him a still from the store's surveillance video. A computer had said that Williams and the man in the picture were one and the same, but it was immediately clear to everyone in the room, including the detectives, that they were, in obvious fact, two different people—far less similar than William and Will West more than a century before. Williams picked up the photograph and held it next to his face. "No, this is not me," he said. "You think all black men look alike?"

That racist computer sure did.

---

16 Steve Lohr, "Facial Recognition Is Accurate, if You're a White Guy," *New York Times*, February 9, 2018.
17 Kashmir Hill, "Wrongfully Accused by an Algorithm," *New York Times*, June 24, 2020.

There are also instances when a statistic designed to measure a certain behavior changes that same behavior—sentient humans become aware that they are being studied and do what they are doing differently to meet the perceived desires of their observers, or to elude them. It's a twist on the dangerous argument that algorithms are somehow independent of us: Not only are algorithms human inventions, but their efficacy presumes that other humans are unaware that they are being watched. One of my favorite quotes about data's behavioral effects comes from Shawn Thornton, a now-retired hockey player with a reputation for passionate play and plain speaking. Time of possession is a key statistic in many sports—if you hold on to the ball or puck for longer than your opponent, that presumably gives you an advantage—and he was asked why his Stanley Cup–winning Boston Bruins were so adept at keeping possession.

"Because not once did anyone ever talk about fucking possession," he said. "Nobody gave two shits or ever even mentioned that stat. We forechecked hard and got the puck back, and we had a lot of skill up front that liked to hang on to the puck, and we had a lot of scary guys who could hang on to it…We didn't have one guy that cheated on the offensive side of the puck, either. I've seen it where guys only change on the backcheck because they don't want it to negatively affect their possession stats. The fucking guy going on after him gets completely fucked. Yeah, *his* numbers look good, but he just gave up a four-on-three. That stat drives me fucking bananas."[18]

---

18 This quote was mined by Eric Engels, a hockey columnist for Rogers Sportsnet in Canada. He posted it on his Twitter account, @EricEngels, on January 14, 2018. I read it and laughed like a goon.

CHRIS JONES

People are increasingly aware how much of their lives are being quantified—Internet "cookies" are just the beginning of the constant surveillance we are under[19]—and that awareness can change how we behave. In *Weapons of Math Destruction*, Cathy O'Neil used a mundane-seeming example to illustrate how deeply AI can alter the human systems it's meant to analyze: the annual ranking of American colleges published by *U.S News & World Report*.

The ranking started innocently enough in 1983. *U.S. News* was struggling, and a standalone ranking of colleges and universities would help prospective students make one of the biggest decisions of their lives and, more important, sell magazines. At first, the ranking was an entirely human construct. A team of journalists pored over opinion surveys sent to university presidents. Not surprisingly, the usual Ivy League suspects finished on top, and there were complaints about human bias and reputation coasting. *U.S. News* sought to make their study more rigorous and resistant to criticism by including hard data in the mix: Numbers, after all, are indisputable measures. But "educational excellence" is difficult to quantify. *U.S. News*, like many modelers, employed fifteen proxies to build their rankings, and they seemed logical enough: the average SAT scores of incoming students, acceptance and graduation rates, student-teacher ratios. Alumni donations were also factored into the equation, because presumably only happy graduates keep paying for an education they've already received. In 1988, *U.S. News* released its first truly mathematical model of higher education in America.

---

19 What diabolical genius named them "cookies"? Of course I accept cookies! Who doesn't want a cookie? Wait, how did you know I was shopping for bed frames?

More than three decades later and still going strong—long after *U.S. News*, the magazine, stopped printing—the ranking has had a calamitous effect on the system it was supposed to measure. Universities have tried to game the rankings by improving their scores in the fifteen proxies. They've had accepted students retake their SATs to lift their scores; they've passed students who should have otherwise failed; several have been caught simply lying about the numbers they submit. Saudi Arabia's King Abdulaziz University finished higher than vaunted Cambridge and MIT in 2014's global rankings by hiring dozens of acclaimed mathematics professors to three-week terms and claiming credit for their publications, bumping how often its name appeared in academic citations, a key quantity in the ranking.

Such distorting effects have their own cautionary axiom among statisticians. First pronounced by economist Charles Goodhart in 1975, it has become known as Goodhart's Law: *When a measure becomes a target, it ceases to become a good measure.* Obviously less eloquent than Shawn Thornton, Goodhart nevertheless saw the inherent problem in tracking possession time or academic citations long before the analytics movement reigned supreme. In the case of the college rankings, what O'Neil described as an "arms race" led to massive tuition inflation and student debt, because schools have tried to spend their way to the top, and cost or the relative value of education has never been a factor on the list. Like other models that exacerbate inequality, the *U.S. News* ranking became lamentably self-reinforcing. Schools near the top of the list became more successful, and schools near the bottom less. The rich got richer. The poor went to the University of Phoenix.

Algorithms designed to reduce crime often have the same effects. American law enforcement has increasingly treated nuisance crime as serious crime, the "broken windows" theory of policing employed by former mayor Rudy Giuliani in New York City: Stop the petty stuff, and that abiding sense of order will "trickle up" and curtail real criminals. It can work, but the question becomes at what cost? Predictive software suggests that nuisance crimes like aggressive panhandling or petty drug use will likely take place in poorer (minority) zip codes. They see greater police attention, which means their populations witness more arrests—not necessarily because their collective behavior is more criminal, but because there are more police there to catch them. That creates what O'Neil described as a "pernicious feedback loop." Crime rates rise, and so the algorithm directs more police to the area. Those populations rack up more charges, which means they spend more time in jail, which means they're even less likely to get jobs, which means they commit more crimes. If you want to make someone behave like a criminal, treat them like a criminal—and the machine will self-justify the further use of machines. "The result is that we criminalize poverty," O'Neil wrote, "believing all the while that our tools are not only scientific but fair."

The *Tampa Bay Times* went deep on the dangerous predictive algorithm employed in Pasco County by Sheriff Chris Nocco.[20] Using a soupy combination of "arrest histories, unspecified intelligence, and arbitrary decisions by police analysts," Nocco's office, which he assumed in 2011, generates a list of "likely"[21] offenders, 10 percent of whom are under the age of eighteen. The *Times* found that deputies then harass the people unfortunate enough to find their names on that list,

20 Kathleen McGrory and Neil Bedi, "Targeted," *Tampa Bay Times*, September 3, 2020. Their investigation is as excellent as it is horrifying, and I encourage you to read it in full.
21 There aren't enough air quotes in the world for this shit.

as well as their friends and families. The police raid houses after dark, perform interrogations without probable cause, and write up tickets for petty offenses like overgrown grass and underage smoking. A former deputy described the purpose of the program succinctly: "Make their lives miserable until they move or sue." One fifteen-year-old was visited by police twenty-one times in four months after the arrest for bicycle theft that had landed him on the list in the first place. The mother of another teenage target was fined $2,500 for keeping five chickens in her yard. Deputies didn't catch her child doing anything wrong, but thankfully they stepped between those chickens and whatever chicken malfeasance they almost certainly had planned.

Nocco's office told the *Times* that it stood behind their "intelligence-led policing," which at the time included a full-time staff of thirty analysts, supervised by former counter-terrorist and army intelligence officers, and a $2.8 million budget to monitor teenage bike thieves. It parroted the usual bullshit that its algorithm was objective and designed to reduce bias in the system. (Much of the platform was built using all-too-human inputs, and the computers provided only a list of suspect suspects. The police determined which ones actually "deserved" visits, and you can imagine how they might have decided.) Nocco's office also provided data showing declines in theft since the program began. "This reduction in property crime has a direct, positive impact on the lives of the citizens of Pasco County and, for that, we will not apologize," the police said in a huffy statement. That's all well and good, except that seven large neighboring counties saw a similar decline, minus the targeting and harassment, and *violent* crime in Pasco County under the program has gone up. Statistics can lie, remember.

171

The *Times* asked actual experts for their opinion on Nocco's system—dubbed *"Moneyball* meets *Minority Report"* by the paper—and they did not mince words. "One of the worst manifestations of the intersection of junk science and bad policing—and an absolute absence of common sense and humanity—that I have seen in my career," David Kennedy, a criminologist at the John Jay College of Criminal Justice, has said. In a twist that would have impressed George Orwell, Pasco County cited Kennedy's own research in crime prevention to justify the program that he so unambiguously decried. Too bad gaslighting isn't illegal.

———

So what do we do? The costs of crime are so high, our desire for accountability so intrinsic, that asking for patience or restraint or prudence or compassion in our application of laws risks seeming soft or naïve or, worse, somehow *tolerant* of criminals. And I want to reiterate: The effort to bring precision to police work has led to serious, significant advances, the use of fingerprint and DNA evidence especially. It's a lot harder to be a serial killer these days. But we sometimes act as though we don't have control of our technology, that it behaves the way it behaves and we have to adapt to it. That's not true. We can keep using what works and stop and dismantle and rebuild whatever we wish to make better.

There are few more effective instruments of terror than bad policing. Pasco County is a terrible example. Reform is obviously needed—the same pseudo-scientific quest that has led to the dehumanization of criminals and innocent suspects has also helped turn police into cogs of a sometimes corrupt and violent machine. Somewhere along the way, we seemed to decide that it was a greater sin for a guilty person to go un-punished than for an innocent person to be unjustly accused. I think that's the wrong choice, and it's led to a ruthlessness, a callousness, that doesn't serve our communities.

I live in a little town. It is bucolic. Yet every member of our local force has received training in long guns—how to be snipers, basically. It took an unfortunate incident with my son Charley for them to receive any training in how to deal with a person with autism, when that's the skill that's far more likely to be required of them. That awful experience changed me. As a white man, I was finally exposed to the gross power imbalance that exists between the police and the populations they are meant to protect—the cynical, authoritarian priorities of even small-town forces. There is no reason in the world for local cops to have tanks or to dress like soldiers. It's all part of our growing problem of labels, of categories, of distance, of facelessness. We're all less human than we were.

I'm not going to pretend I know the answers. Crime and punishment is a messy, messy practice. We need to acknowl-edge that, rather than try to pretend that it isn't. Human cops can be as deeply flawed as algorithms, as uncaring as any robot. It was a human cop's knee that suffocated George Floyd; it was a human cop's arm that choked Eric Garner. I'm not sure the response to that obvious injustice is to put more of our faith in equally imperfect machines. As naïve as it might sound, I believe we should try to make better humans. We should be more careful about who we turn into police, what training they receive, what of their behavior we validate and what we condemn, and what tools we give them and what tools we take away. Our fight against crime is often portrayed as a war between opposing armies, good and evil, but that's not right: Crime is more like an infection, and we should be working humanely to limit its spread. Our entire system of justice was built on the premise of *reasonable doubt*. Think of the subtlety and nuance, the intellectual gentleness, those two words imply. They are the definition of *human discretion*. And yet the same modern intractable side-choosing, the same imaginary certainty to which too many of us subscribe, has also contaminated our dispensation of law and order.

Conversely, there aren't many people worthier of our veneration than a good cop. We've put police into buckets, too. Good cops do exist, and we need to celebrate them if we want more of them. I wish here to celebrate one good cop.[22] His name is Detective Sergeant Jim Smyth of the Ontario Provincial Police. He is a master of the Eye Test, and the sort of cop we should want all of our cops to become.

———

On January 28, 2010, a twenty-seven-year-old woman named Jessica Lloyd went missing from her home in lakeside Belleville, Ontario. The night of her disappearance, two men driving past her house had noticed an SUV parked in a nearby field. They told police, who then found tire tracks and boot prints in the field: solid, old-fashioned evidence based on eyewitness testimony. Police began conducting random stops of vehicles driving on the highway in front of her house: gumshoe work that would have made Robert Caro proud. On February 4, they stopped an SUV driven by Colonel Russell Williams, the forty-six-year-old commanding officer of Canada's largest air

---

22 The rest of this chapter is dark, detailing sex crimes, and if you don't wish to read it, please do not. Just know that the premise here is the premise of this book: We do our best work when we remember our humanity, especially when it's hard to remember it.

force base in Trenton, Ontario. His tires were a match. Police let an unsuspecting Williams go, but he was kept under surveillance while they continued their investigation. They found geographic connections between Williams and the previous, unsolved murder of Marie-France Comeau, a military flight attendant at the base, and the sexual assaults of two women who lived near his cottage in the hamlet of Tweed. He drove to his home in Ottawa, where his wife lived full-time and he lived when he wasn't on the base. On February 7, he was asked to come into the city's police station to answer a few questions. It was three o'clock in the afternoon. He told his wife he would be home for dinner.

Williams was an unusual suspect. He had served in the military for more than twenty years and was considered a model officer. He was highly intelligent and disciplined, an excellent pilot who had flown Queen Elizabeth II during his duties. He was direct, physically unremarkable, and had no criminal history. But profiling—data-mining by a different name—has never been particularly useful in such crimes. I loved *Mindhunter*, too, but the sample size of true psychopaths is small, thankfully, and there is no killing "type." They are usually outliers even when compared to other outliers. Michelle McNamara, in her posthumous bestseller *I'll Be Gone in the Dark*—about her obsessive search for a serial rapist and murderer she dubbed the Golden State Killer[23]— wrote that serial sex offenders "are not only rare but also so varied that generalizing about their backgrounds and behavior is unwise." Paradoxically, the richness of our modern instruments, the volume of seemingly relevant information, can

---

23 Michelle McNamara, *I'll Be Gone in the Dark: One Woman's Obsessive Search for the Golden State Killer* (New York: HarperCollins, 2018).

leave investigators with tunnel vision. "The feast of data means there are more circumstances to bend and connect," she wrote. "You're tempted to build your villain with the abundance of pieces. It's understandable. We're pattern-seekers, all of us. We glimpse the rough outline of what we seek and we get snagged on it, sometimes remaining stuck when we could get free and move on."

By the time Williams had arrived at the police station, Smyth had done enough research to know that his suspicions were reasonable. The thumbtacks in his mental maps made sense, at least. But he also knew that his evidence was circumstantial. The base in Trenton is massive, and there were hundreds of other men who worked there and lived nearby. Even if Smyth could prove that Williams had driven in that field beside Jessica Lloyd's house, he didn't have proof that he had murdered her, or had anything to do with the other crimes. Smyth wasn't even certain Lloyd was dead. No body had been found. Officially, she was still missing.

More than a decade later, the ten-hour interrogation that followed is still upheld as a stunning example of the art. The Canadian TV news documentary *The Fifth Estate* devoted an entire program to the conversation;[24] much of it is available on YouTube and has been watched by millions, including untold numbers of detectives yearning toward self-improvement. In the beginning, Williams, wearing jeans and a blue golf shirt, seemed relaxed. He smiled. He chewed gum. Smyth wore a dark suit. Setting up the room, he had followed the rules of effective interrogation. He made sure there was no furniture, no table or desk, between him and his suspect. He sat close

---

24 The episode, reported by Bob McKeown, was titled "The Confession." It originally aired on the CBC on October 22, 2010.

and would move closer. He also was calm, friendly, measured in his speech. There was no bare light bulb swinging overhead, no raised voices, no physical threats, none of the hallmarks of coerced confessions. Smyth knew that his suspect would think he could outsmart him, and he shelved his own ego, giving Williams no indication that he was wrong in his assumptions. The detective called the colonel by his first name, and he reminded Williams that he wasn't under arrest and could leave at any time. If he wanted to stop and get a lawyer, that was his right. Smyth told Williams he was hoping only to clear him from a list of possible suspects.

Smyth started with broad strokes before narrowing his focus. His first priority, apart from learning the whereabouts of Jessica Lloyd, was the acquisition of more physical evidence. "What would you be willing to give me today, to help me move past you in this investigation?" he asked Williams.

"What, um, what do you need?"

Smyth named blood samples, fingerprints. Williams agreed to supply them: "Sure." Then Smyth mentioned, almost as an afterthought, "Footwear impressions." As soon as the words left Smyth's mouth, Williams looked down at his boots.

Smyth had made a long study of physical behavior. Now, again—we have made physical tells seem more conclusive than they are. They are not *definitive*. But under certain circumstances, they can be *indicative*. Any reasonably experienced poker player will tell you that when an opponent looks down at his chips after he looks at his hole cards, he likes what he's holding and is calculating the bet he is about to make. Williams did not like what he was wearing on his feet.

But Williams, unaware that the police had lifted boot prints from the field, wanted to appear as though he had nothing to hide. He gave an impression of his boots. Smyth asked him if they would learn something about him that would upset his wife. "Absolutely not," Williams said. Smyth moved victim by victim, location by location, asking Williams each time if there was any reason for his DNA or any other piece of him to be there, giving him the potential out of a consensual affair. "No," Williams said. Smyth burrowed in. He asked Williams if he had parked in the field next to Lloyd's house. Williams again said no.

The ironclad denials were useful. Smyth did have DNA evidence from three of the crimes; he had good science on his side. Now if Smyth proved Williams had been near any of the four victims, then he had caught Williams in a lie. With that trap set, he made a textbook turn, to what investigators call *the confrontation*. Smyth's voice didn't change. He stayed soft-spoken, almost conciliatory, as though he was sorry to be the bearer of bad news. He showed Williams photographs of the boot prints behind Lloyd's house, and how they matched the boots worn by Williams into the police station. "They are identical," Smyth said. He showed how the tire tracks had matched, too. "This is getting out of control, Russell," Smyth said. "Really, really fast."

It didn't take a forensic specialist to watch Williams in that moment, his body language, his facial expressions, and see a man who realized he was in trouble. But Smyth didn't revert to some blunt, universal tactic; he continued to tailor his approach to Williams. He banked on his suspect's conceit, on his faith in his own persuasive abilities, to talk himself out of the corner in which he found himself. Shockingly but tellingly, Williams didn't end the interview. He didn't ask for a lawyer.

"I wanted to give you the benefit of the doubt," Smyth said. "But you and I both know you were at Jessica Lloyd's house."

Williams went silent for long stretches—processing, calculating, trying to remember what he had done and invent ways to explain his behavior. In the meantime, Smyth appealed to the parts of Williams that mattered to him: his reputation, his intelligence, his marriage. He even tried to appeal to Williams and his lingering humanity, raising the specter of Jessica Lloyd's family, somewhere out there, desperate to learn what had happened to their missing daughter.

"Russell, what are we going to do?"

"Call me Russ, please."

"Okay. What are we going to do, Russ?"

Smyth again laid out the evidence. The tire tracks. The boot prints. And the DNA match that both men knew would soon come.

"So what am I doing, Russ? I put my best foot forward for you here, bud."

"I want to minimize the impact on my wife."

"So do I."

"How do we do that?"

"We start by telling the truth."

"Okay."

"Okay. So where is she?"

Four hours, forty minutes, and ten seconds after the two men sat down together, Williams broke.

"Got a map?"

Later, the detective offered the murderer his hand. "Russ, you're doing the right thing here," Smyth said. Williams took it. Smyth knew there was still more work to do. The rest of the time in that room would be spent making an inventory of horrific events. "Do you want to work forwards or backwards?" Smyth asked.

"Doesn't matter."

They started with Jessica Lloyd.

Russell Williams has a mind for detail, and he remembered everything about his crimes. He told Smyth precisely where Lloyd's body could be found, and then he told him everything else. No one would have to wonder what happened. Smyth's graceful, measured, seasoned approach to his grim work, bolstered by legitimate forensic science, had given us a picture that was all too complete. In fact, Williams knew the answers to all of Smyth's questions but one. Even though the interview was nearly over, Smyth still used the passive language that he had practiced using, allowing his suspects to escape responsibility even as they confessed to their sins.

"Why do you think these things happened?"

"I don't know," Williams said.

We often turn criminals into something other than human. The worst of them become creatures, fiends, ghouls—the monsters who live in our closets and under our beds. We similarly disassociate ourselves from the victims of crime, divorcing ourselves from their fates by telling ourselves that it can't happen here, and if it does, it won't happen to us. They made mistakes that we wouldn't make. Maybe they even deserved it. But those are lies that we tell ourselves in pursuit of false comfort, the way we employ make-believe certainty to insulate us against the randomness of our doubt-filled lives. Murderers and rapists and those who suffer at their hands—and the police and lawyers and judges we ask to punish one and bring peace to the other—are human beings. We might not always like to think so, but we would be wiser to treat them that way. That's maybe the hardest but most essential part of passing the Eye Test, of becoming a better beholder. If you want to behave more like a human, to see and use the advantages of your distinctly personal experience, you have to fight to see your fellow humans as humans, too. You can't pick and choose who to treat like a person and who to discard like a remainder. You either practice compassion or you don't. You either think generously and expansively or you don't. Like our technology, criminals and their victims aren't alien machines visited upon us by some mysterious external force. They are our friends and neighbors. They are our insides, turned out.

MONEY

Market Corrections.

*There is no competitive advantage in follow-
ing the crowd. In finance, as in the rest of
our lives, the pendulum has swung too far in
favor of analytics, which has left a vacuum,
and an opportunity, at the other end of
the methods spectrum: the singular work of
courageous humans. The same holds true for
every aspect of creative enterprise. Do you
remember the Hartford Whalers logo? One
man made it, and it's perfect and immortal.
That's the goal.*

Kenneth Feinberg had always been careful about his decisions.
A Boston lawyer who had done pretty well for himself as a
mediator in high-stakes civil and corporate disputes, he and
his family began shopping for a getaway in 2002. They had
narrowed their possible retreats to Martha's Vineyard and
Nantucket, two rarefied islands out to sea, but not too far out
to sea. Feinberg isn't—or wasn't then—the sort of man who
would leave such an important binary choice up to whim or
fate. His selection of a vacation retreat required a scientific
approach. His course was evidence-based.

He studied reams of historical weather data and the prevailing ocean and air currents. (We've discussed how past climate

isn't as useful in predicting future weather as it was, but it's still superior to a hunch.) Feinberg found that Nantucket's airport was nearly twice as likely to be closed by fog on any given day. A man forever on the move, Feinberg soon bought five acres of woods on Martha's Vineyard. "I got a chance to buy property that wasn't on the market that I thought was a very good price," he told me years later, in 2013. We were sitting on a small upstairs porch in the stunning house that he and his wife, Dede, had built among the trees.

When Feinberg was making his careful and considered property purchase, he was in the earliest days of his newest work—the work that would consume the rest of his career and much of his life. He had been named the special master of the September 11th Victim Compensation Fund, responsible for allocating billions in federal money to the injured and the families of the dead.

Feinberg already had a history of reaching settlements for victims of pain and suffering: He had helped two sides agree on the financial fallout for Agent Orange, asbestos, and the Dalkon Shield, the tragically flawed IUD. But the September 11 fund was without precedent; he had no case history on which to rely. The federal government hadn't thought to compensate victims after the first World Trade Center bombing in 1993, or after the Oklahoma City bombing in 1995. That's because the federal government was only now concerned that two major domestic airlines, United and American, would be sued out of the sky.

Like many Americans, Feinberg had felt helpless watching the attacks but wanted to help. He had read about the emergent fund in the newspaper and within days had asked to administer it *pro bono*. Feinberg's faith factored into his volunteerism. In Israel, there is a team of strong-stomached Orthodox Jews, a volunteer group known as ZAKA. After bus bombings and airport shootings, they comb the wreckage and ruins for body parts, even sopping up blood, ensuring the dead are made as complete as possible before burial. Feinberg was not Orthodox, but he believed in the Jewish practice of *tikkun olam*, a Hebrew phrase for "repairing the world." He saw himself as the closest American equivalent to ZAKA, both blessed and cursed with a tolerance for misery and a need to fix unfixable things. He could not yet see that he would become the nation's leading expert in picking up the pieces.[1]

"Be careful what you wish for," Senator Ted Kennedy told Feinberg before he set about his sad business.

Feinberg's task was impossible. The fund would prevent the bankruptcy of the airlines only if the vast majority of victims and their families agreed to the compensation they were offered. (Taking money from the fund meant waiving your right to sue, leaving each family with their own calculating to do: Was the offer more or less than they would receive in a civil suit, and if it was less, would it be worth the time and emotion of a court fight to make up the difference?) But few people in the throes of grief look at the same set of facts and draw the same conclusions. "It's amazing, the spectrum of emotion," Feinberg told me. "As diverse as human nature itself."

One of the few early unifiers of the September 11 families was their hatred of Kenneth Feinberg. Nearly a year into his

---

1 I first wrote about Kenneth Feinberg for *Esquire* in its January 2014 issue. The story was titled, in fact, "The Nation's Leading Expert in Picking Up the Pieces."

mission, very few families had signed. He risked overseeing a colossal failure: If he spent billions in government money to sign half the families, but the other half sued, then what had he accomplished? On the first anniversary of that terrible day, a desperate Feinberg held a town hall on NBC alongside Tom Brokaw. He was surrounded on three sides by grieving families, many of them holding portraits of their lost loved ones on their laps. They screamed at Feinberg, who had approached his work the way he approached every decision: with an unerring, almost robotic rationality. That approach had not found much purchase in wounded people.

Feinberg's principal mistake was not of his own making. The government had mandated that no two deaths be equally valuable, financially speaking, because neither are all careers. Unequal payments are a standard practice in mass torts, and they make a certain mathematical sense. In the case of the September 11 fund, a young stockbroker's family would receive more than the family who had lost a middle-aged police officer or firefighter, and they would receive more than the family of an older custodian. Years of earning potential, multiplied by expected annual incomes, resulted in a proposed settlement.

But at that town hall, surrounded by those devastated families, Feinberg saw the error inherent in his cold calculations, however reasonable they might have seemed in the abstract. A man in the audience named Nick Chiarchiaro put voice to the objection. He had lost his wife, Dorothy.

"Why not just set a flat number? Why all the calculations?" Chiarchiaro asked.

Feinberg lifted his hands. "As I've told the families," he said, "I can only administer the law that is before me."

Chiarchiaro pressed. "Is my wife worth less than the bond

trader? Well, not to me. I was married for thirty-seven years. She's worth a gazillion dollars."

Feinberg left the town hall and made what, for him, was a hasty decision: He would meet personally with every family unsatisfied with their offer, hear their arguments, and decide whether to change it. "It wasn't empathy," he said. "It was strategy." He had to maintain some sense of fairness, otherwise he might lose the upper end of the income spectrum. "People always count other people's money," he said. But he realized that most people would never sign if they felt the lives of their loved ones had been reduced to simple math. He became his own court of appeal, with potentially 2,977 cases to hear.

He was surprised when the first person to visit him, a young firefighter's widow with two children, aged six and four, didn't appeal the amount of her award. It was close to the average final settlement: $2 million, give or take. (The maximum was about $7 million.) Instead, she asked for her check to come more quickly than it was scheduled to arrive. She needed it within thirty days.

Feinberg blanched at the request. Thirty days just wasn't possible. He had to justify his figures to the Treasury Department, which could accept or veto any settlement at which he'd arrived. Bureaucracy doesn't move that quickly, especially when it comes to the apparatus that writes checks. "Why do you need it so fast?" he asked.

"I have terminal cancer," she said. "My husband was going to survive me and take care of our two children, and now they're going to be orphans. I've got to get that money to set up a trust fund, because I'm not going to be around much longer."

That was the instant the old Feinberg began making way

for a new, less mechanical, more bespoke version of Feinberg. The widow got her check. She died eight weeks later. "That was the first one," he told me. "I knew after that one, I'm in for rough sledding."[2]

In the end, Feinberg settled with 97 percent of the families, distributing about $7 billion. Because tragedies and the funds we set up in response to them have become unceasing, so have the demands for Feinberg's singular expertise. He has since helped compensate the victims and their families of the Virginia Tech massacre, the *Deepwater Horizon* oil-rig disaster, the stage collapse at the Indiana State Fair, the crash at the Reno Air Races, the Aurora movie theater mass killing, the school shooting at Newtown, the Boston Marathon bombing, and Boeing's 737 MAX crashes. He has developed best practices that he faithfully abides: He always meets one-on-one with the victims; he has never again valued one person's life more than any other; he has decreed that a lost arm is worth the same as a lost leg; rather than try to measure pain, he grades the seriousness of an injury based on how many nights someone spends in the hospital. None of it is routine; all of it has become more like routine. I was with him for an hour once when he hadn't checked his email. He pulled out his phone. In that short time, he had received requests for his assistance for two more calamities: the shootings at Fort Hood, and the deadly wildfire

---

2 Feinberg later met with another lost firefighter's widow and three semi-orphaned children. She was crying so hard during their meeting he was worried she was going to collapse. "My life is over," she told him. "I'll never be the same." She had lost the perfect man. The next day, Feinberg received a call from a lawyer representing that same firefighter's secret second family—another widow, absent only the ring, and another two fatherless kids. Feinberg debated telling the first family about the second, perhaps abetting the first wife's grief, or preventing half-siblings from unknowingly meeting and dating. He kept quiet and wrote two identical checks.

in Prescott, Arizona. It was as though he carried a graveyard in his pocket.[3]

Feinberg was resistant to the idea that his work had changed him very much. But those who knew him best saw the differences before and after. He listened to opera at loud volumes almost constantly, as though trying to drown out other sounds. (For a while he found the only way he could sleep was by buying a ticket to the actual opera, where he would collapse in his seat, washed over by what he called "the height of our civilization.") Dede told me that her husband was far more empathetic than he had been, a more compassionate man. Camille Biros, who had worked with him for more than thirty years as his right hand, believed that his grief-soaked meetings had turned him into one of the world's most gracious listeners. His son, Andrew, said that he saw his father age dramatically over the thirty-three months he spent distributing the September 11 fund. He could see in his father's face the weight that he carried, even if Feinberg himself tried to shrug it off.[4]

There is a case to be made that by meeting with the families of the victims, Feinberg made a profound mistake—not personally, or not only personally, but professionally: that their tears and scars were the worst kind of prejudicial evidence, robbing him of his former objectivity, his clinical strengths and the coolness of his judgment. It was the opposite of analytical. "That's probably right," he said when I raised the possibility with him.

---

3 Feinberg has written two books on his work: *What Is Life Worth?: The Inside Story of the 9/11 Fund and Its Effort to Compensate the Victims of September 11th* (New York: PublicAffairs, 2006), and *Who Gets What: Fair Compensation after Tragedy and Financial Upheaval* (New York: PublicAffairs, 2012).
4 Rapid, premature aging has been associated with scapegoats and sin eaters for centuries.

But later I saw him teaching a class at Harvard Law School, which, like opera, he had taken up as an antidote to his other work: Teaching is an act of hope. On that sunny afternoon, he spoke about the limits of numbers. Statistics, he said, might work wonders in ballparks. An increase in class sizes might be all the argument you need in front of a school board. Not, he said, in a court of law. He brought up the example of a late-night hit-and-run involving a bus. Only one bus company operated a bus on that route at that time of night. The odds overwhelmingly suggested that a bus from that company was the one involved. Was that enough evidence to bring the company to trial? Some of his students began to nod. Others weren't so sure.

"Absolutely not," he shouted, and he slapped his desk so hard that a few of his students jumped.

I'm convinced that a large part of Feinberg's success is attributable to the power of his voice. It's thick and loud and warm; if anyone on Earth could hold a conversation with thunder, it would be him. Now he continued to shout, as though he were making a declaration from rooftops, commanding people on the street below to stop and hear him. That classroom was *listening*, as rapt as any courtroom on the verge of a verdict, waiting to hear whatever it was he said next, because there was a chance that it might change everything.

"We want witnesses, not just statistics," Feinberg said, his voice continuing to rise like his audience. "We want human beings. We are not calculating machines. We are not some assembly line of math." He hit the desk again. I don't think he was really talking about buses.

———

In 2019, *Logic*, a smallish, excellent magazine dedicated to technology, published an interview with an anonymous algorithmic trader.[5] Following the economic collapse of 2008, the financiers responsible weren't held remotely to account, but one of the so-called corrections was an increasing reliance on machines to do our trading for us. "Part of the shift involved removing human decision-making when it wasn't perceived as adding any value," the anonymous trader said. Striving to make a market more efficient makes ruthless sense: If something doesn't add value, you get rid of it, like astronauts and their heel calluses. But I was intrigued by the trader's use of the word *perceived*. Data is meant to lessen our reliance on perception, to help us replace our beliefs with facts. But here was an algorithmic trader, one of the Robespierres of the Data Revolution, talking about dramatic changes that happened because of how something *seemed*.

The financial markets were supremely inclined to see the potential benefit and feel the wide-ranging effects of analytics, because inside the blackest of black boxes, the numbers were all that ever mattered. Interestingly, however, a lot of investors have needed something more than numbers from fund managers. Return on investment obviously reigns triumphant, but people still want to *understand* where their money is going, and funds often explain their strategies with stories. (One algorithmic trading strategy involves trawling social media to divine "sentiment" about the markets or a particular product—using data to understand how people *feel*, because feelings still have their influence.) Lately, more funds have told

---

5 No byline, "Money Machines: An Interview with an Anonymous Algorithmic Trader," *Logic*, Issue 6, January 1, 2019. The entire transcript is worth reading. Our anonymous trader explains complicated things simply.

the story that they have better quantitative methods than any-one else—better algorithms, better computers, better nerds, better access to better data. The number-crunching has *become* the narrative. Take the billion-dollar rise of a consultancy like Mu Sigma, the world's largest "pure-play data analytics firm." The first question their site asks visitors is: "Do you have the people, processes, or platforms to keep up with the data deluge? We do." They exist to help other firms do the math they can no longer do on their own.

That "data deluge" raises a couple of serious problems. (Let's set aside the fact that many people are lying about their mathematical abilities, or, like Ryan Kavanaugh at Relativity, at least exaggerating their prowess.) As we've seen, data mining relies largely on history repeating itself, and it doesn't always. Unfortunately, quantitative models believe what they're told. "As these techniques become more widespread," the anony-mous trader said, "the assumption that the world will behave in the future the way it has in the past is being hard-wired into the entire financial system." Making a system that affects our reality while also ignoring it does not seem like a good idea.

One of the interesting effects of COVID-19—the sort of unpredictable flash event that algorithms have trouble reconciling—was the puzzling buying behavior that humans, as a species, demonstrated upon its arrival. Like weather models, financial markets get confused when their inputs—otherwise known as "us" and "our lives"—change too quickly or too radically; they tend to break when both happen at the same time. The panic buying in the early days of the pandemic took even the most robust AI by surprise.[6] What model

6 Will Douglas Heaven, "Our Weird Behavior during the Pandemic Is Messing with AI Models," *MIT Technology Review*, May 11, 2020.

could have foreseen the skyrocketing demand for toilet paper? Or the enigmatic run on chest freezers? Or punching bags? Putting too much of our collective faith in data can leave entire markets looking like empty grocery store shelves.

I live on a lake, and our local canoe and paddleboard supplier couldn't keep anything that floats in stock during the pandemic. That makes sense to me in retrospect. With regular sports canceled and fear of plague in the air, more and more people chose to stay fit and isolated on the water. But I refuse to believe that in February 2020, say, any predictive model knew that it was time to sink all of your money in canoes. Of course, not many people would have known to make such a smart bet, either. Placing it would have required a special kind of intuition, or at least quick reactions. That means only a *certain* kind of person could have: the creative, imaginative free thinkers this book celebrates.

That brings us to the other problem with the current state of data-driven conformity. Machines might not panic like humans, but they do act increasingly in unison. If too many funds follow the same approach—presumably the consultants at places like Mu Sigma don't give contradictory advice to each client—crests and troughs will be more extreme. Tying everyone together works well enough when markets are happy and calm; a rising tide lifts all boats. But when the inevitable storm comes, everyone goes down together.

We've reached a state of systemic fragility, one that means a single wrong number can decimate an entire industry. (Or, as the GameStop debacle proved, a few rogue traders with a Reddit account can blow up hedge funds worth billions.) A 2018 lawsuit against Facebook exposed either an honest flaw in the social media giant's internal accounting or, its claimants argued, a sinister plot to deceive: It had overestimated the "average duration of video viewed" metric, making it seem as though people were watching videos for longer than they actually were. (Any video watched for less than three seconds wasn't included in the data. Facebook told its advertisers that eliminating the low end had inflated viewership numbers by about 80 percent; its advertisers argued that the numbers were off by 150 to 900 percent.)[7] By then the damage was done. Media companies—whose traffic had already become so dependent on Facebook shares—had stampeded toward an ill-fated "pivot to video," laying off writers and editors to make room for videographers and producers. MTV News, Vice, and Vocativ were among the companies that underwent seismic shifts in how they delivered their news. When not nearly as many viewers watched the videos as had been expected, more layoffs came. Mic, for instance—a New York media company that reached nearly 20 million mostly millennial visitors by 2014—made a massive bet on video; its traffic and valuation each plummeted by tens of millions, until it was finally sold off for a fraction of its former worth.[8]

Trading, similarly, doesn't allow everyone to be right at the same time, even given a sounder statistical underpinning. Money that appears somewhere has disappeared from somewhere else. In today's remorseless markets, if you do what everyone else is doing but a little worse, you'll lose. (And again, if you're all wrong, the world will tilt on its axis.) Like the slight edge that a casino holds over its patrons, that sliver of weakness will be found out. That's what happened in baseball, when the reveal of Billy Beane's "secret" led to a more

---

7 Maya Kosoff, "Was the Media's Big 'Pivot to Video' All Based on a Lie?" VanityFair.com, October 17, 2018.

8 Mathew Ingram, "Mic Shuts Down, a Victim of Management Hubris and Facebook's Pivot to Video," *Columbia Journalism Review*, November 29, 2018.

efficient market; the teams that spent more money did better again. The Red Sox and Cubs, not the A's, won the World Series. The giants reasserted their place.

In the movie version of *Moneyball*, Brad Pitt, playing Beane, explains the flip side of the same premise to his room of befuddled scouts: "We've got to think differently," he says. "If we try to play like the Yankees in here, we will lose to the Yankees out there."

"Boy, that sounds like fortune-cookie wisdom to me, Billy," his chief scout says back.

"No," the Pitt version of Beane says. "That's just…logic."

Why wouldn't the same hold true for analytics and their application? "One of the fallacies that people have is the assumption that because the people who are working at certain firms are smart, they must be successful," the anonymous algorithmic trader said. "But the fact that they understand artificial intelligence or machine learning or big data is somewhat useless as a competitive advantage if everyone else understands it as well." Advantage, as ever—not just in finance, but in business, in baseball, in whatever competitive situation you might imagine—comes by doing something better than everyone else, or by doing something different from everyone else.

There can be only one "best." Fortunately, there are countless ways to be different.

———

In May 2018, Jason Witten, one of the great tight ends in football history, retired from the Dallas Cowboys. He was thirty-five years old when he appeared in a blue suit at an emotional news conference in Frisco, Texas. His decision to leave the game after fifteen seasons was not easy; those few athletes who choose when to go—unlike the hobbled, marginal majority whose fates are dictated for them—often find it the most difficult decision of their career. "No man knows when it's the right time to walk away," Witten said. "And I'm no different. It's been said, whether it's right or wrong, it's better three hours too soon than a minute too late. The man who insists on seeing with perfect clearness before he decides—he never decides."[9]

Witten's struggle to know what to do next seemed unlike him. He appeared clairvoyant on the field, displaying the same "sense of where you are" that Bill Bradley famously and beautifully expressed on the basketball court.[10] At Witten's farewell, his admiring coach, Jason Garrett, also in a blue suit, sat beside him and told a story to illustrate his tight end's singular understanding of how things work. It revolved around Witten's signature play, the Y Option.

Sports can be complicated, football especially, but the Y Option is the simplest of routes. ("Simple, but not easy," Witten said.) The target—usually a tight end, but sometimes a traditional receiver; Julian Edelman frequently ran it for the New England Patriots—sprints five or ten yards from scrimmage, dead ahead, and then chooses whether to turn inside, toward the middle of the field, or outside toward the sideline. The Y Option presents a relative rarity in sports: an almost purely binary choice. Inside or outside? How much thought can go into that?

At their preseason camp in 2015, Garrett had asked Witten

---

9 Witten later changed his mind and returned to the Cowboys in 2019 after an unsuccessful season in the broadcast booth for ESPN's *Monday Night Football*. "It sucked," he said.
10 John McPhee, *A Sense of Where You Are* (New York: Farrar, Straus and Giroux, 1965).

to answer that question in front of the team at their night meetings. "It was simply the greatest presentation I've ever seen in football," Garrett remembered.

The coach estimated that half of Witten's career receptions — 1,152 at the time—came on the Y Option. Witten himself guessed about 500 of them had. Whatever the actual number, the way Witten ran the Y Option made it almost impossible to defend. Witten's advantage was foreknowledge. He *chose* which way to go; the defender—his competitor, in business parlance—could only react to that choice. Each Y Option was a microcosmic illustration of the benefits of leading over following. Witten never followed.

First Witten told his team about his preparation before the ball was snapped: his stance, the placement of his hands, how he shifted his weight. Then he spoke about everything that went into his decision to run inside or outside, his years of practice and experience that gave the illusion of providence. Witten told his enraptured teammates how he angled his release depending on the inclinations of the defender, how he allowed himself a precise number of steps to make his choice, how he could feel the alignment of his opponent in his core and whether that doomed man—not wanting to lose the half-step it would take him to respond to Witten's move—was leaning inside or outside based on small tells in his eyes, his hips, his feet.

Witten finished his presentation, Garrett said, by playing a piece of film from the previous season, a clip of one play during a playoff game against the Detroit Lions. With just over six minutes left and the Cowboys down by three, they faced a 4th-and-6 on Detroit's 42-yard line. "The play of the game," Garrett said. He called for the Y Option. Detroit's two-man coverage was tailored to prevent its success, because it almost always forced the receiver to break outside. Garrett estimated that against that look, the receiver was pushed to the sideline ninety-five times out of a hundred. Given those percentages, the defender would not have to guess where his man, or the ball, was headed. He'd know with an almost unassailable certainty that Witten was headed outside, eliminating his advantage.

When the ball was snapped, Witten steamed about twelve yards forward. Witten was quick rather than speedy; his defender stayed with him. Then Witten—"who knows this play better than anybody on the planet," Garrett said—felt his man move underneath him, assuming that Witten would be playing to the outside. That was a good assumption; the percentages overwhelmingly supported it. But Witten, faster than any machine might calculate, in the middle of a professional football game's madness, processed all of that information and turned it into artistry. He *faked* the predictable move outside, taking a big step with his right leg and nodding his head in the same direction. The defender bit, and Witten turned back inside, now with daylight between them. He received a perfect pass from Tony Romo for a twenty-one-yard gain, first down. Six plays later, the Cowboys scored a touchdown and won the game.

"I'll tell you why this play really worked," Witten said to his team, and Garrett, relating the story in front of an already tearful audience, now lost his voice. He gathered himself and said that Witten ran the film again. This time, Witten ignored what he was doing, and instead went through how every man on the team contributed to that completion—how every Cowboy had his own role to play, and each man had played it perfectly: Dez Bryant, Dallas's obscenely talented wide receiver, drew double coverage; the offensive line gave flawless protection to Tony Romo; Romo's throw was right between the numbers.

Garrett reached the end of his account of Witten's speech. The coach's eyes were still glistening. "So it struck me," he said, "that this play, his signature play, where he made it at the critical moment, he didn't make it about him. He did what he always does: He makes it about everybody else." Garrett again lost his voice, and he reached for a bottle of water to give himself time to find it. "He made it about the team."

I've watched the video of that news conference probably a hundred times, and it never fails to move me. It's not just Garrett's obvious love for Witten that chokes me up, or that we get to see someone do something as well as it's ever been done. It's the levels of the game that can be seen in that single play, like the layers of rock in a canyon wall. The Y Option is simple, yes. Absent close attention, it's completely uninspiring. "It's not sexy, and really, it's tough to make an eight- to ten-yard route look sexy," Witten said.[11]

But that same simplicity makes it a wonderful departure gate for the imagination. You can watch that play and see whatever you want to see. It's the blankest canvas. You can see the value of teamwork or one man's particular excellence. You can admire the concreteness of numbers or the cracks of their limitations. You can isolate the pass or look at the mayhem that surrounds it. I don't really go for the idea that sports are metaphors for human existence; they are games that we play, and life's big decisions have far greater consequences than whether we catch a ball or not. Still, that film is a good reminder of the scope of *opportunity* that exists in a single play in a single football game, never mind in the maelstrom that is life on Earth. How you watch that film—what you see, with

---

11   Jason Witten, "The Route You Can't Defend: Inside the Y Option," ESPN.com, September 20, 2018.

your particular set of eyes—demonstrates that abundance of possibility. The same situation, the same players doing the same things at the same times, reveals something new with every viewing.

For me, watching Jason Witten run the Y Option is proof that seemingly binary outcomes can be more than a choice between two paths. The Y Option isn't just inside or out-side. Watch that film. Watch it again. Watch it again and again and again. Each time the ball is snapped, each time Witten explodes over the line of scrimmage, there are any number of destinations available to him. With passion and practice and his unerring attention to detail, he has success-fully bent what might have been a constricting reality and made it his to control. The rules that everyone else has to follow no longer apply to him. He is permitted every possible outcome, because he has given himself so many ways to break free.

———

It's perhaps telling that one of the few negative uses of the word "creative" is associated with money: "Creative account-ing" means cooking the books. Smarter people than me have decried the "intellectual sterilization" of STEM grads that has taken place alongside the rise of Big Data. Because the pay at tech giants is so lucrative, young intellectuals tailor their edu-cations and experience to earn the typical roles at the typical places—"to work on irrelevant features for long-tail products that impact very few or stale, irrelevant features for products that are already at scale." So wrote Chamath Palihapitiya, the CEO of Social Capital, chairman of Virgin Galactic, and a minority owner of the supremely analytical Golden State

Warriors.[12] He argued that the same "lobotomization" that led to the 2008 financial crisis—when physics graduates who should have been working in space exploration or materials science were instead building identically catastrophic trading models—now occurs in technology. Too many smart kids are doing the same dumb things.

People have been exhorting other people to think more creatively since people began thinking. I'm slightly embarrassed to be adding to an already tottering pile. In 1967, Edward de Bono encouraged people to think laterally; in 2005, Malcolm Gladwell wanted you to think without thinking. In between, you were told to think different by Apple, to think like Leonardo da Vinci by Michael J. Gelb, and to think outside the box by several thousand overpriced management consultants. It's vaguely hilarious to presume that you can change the way someone thinks by telling them not to think the way they think anymore. It's a bit like telling someone that the cure for depression is to stop being sad.

I'm more inclined to suspect that if you're old enough to read this book, your brain is your brain, and it's going to continue working the way it works. I'm more interested in encouraging you not to succumb to the tyranny of numbers, and to see worth in your abilities even if you don't know anything about advanced mathematics. I'm not an especially creative thinker myself. There is a reason I write nonfiction rather than novels. I still believe there is a value in observing creative people at work. Not because you'll end up thinking like them, exactly,

---

12 Specifically, Palihapitiya wrote this and many other interesting things in his impassioned 2019 Annual Letter to Social Capital's stakeholders. He made the letter publicly available via his Twitter account (@chamath) on March 9, 2020. It's one of the few financial documents I can say I enjoyed reading. And pretty much fully understood.

or like anyone else—but because you might feel more inspired to think like yourself, in ways that only you do.

Of all the books on creativity, my favorite is perhaps Ed Catmull's *Creativity, Inc.*, written with Amy Wallace.[13] (Yes, she's my friend.) Ed is the president of Pixar Animation and Disney Animation. *Creativity, Inc.*, is a bit of a Trojan horse, packaged like a self-improvement book, but it's essentially the memoir of a man who has surrounded himself with inspirational people, and together they have made some unbelievable shit.

Pixar's first full-length movie was *Toy Story*. It came out on November 22, 1995, and was the top-grossing film of the year. It was also a piece of incredible invention, the first proper film to be animated entirely on computer. I'm sure there are lots of animators who hate it for that same reason. They can probably see a coldness in it, the way Christopher Nolan refuses to use digital cameras, or an audiophile deplores MP3s. But the way Ed told it, the making of *Toy Story* was a kind of Platonic creative ideal: a group of people shared an obsession with a fairy tale—the story of a lonely toy cowboy named Woody who just wants to be loved—and used the best modern tools to make it come true.

It wasn't easy. *Toy Story* took a team of about 100 people five years to make. Pixar nearly capsized under its all-consuming weight. Ed and his team answered to Disney, and Disney had its own, intractable ideas of what made a good story. I've worked for divisions of Disney and hope I do again; they are the best at what they do well.[14] They are also a machine,

---

13 Ed Catmull with Amy Wallace, *Creativity, Inc.: Overcoming the Unseen Forces That Stand in the Way of True Inspiration* (New York: Random House, 2014).

14 When you work for Disney, your paychecks have Mickey Mouse on them. I look more like a drug dealer than someone who might work

and *Toy Story* was constantly in danger of being devoured by it. Disney had enjoyed great success with musicals, and, not surprisingly, they wanted *Toy Story* to be filled with songs. (Ed did not.) The folks at Pixar also received story notes that they felt compelled to incorporate, because they came from important people like Jeffrey Katzenberg. He felt Woody needed more edge. "Gradually, over a period of months, the character of Woody—originally imagined as affable and easygoing—became darker, meaner...and wholly unappealing," Ed remembered. "He had, in short, become a jerk." On November 19, 1993, Ed and his team showed Disney a mockup of the film with a fiery Woody, including a scene in which he unceremoniously defenestrated Buzz Lightyear. Repelled by the monster they had helped make, Disney immediately shut down production. That day is still known within Pixar's walls as "Black Friday."

But a little over two years later, *Toy Story*—the real *Toy Story*, the original *Toy Story*, the *Toy Story* that was made by people who used machines rather than people who obeyed them—came out and made its own history. "Despite being novice filmmakers at a fledgling studio in dire financial straits, we had put our faith in a simple idea: If we made something *we* wanted to see, others would want to see it, too," Ed wrote. "Now, we were suddenly being held up as an example of what could happen when artists trusted their guts."

That faith was shaken when Pixar began their inevitable work on *Toy Story 2*. The first installment had made $358 million

---

for Disney, and a bank teller once asked me what I did for them. (She omitted "What on Earth..." from the start of her question, but I still heard it.) I convinced her that I was the voice of Pluto. In fact, she'd shout "Pluto!" whenever I walked into the bank. I never had the heart to remind her that Pluto does not talk.

worldwide; of course there was going to be a sequel. Originally it was envisioned as something slapdash and direct-to-video, to capitalize quickly on the success of its groundbreaking predecessor. Thankfully, history tells a different story. Ed and his team realized that setting out to make a pale imitation of something great ("Shadows") is the same as admitting that you want to make something bad ("Rose & Her Shadow"). Pixar adopted a new motto: "Quality is the best business plan." At the time of this writing, the studio has made twenty-three full-length animated films. Eleven have won the Oscar for Best Animated Feature, including *Finding Nemo*, *WALL-E*, *Up*, *Inside Out*, *Coco*—and *Toy Story 4*. Their average box-office gross approaches $700 million.[15]

But here's what I like best about the lessons of Ed Catmull: He doesn't pretend what he does is particularly complicated. A lot of people have tried to portray creativity as a mysterious, impenetrable process, to make their own work seem more insightful or important than it really is. Honestly? Love something as hard as you can. Be voracious in your appetites. Take your time. If you have good taste, trust it. Don't worry about your process; worry about your discipline. Recognize that sometimes your work won't love you back, and that sometimes you will feel alone in your pursuits. Resist the urge to compromise, especially if a machine is the one asking for concessions. Try to make good things, and try to make good things better. And try to do that unlike anyone else.

---

15   Take a bow, Robert McKee.

CHRIS JONES

Let's take the most boring thing imaginable and try to re-imagine it. Concrete is the most popular building material in the world because it's cheap, durable, and easy to make and pour. It has four ingredients, each fundamental and as essential as the others: water, sand, gravel, and cement. The first three, obviously, are natural; cement is a binder, like brick mortar, made of kiln-baked lime and clay that constitutes about 15 percent of the mix. That's been the recipe for concrete for centuries, and it's been used to build the Roman Colosseum and Burj Khalifa in Dubai and millions of buildings, dams, and sidewalks in between. Concrete is the ultimate volume business: We pour enough every year to cover the whole of England.[16] The only obvious way to gain an advantage in the concrete market is to make more of it than anyone else, so you can make it cheaper than anyone else.

That volume has led to some significant problems, as volume so often does. Were concrete a country, it would rank third on the list of world polluters, after China and the United States. All told, concrete production is responsible for as much as 8 percent of carbon emissions. Its powdery mixers are also a significant contributor to air pollution; in Delhi, for instance, a tenth of the city's chronic air pollution comes from construction dust. Concrete's raw materials, while seemingly plentiful, are also finite resources, especially when we use 40 billion tons of them each year. The concrete business accounts for 10 percent of industrial water use. Even sand is becoming a scarce commodity. Desert sand doesn't work in construction, because grains shaped by wind rather than water are too smooth and round to bind together. (That's why Australia exports sand to the Middle

---

16   Jonathan Watts, "Concrete: The Most Destructive Material on Earth," *Guardian*, February 25, 2019.

2 0 4

East.) Illegal sand mines and criminal control of an increasingly dark trade have become commonplace. Sand mining has erased dozens of islands in Indonesia and sand divers in India have carved new rivers fifty feet deep.[17]

What can be done? *Use less concrete* is the obvious solution, and alternative building materials such as bamboo are being explored—there's a good and understandable reason for that market to exist. But realistically, concrete will continue to be poured at record rates, and the construction industry hasn't been given a lot of incentive to change.

In a way, the concrete market has the same constraints familiar to Canadian dairy producers and processors. Since the 1960s, farmers there have been given provincial quotas to meet, and in return they receive board-set prices for their milk, which both props up small markets and keeps the product and prices stable. The product stability means that consumers aren't brand loyal. The price stability means that across the country, milk costs a little less than a dollar a liter, give or take. There isn't any way to gain a cost advantage or capture more of the market with a superior product: Milk is milk the way concrete is concrete.

Unless, that is, producers add a little something extra to their milk, like chocolate and other flavors. If that chocolate is branded, then consumers will favor some over others and pay a premium for them. Nestlé makes a single-serving "milkshake" flavored like its popular Coffee Crisp[18] candy bar and charges $2.50 for less than a half-liter. Take milk, add a shot of flavor and color, and you can more than double its price—as

---

17 Vince Beiser, "The Deadly Global War for Sand," *WIRED*, March 26, 2015.
18 It's Canadian, and it's delicious. A very adult chocolate bar, for refined, polished palates.

well as increase the chances that consumers will buy *your* milk, even though at bottom it's the same as everyone else's.

In a space where it's seemingly impossible to innovate, the concrete industry has, at least at its more advanced margins, become a hive of creativity. Several manufacturers are trying to make it a contest between chocolate milks. The process began decades ago, when they started using fly ash and slag—waste products of the coal and steel industries, respectively—in place of cement, which is the most expensive and polluting ingredient because of the heat required to fire it. A newer addition to the mix is crushed post-consumer glass, "ground-glass pozzolan," which replicates the jagged edges of water-eroded sand. The understanding that concrete can trap pollutants rather than create them has led to another alternative concrete ingredient: carbon itself. Some manufacturers have found that injecting liquid carbon into their concrete makes it stronger, reduces the amount of cement required, and keeps that carbon out of the atmosphere; others have started collecting smoke from their stacks and turning it into artificial limestone, which can then be used to make cement.[19]

There is no machine that can replace that eye for opportunity. Algorithms don't experiment. You beat them by refusing to follow their rules. The most enterprising of us never look at something and see it for what it is; they ask why it's that way and then wonder what else it might be, even when it comes to something as seemingly inalterable as concrete. They are the doctor whose patient presents the usual symptoms of aging—hypertension, diabetes, creaky joints—

---

19 Jane Margolies, "Concrete, a Centuries-Old Material, Gets a New Recipe," *New York Times*, August 11, 2020.

but also widening spaces between his teeth, and tests him for acromegaly.[20] In the mundane, creative people see the potential for giants.

Chrissy Teigen, who learned the nature of refinement as a *Sports Illustrated* swimsuit model, turned her own eye to a product that sometimes can be confused for building material: banana bread. It took her a year to perfect her recipe, which, unusually, included chocolate, coconut, and a box of vanilla pudding mix; it has helped turn her *Cravings* cookbooks into bestsellers and seen runs on Bundt pans. Cat Bordhi built her own domestic empire out of extraordinarily innovative knitting.[21] She found new ways to knit socks (starting unconventionally at the heel rather than the toe or cuff) and physics-defying "Moebius" cowls, twisting scarves without end. Shortly before she died in 2020 after a long fight with breast and endometrial cancer, she wrote: "Knitting has the most marvelous ability to free up the knitter as a human being, while masquerading as innocent knitting."[22] Cancer finally claimed her, but UCLA's Dr. Dennis Slamon saved millions of other women from similar fates—despite significant scientific skepticism—by injecting them with the antibody Herceptin. Caitlin Flanagan, a fierce, funny writer for the *Atlantic* and the mother of twin boys, earned eleven years of breast cancer remission thanks to Dr. Slamon's determination. "Do you know what it's like for a mother of school-age children to be given an eleven-year remission?" she wrote. "And it was

---

20 Lisa Sanders, "The Patient Had Pain When He Walked, but There Was a More Telling Change," *New York Times Magazine*, July 27, 2018.

21 Yes, there is such a thing, and yes, there is a demand for it. Bordhi's self-published first book, *Socks Soar on Two Circular Needles*, sold more than 100,000 copies.

22 Ann Shayne, "A Note from Cat Bordhi," *Modern Daily Knitting*, September 16, 2020.

the direct consequence of the UCLA scientist who never gave up."[23]

I'm not advocating that you "trust your gut," which is too often used as shorthand for gambling, or indulging your biases. We're not talking about blind faith or dumb luck or raw animal instinct here. (Trust *that* when you're in physical danger.) My gut would be useless when it comes to many things, because there are many things that are mysteries to me—like trying to referee a sport I've never seen. I want you to have faith in your earned, valid experience. The pressure to conform is real, and it's hard to resist the supposed infallibility of analytics. But you have advantages, especially if you study and practice and experiment and observe, and that expertise is special to you. That's not gut. That's *embodied analysis*. Use it to make something different and beautiful and human. Try to build something that lasts.

In 1979, Peter Good was thirty-eight years old and fairly early in his graphic design career—"not a star," he said—when he received a call from a friend at an advertising agency: Did he want to design the logo for a hockey team?[24] The New England Whalers of the World Hockey Association were poised to become the Hartford Whalers of the National Hockey League, and they needed a new identity. Peter and his

---

23 Caitlin Flanagan, "I Thought Stage IV Cancer Was Bad Enough," *Atlantic*, June 2020.

24 I spoke with Peter Good on October 7, 2020. Apart from being a wonderful designer, the man has a beautiful voice. He and his wife's design firm, Cummings & Good, still operates in Chester, Connecticut. All logos included here have been reproduced with their kind permission.

wife, Jan Cummings, had opened their own firm in Chester, Connecticut, and together designed a number of corporate logos, as well as objects like posters and book jackets. Neither had worked in sports. Peter wasn't even much of a hockey fan. "I used to play hockey on ponds," he said, "but the only thing I knew was, you were supposed to get the puck in one net or the other."

Peter told his friend: "Sure."

The Whalers didn't present him with a design brief. They made no specific demands. Peter's only guide was the team's old logo, in green and white. It consisted of a large "W" bisected with a harpoon. The rest was up to him.

"It will never happen that way again," Peter said, although it could happen exactly that way again if only someone, somewhere made those same choices. Couldn't it? "A major sports team coming to a single designer?" Peter said. "Today they would go to Nike or some sports marketing company and have ten designers working on it."

Like so many of our pursuits, graphic design was not always the complex industry it is today; until the 1960s, logos were still largely functional rather than a means of potentially iconic expression. In 1965, Peter Good was the first graphic design major to graduate from the University of Connecticut, the only one in his class. He learned more on the job, including valuable years at legendary Chermayeff & Geismar Associates in New York City. They had made one of the first abstract corporate logos in America: the Chase Manhattan octagon that the bank still uses. Peter became a typography obsessive and consumed every design journal and periodical he could find. He saw inspiration whenever he opened his eyes. He never wondered whether he had found his calling. He was one of those lucky people who did what they were *born* to do.

Now handed the Whalers' nonexistent brief, Peter did what he was *taught* to do: He pulled out a pad of paper and a pen and began sketching. That's how his mentors worked, and those simple, manual tools served them with grace. "Basically it starts with the mind coordinating with the hand and the eye," Peter said. When I spoke to him in the fall of 2020, he was seventy-eight years old and still working; his life and business partnership with Jan had lasted fifty-five years and counting. While computers had become an integral part of their operation, Jan was the techie between them, the more analytical mind. Peter remained an intuitionist, and he still began his work with paper and a pen. Any idea that popped into his head, he'd sketch, even if it was awful, even if he knew it was useless. He didn't want to shut the door to any possibility.

He winnowed hundreds of ideas down to nine for his opening presentation to the Whalers. They included whales paired to form either an H for Hartford or a W for Whalers; two versions of a whale's fluke; the tip of a harpoon; and one that turned the W into a trident, with three points on top. In the negative space, there was an H:

Peter Good

Peter was lucky that he wasn't serving many masters. In his experience, design by committee often ended up watered down. Pass a logo around a table and everyone felt like they had to have something to say about it; "Looks good to me" made them sound uninvolved. Take all of those inputs and you end up with something flat and compromised. Over the last forty years, Peter has grown only warier of the clumsy influence of market research and focus groups. "The more requirements you have to address, the more diluted the solution becomes," he said. People tend to be repelled by unfamiliar things. Graphic design that gets filtered through a crowd often ends up feeling familiar, because people tweak it to resemble something they've seen before. They immediately like that better. "But if you do something familiar right away," Peter said, "it might be comfortable, but it will be forgotten. A lot of good ideas would never get past a focus group." Focus groups famously hated the first episode of *Hill Street Blues*, a series that changed how we watch television.[25] Focus groups are vaccinations against bravery.

In the case of the Whalers, owner Howard Baldwin had the first and final say. He looked at Peter's nine possibilities and picked the trident. "That's fine," he said. "Let's go with that." Peter asked him why he liked it, and Baldwin said he liked the H. Having been given that fragment of guidance, Peter asked if he could work on the logo some more. He thought the trident was a bit top-heavy—"rather crude," he said—and he'd never liked the idea of incorporating a harpoon into his design. The team's mascot was a whale, after all. Peter

---

25 Brett Martin, *Difficult Men: Behind the Scenes of a Creative Revolution* (New York: Penguin Books, 2014).

remembered thinking: "Why would you have a symbol that kills your mascot?" Baldwin agreed, and Peter returned to his studio.

Here began another small battle in the endless war between mechanics and feel. Remembering our discussion about screenwriting in the first chapter, following precise instructions from experts can yield respectable results. Since you've read this far in the book, I'd rather imagine you're in closer league with the geniuses—golfer Rory McIlroy, for one. In 2018, he fell to thirteenth in the world rankings and sought help from legendary putter Brad Faxon to ease his woes. After McIlroy sank one of three eight-foot putts on the practice green, Faxon asked him to try putting with his 5-wood instead: McIlroy dropped all three. "I wanted to prove something to you," Faxon told him. "A lot of putting nowadays is very technical and mechanical. It needs to be instinctive." McIlroy won Bay Hill his next time out, after what he described as the best putting week of his career.[26] Guitarist Eddie Van Halen, for another, famously did insane things to his rigs, driven by the pursuit of an elusive, perfect tone he called "brown" sound. He soaked his pickups in paraffin wax and drilled them directly into the bodies of his guitars, believing in the power of a more direct connection; he maxed out his amps so courageously, the editors of *Guitar Player* warned its readers that attempting the same modifications risked frying them— both the amp and the person plugged into it. Van Halen took that same lethal combination and wrote "Ain't Talkin' 'Bout Love."

---

26 Paul Kimmage, "Rory Revisited: No Questions Off Limits, No Subject out of Bounds as Paul Kimmage Meets Golfer of the Decade," Independent.ie, February 2, 2020.

Peter Good realized he had been given the great gift of working with two symmetrical letterforms—W and H—and he had always been mindful about the use of negative space in design. (The most famous modern example might be the arrow in the iconic FedEx logo; if you haven't seen the arrow, it's between the E and the X. It will be the first thing you see from now on.) "Negative space tantalizes the eye," Peter told me. It gives a static image a subconscious energy, a sense of movement that we *perceive* even if we don't see it, exactly. But maybe the H in his logo needed to be a little more elusive, more of a discovery. He began playing with ideas involving a whale's tail rather than a harpoon or trident—also symmetrical, and more positively symbolic. "The tail propels the whale," Peter said. "It gives it power, direction, thrust, all great metaphors for a sports team."

In 1979, making a logo was messy handwork.[27] Paper soon littered the walls and floor of his office. He took Rapidograph pens to vellum, sandpaper to acetate. "It's trial and error, essentially," Peter said. "You keep on trying—trying to find that solution that's eluding you. It rarely comes from a conscious kind of analytical thinking. You have to do something and then put it away. You might be walking down the street and something occurs to you that makes that work. You might hear a phrase that triggers something that will alter that design. It's about being open. It's the process."

---

27 If you look closely at the four corners at the bottom of the H, you'll see "light traps," a tell that a design is analog rather than digital. At the time, logos were reproduced with Photostats, which tended to round corners with use. Light traps kept them sharp. I love very much that a hockey sweater worn by Gordie Howe included Peter Good's hand-drawn light traps.

Peter Good's process ended here:

Peter Good

The Whalers were never much of a hockey team, but their logo—singular, uncompromised, handmade—was met with almost universal acclaim. It's simple, beautiful, reproducible at any scale, and instantly recognizable.

Sadly, the Whalers played their last game in Hartford in 1997; owner Peter Karmanos Jr. moved the team to Raleigh, North Carolina, where they became the Carolina Hurricanes. Peter Good's design disappeared from the ice, seemingly forever. But in 2010, thirteen seasons after the Whalers had left Hartford, their timeless logo remained among the National Hockey League's top five sellers. Carolina's far more carefully vetted iconography was ranked the worst in the league by the *Hockey News*, and fans routinely showed up wearing the old sweaters as though they were supporters of another team, from a different city. "What have you done, Carolina?" the *News* asked. The Hurricanes crest was meant to look like the eye of a storm but is more often likened to a flushing toilet. Where once there was art, now there is another familiar, forgettable machine.

MEDICINE

Every Sickness Asks a Question.
The Only Answer Is a Cure.

*We have made even treating our sicknesses
a mechanical, unfeeling process, which hurts
both patients and doctors. Why would we try
to make the world such a cold, dark place?
We need to take a less clinical approach to
medicine—and to the rest of our lives. Ask
yourself: What brings you comfort? What
brings you happiness? What do you want to
make? How do you want to be remembered?
I imagine you'd like to be someone who can
pass the new Eye Test. Imaginative. Creative. Expert. Human. Now: What's your
four-leaf clover?*

The U.S. hundred-dollar bill is the closest thing we have to a
global currency. The United Nations recognizes 180 currencies
as legal tender, but none is *more* recognized than the American
greenback—specifically the one featuring Benjamin Franklin's
tight-lipped visage. There are tens of billions of American
hundreds in circulation—billions of pieces, not dollars—and
at any given moment, about 60 percent of them are changing
hands outside U.S. territory. Not surprisingly, the Benjamin
is also the most counterfeited bill in the world, giving it the
contradictory distinction of being the most trusted and suspect

of banknotes. Behind that sturdy, familiar face lives a great irony: From gamblers in Las Vegas to taxi drivers in Taipei, we've put our universal faith in the single denomination most likely to betray us.[1]

For several prideful and hegemonic reasons, the U.S. government wishes to maintain that tenuous-seeming trust, and it has repeatedly asked the three bodies that oversee the production of American currency—the Treasury Department, the Federal Reserve, and the Secret Service—to improve its robustness. The most recent version of the hundred, which first appeared in 2013, is filled with technological wizardry that seems impossible to replicate. ("We can't say that," one senior member of the Secret Service told me, because forgers have proved equal to almost any challenge. "But it will be very, very difficult.")

The newest bill is less a banknote than a tiny, complex machine, the product of computer-enabled advances in manufacturing and design. It contains watermarks and security threads, raised printing and color-shifting ink, secret features revealed by ultraviolet and infrared light, and a mysterious internal trigger that instructs photocopiers not to reproduce it. But among its most vanguard defenses: the blue plastic ribbon threaded through the paper it's printed on. Each ribbon is less than five-thousandths of an inch thick and contains 875,000 microscopic lenses. They magnify iconography—Liberty Bells and the numeral 100—printed behind them with such microscopic specificity that lettering of the same size could fit every word in the Bible on the face of a dime, twice.

---

1 I spent a long time researching currency design for a story about the new U.S. hundred for *Esquire*. ("The Benjamin" appeared in the September 2013 issue.) Spending time at the Bureau of Engraving and Printing was proof to me that wonders sometimes exist behind the most everyday objects. Someone made them. That someone probably has a story to tell.

Like smartphones that contain the sum total of human knowledge, these are remarkable technologies that we slip into our pockets without much thought.[2] But one aspect of the U.S. hundred remains familiar enough to occupy a place deep in our subconscious: The paper we chase hasn't changed since 1879. Other national currencies are made increasingly of slick, shiny polymers. Plastic banknotes were first introduced in Australia in 1988, both as a deterrent to forgery and because they're more durable than paper. The U.S. government has periodically considered switching but has kept using its unique paper stock, the only one in the world made of cotton reinforced with linen. There's good reason to believe we'd notice pretty quickly if it did change, because of how fast we think with our hands.

Crane & Co., a small, family-owned company in Dalton, Massachusetts, has made that paper for five generations. Every dollar printed today is born in the same rotary boiler, a beast of a kettle that spins like a planet before it vomits another pile of scalding raw cellulose onto the floor. (Sometimes the cotton comes from offcuts from denim factories, which explains why American cash ages like jeans.) That boiler seems a relic of a spitting industrial age, like the broad-backed men who sweat in its shadow. But those men and their groaning machine remain the spark behind the most modern of processes; their ancient ways serve, as they so often do, as the foundation for our ever-evolving new. Set aside the latest hundred's microscopic technology and its shielding artistry. Its life still begins in cotton and flax fields, and next comes a flame.

---

2 An exception: The dollar bill has been left untouched for more than fifty years, and in 2015, it was protected by Congress from any future redesign. That's not because the design is particularly venerated. It's because the vending machine lobby doesn't want to change its machine readers every time a new currency design comes out.

In the late 1980s, a counterfeit hundred began circulating that was difficult even for the professionals to detect. It looked identical to the real thing, betrayed visually by only the most rigorous forensic testing. After enormous copies of the phony bill were made, detectives found some minor imperfections in its engraving, but the rest of the work was so flawless, they decided those defects were intentional. Its makers didn't want to get duped by their own handiwork. Since then, new generations of the same counterfeit have floated into currency markets, including a "Big Head" version, mimicking the redesigned hundred that first appeared in 1996.

The bogus note was first delivered to America on boats by Chinese gangs. Its origins were ultimately traced to North Korea, and it's believed to have been manufactured by the North Korean government on its own presses, but there's room for doubt: A British crime syndicate also printed about $35 million in high-quality copies. The family of linked fakes has been given its own title, one that befits its legendary stature: the supernote.

The Secret Service won't acknowledge its existence. (When I asked my agent about it, he refused to say a word in response. He just looked at me until I asked a different question.) Some stories about the supernote have assumed the quality of myth, and they are impossible to confirm. There have been reports that it was first laundered by a bank in Macau; several bricks of them allegedly appeared in Lima overnight, threatening to tip over the entire Peruvian economy. But there is one truth about the supernote that the American government and its agencies have never forgotten: It was first detected not by a computer or some other forensic instrument, but by an ordinary teller at the Central Bank of the Philippines, hand-counting a stack of bills. The supernote might have *looked* flawless, but its makers did not have access to a very particular rotary boiler in Dalton, Massachusetts, which meant they couldn't make a perfect copy of Crane & Co.'s soft yet substantial paper. What stopped that teller in the middle of her stack was an unfamiliar sensation in her fingertips.

Something just didn't feel right.

––––––––––

When COVID-19 began its own grim spread in late 2019 and early 2020, many of the warnings came in the form of technical, statistical projections, nightmarish to the point of abstraction—millions dead, tens of millions more infected. Whether the projections were ultimately accurate or inaccurate is impossible to prove: the inputs changed, and so the outputs did, too. Exponential growth is hard to predict, and a small, early intervention can drastically change the result. Dr. Anthony Fauci, the weary public face of the fight against the virus in America, cautioned against the efficacy of models from the start: "I just don't think that we really need to make a projection when it's such a moving target, that you could so easily be wrong," he said.[3] New York governor Andrew Cuomo expressed similar reservations: "The projection models have a number of alternatives," he said. "No one can tell you which will occur."[4]

It's also uncertain how useful the models were in motivating

––

3 Dr. Fauci said this to Jake Tapper on CNN on March 29, 2020, after suggesting that the U.S. could see millions of cases and between 100,000 to 200,000 deaths—projections that proved, sadly, significant underestimates.

4 Joseph Goldstein, "When Will N.Y.C. Reach the Peak of the Outbreak? Here's What We Know," *New York Times*, April 6, 2020.

changes in human behavior. (The answer seems clearest in the United States: *not very*. It arguably mattered more that Tom Hanks came down with it, in no small part because he's more relatable than a hypothetical curve.) COVID-19 data was compromised in the standard ways humans corrupt supposedly incorruptible data, and that didn't help. Two studies were retracted when one of their authors, Dr. Sapan Desai, proved a suspect source, helping to "sow confusion and erode public confidence in scientific guidance."[5] Certain American states used statewide hospital data—combining urban and rural hospitals—to present more optimistic pictures than were true in cities, where some hospitals were overwhelmed.[6] Florida's COVID-19 data scientist was fired, she said, when she refused to cook the positivity rate to help the state meet federal guidelines for reopening.[7]

Even when the data and its application was more rigorous, it never offered a complete picture. Big Data, including the quant armies at Google and Facebook, sought to monitor virus spread through cell phone usage, but COVID-19 disproportionately affected poor and marginalized populations with limited access to mobile networks, meaning the people most likely to get the virus weren't among those tracked.[8] "In the fog of the pandemic," one analyst wrote, "every statistic tells a story, but no one statistic tells the whole truth."[9] That's

5 Ellen Gabler and Roni Caryn Rabin, "The Doctor Behind the Disputed Covid Data," *New York Times*, July 27, 2020.
6 Jim Salter and Lindsey Tanner, "As Virus Grows, Governors Rely on Misleading Hospital Data," Associated Press, June 26, 2020.
7 Marisa Iati, "Florida Fired Its Coronavirus Data Scientist. Now She's Publishing the Statistics on Her Own," *Washington Post*, June 16, 2020.
8 Amos Toh, "Big Data Could Undermine the COVID-19 Response," *WIRED*, April 12, 2020.
9 Derek Thompson, "COVID-19 Cases Are Rising, So Why Are Deaths Flatlining?," *Atlantic*, July 9, 2020.

because a plague isn't any more perfect in its behaviors than we are. It often but doesn't always follow patterns, and its otherwise linear paths are inevitably altered from within, by variants, and without, by outside forces and interruptions. Viruses are living things—sort of—and like all living things, their first and sometimes only loyalty to math is that they will do whatever it takes to multiply.

In March 2020, Dr. Michael J. Ryan, the executive director of the World Health Organization's health emergencies program, was asked what he'd learned fighting Ebola outbreaks in Congo, and how his wisdom might be applied in the global battle against COVID-19. Dr. Ryan is Irish, which perhaps gives him an innate understanding of complications. He began his answer equivocating: Sometimes we take lessons too closely to heart and believe they will protect us against every possible future, and sometimes we forget too easily what we have only recently suffered.

Then his voice became sterner, and he spoke with the certainty of a man who has stood too close to the dangers of uncertainty. He painted a picture of the world as it is—chaotic, random, extreme—not as the orderly, predictable system we wish for it to be. Sometimes you don't have time to do the math, and sometimes the math won't give the right answer anyway. You need to trust your experience, your wisdom, and reach some internal, *felt* conclusion faster than even a computer might: "You need to react quickly," he said. "Be fast. Have no regrets. You must be the first mover. The virus will always get you if you don't move quickly…If you need to be right before you move, you will never win. Perfection is the enemy of the good when it comes to emergency management. Speed trumps perfection. And the problem in society we have at the moment is everyone is afraid of making a mistake. Everyone is afraid of the consequence of error. But the greatest error is not to move. The greatest error is to be paralyzed by the fear of failure."[10] The worst answer is no answer.

Science denialism is its own plague, of course. *Of course.* But in healthcare, more than most fields, practitioners have to make enormously consequential decisions based on incomplete pictures and the suspicions that arise from them. "When we have a lack of scientific evidence, then we have to use our judgment on what might be the best thing to do and what's at stake," Benjamin Cowling, a professor of epidemiology and biostatistics at Hong Kong University, has said.[11] It's alarming to think how routinely doctors are forced to make best guesses; the imminence of sudden death doesn't always allow them perfect understandings. Dr. Sara Seager, the astronomer, told me that I'd be surprised how much science—the sort of science that changes our lives, and sometimes saves them—begins as a hunch, as a feeling: a sixth sense, derived from some larger, expert familiarity with both the positive and negative natures of progress.

Maybe it's a coincidence that the countries with the best COVID-19 responses—Iceland, say, or New Zealand—eschewed modeling for a profoundly human, case-by-case approach to the virus. Maybe it mattered more that they are islands, or have small populations, or are led by women. Maybe it's a coincidence, too, that some of the leading American plague hunters—Dr. Fauci, but also Dr. Francis Collins, the director of the National Institutes of Health—are deeply religious, equally reverent in labs and churches. Both men have

---

10 Dr. Ryan made his statement during the WHO's daily briefing on March 13, 2020.

11 Maggie Koerth, "Science Has No Clear Answers on the Coronavirus. Face Masks Are No Exception," FiveThirtyEight.com, April 6, 2020.

talked about the humility that their faith gives them—their understanding that their understanding will have its limits—but also that it's within their mortal reach, and in fact is their moral duty, to try to improve the lives of their fellow humans. Indisputably, however, their kind of science, like every search for a solution to a problem, begins with a hard-wired, almost animal reaction to something undesired: *I don't like what's happening here.* Next comes what you're going to do about it, and how you're going to do it. Seeking a solution through analytics is one possibility. Maybe you want to build a better machine. Or maybe you want to find at least part of the answer in your fellow humans: in those who are suffering, and in those who might heal them.

———

In 2016, Michael Lewis published *The Undoing Project.*[12] It was a departure for him, except that it became yet another bestseller. (That sounds more bitter than I would like. I'm sure he's a very nice man.) Like *Moneyball*, it's about the limits of our capacity for reason and the limitlessness of our appetite for self-delusion. But rather than casting a lonely man in a fight against idiots—rather than viewing change through the lens of conflict—*The Undoing Project* reads more like a love story.

Two revered psychologists reside at its heart: Dr. Danny Kahneman, a quiet, serious Holocaust survivor given to crushing bouts of self-doubt, and Dr. Amos Tversky, Dr. Kahneman's brazen opposite. They met at Hebrew University in Israel in the late 1960s, and at first they did not enjoy each

---

12 Michael Lewis, *The Undoing Project* (New York: W. W. Norton & Company, 2016).

other's company. Their personalities clashed, and so did their approaches to their studies of human behavior. Dr. Tversky was more mathematically inclined, and statistics-based in his approach. Dr. Kahneman was less dogmatic and certain. But they were soon inseparable, equally fascinated by the same deeply mysterious human process: decision-making.

Their foundational work began at a time of looming suspicions about experts, including medical doctors. A psychologist named Dr. Lew Goldberg at the Oregon Research Institute had published a damning paper in *American Psychologist* about the relative quality of professional radiologists when they were pitted against an algorithm designed to diagnose stomach cancer. The algorithm was built upon what the doctors agreed were seven signs of trouble, including the shape of an ulcer, and the size of the crater that it made. Researchers gave the doctors (and the algorithm) nearly 100 images of ulcers and asked them to decide whether they were obviously benign, malignant, or something in between. Some of the images were repeats, inserted into the mix to see how consistent both the doctors and the algorithm were in their judgments.

The model proved nearly as effective as the doctors, in part because every doctor in the study gave differing opinions of the same ulcer at least once. In a subsequent study, Goldberg found that the doctors performed less well against the algorithm because it was better than they were at following their own guidelines: The doctors made errors when they disobeyed their own rules. Unlike them, the machine was unwavering. It didn't freelance or have off days. It never got tired or hurried or bored. If it wasn't perfect in its assessments, it was consistent in its imperfections.

Over their decades of research in psychology and behavioral economics, Drs. Kahneman and Tversky gave name to a litany of human missteps, everything that makes us behave more erratically than machines. "Recency bias" was one: our tendency to weigh recent events as more significant than historical ones, particularly when it comes to predicting what will happen next. Or "selective matching," when we might relate two occurrences—bad weather and joint pain, for instance—because they coincided once but memorably. Or "creeping determinism," a common affliction among historians, who tend to link and derive larger meaning from events that were, in fact, random and unrelated. Each was more evidence that we were clumsy about something at which we thought we excelled. Asked whether their work might be applied to the burgeoning field of artificial intelligence, Dr. Tversky demurred: "You know, not really. We study natural stupidity instead of artificial intelligence."

Interestingly, their own methods could never be replicated by machines. Drs. Kahneman and Tversky worked mostly by locking themselves in a room and barking at each other in excited streams of Hebrew and English, making points and counterpoints until they reached unimpeachable conclusions. In his book, Lewis quoted one of their more admiring colleagues, Dr. Paul Slovic: "They had a certain style of working," Dr. Slovic said, "which is they just talked to each other for hour after hour after hour." They often made each other laugh; they always made each other think. It was helpful, at least at first, that they so often disagreed.

Knowing what they knew about human behavior didn't prevent Drs. Kahneman and Tversky from behaving similarly in time. Ideals are hard to uphold even for the people who set them. They weren't robotic thinkers, and they weren't robotic about their feelings, including how they felt about each other. Despite their undeniable accomplishments—Dr. Kahneman won the Nobel Prize in Economic Sciences in 2002—they exhibited the same weaknesses of character that, at one time or another, every one of us has betrayed: regret, anger, pride, envy. By the time Dr. Tversky died of cancer in 1996 at age fifty-nine, they had fallen out completely.

Algorithms might not fall in or out of love, but they aren't as obviously superior to their human counterparts as Drs. Kahneman and Tversky might have believed, at least today.[13] A 2017 study pitted the diagnostic abilities of twenty-one board-certified dermatologists against an algorithm that had been trained with nearly 130,000 pre-labeled images of the most common and deadliest skin cancers. By the lights of that study's authors, the machine and the doctors did equally well— a "comparable" level of competence.[14] In 2019, researchers at the Medical University of Vienna trained a different algorithm using thousands of images of benign and malignant skin conditions. Their AI proved slightly better than human doctors at diagnosing a few specific maladies—such as pigmented actinic keratosis, patches of scales caused by sun damage—because the machines paid closer attention to the skin around the blemish.[15] Mostly, however, there wasn't much between them.

That doesn't make either of them failures; both are effective diagnosticians. In a wider study, the Viennese tried a more cooperative method of diagnosis rather than an either/

---

13 Algorithms are constantly improving, and what's true of them today will not necessarily be true of them tomorrow. Of course, the same is true of us.
14 Andre Esteva, Brett Kuprel, et al., "Dermatologist-Level Classification of Skin Cancer with Deep Neural Networks," *Nature*, January 25, 2017.
15 Philipp Tschandl, Noel Codella, et al., "Comparison of the Accuracy of Human Readers versus Machine-Learning Algorithms for Pigmented Skin Lesion Classification: An Open, Web-based, International, Diagnostic Study," *Lancet*, June 11, 2019.

or approach: Why not examine worrisome lesions multiple ways? Emboldened by their clearly insane notions, the researchers gave 300 doctors three kinds of machine assists: one that provided a list of diagnoses ranked by probability; another that offered a specific probability whether a lesion was malignant; and a third that provided images of conditions that the AI thought were similar. The latter two did not help the doctors; their diagnostic accuracy remained unchanged. But the first, the probability rankings, improved some doctors considerably. The collective accuracy of the team of human doctors rose 13 percent.[16]

There are provisos. The machine, not surprisingly, proved particularly helpful to young and inexperienced physicians. Seasoned doctors, passers of the Eye Test, knew at least as much as the AI. If anything, better dermatologists were prone to being led astray by the algorithm, changing their correct diagnoses because the machine suggested different ones. They didn't trust enough their own expert eyes, a modern malady of its own. (In a devious move, the researchers tweaked their AI to give it a glitch, spitting out incorrect probabilities. Some doctors were tripped up by it, having been too quick to put their faith in their automated assistants.) And there remain so many things that human doctors do that machines can't, like plan tailored courses of treatment or tell someone who's worried that everything will be okay.

But for non-specialists, or for doctors-in-training, the AI provided a boost. Because skin cancer is so widespread and treatable, a 13 percent improvement in diagnosis is considerable: Over time, that elevation will save thousands of lives and

---

16 Philipp Tschandl, Christop Rinner, et al., "Human-Computer Collaboration for Skin Cancer Recognition," *Nature Medicine*, June 22, 2020.

prevent thousands of needless surgeries. Who would choose for their doctors to be less accurate than they might be? Dr. Sancy Leachman, a professor of dermatology at Oregon Health & Science University, said of the study: "This is not about who does the work, human or machine. The question is how do you successfully use the best of both worlds to get the best outcomes."[17] Her Austrian counterparts reached the same conclusion: "Collaboration is the only way forward."

Before the end of their relationship, Drs. Kahneman and Tversky also studied "framing," the idea that we're more inclined to choose one option over another equal option because of the way it's presented. Most people will choose a surgery that has a 90 percent chance of saving them over a surgery that has a 10 percent chance of killing them. Which returns me to my original problem with how the analytics revolution has been *framed*: that you're either for it or against it, and the other side is hopeless or blind. Among everything else we frame, we also frame our perceptions of ourselves and each other. When people don't behave the way an algorithm might, we've been taught to think of their behavior as flawed. The opposite of "rational" is "irrational," and irrationality is almost always expressed as a negative. (Or as "human stupidity.")

I understand the attraction of extremes. They offer clarity, however illusionary and dangerous that conviction might prove. It can be hard to accept how much of our lives are accidents. A world of chaos is an uncomfortable cathedral in which to sit, and it's appealing to imagine we have more control over the future than we do. But life on Earth doesn't run like a clock. If it did, its surface wouldn't be swept by hurricanes.

17 Tom Simonite, "This Algorithm Doesn't Replace Doctors—It Makes Them Better," *WIRED*, July 17, 2020.

The ground wouldn't occasionally move beneath our feet. And yet some people who admonish the more magical thinkers among us for being *irrational* also somehow believe that we're capable of having nearly perfect control of our fates, so long as we're smart enough to do the math. What? That's *nuts*. Besides being illogical—a different version of the sin of being human— it presumes the rest of us should *want* to be robots, as though we should aspire to be a *what* instead of a *who*. Kenneth Feinberg is right: "We are not assembly lines of math." If human beings are, by our nature, irrational, then it's far more rational to think of ourselves as acting *reliably* human rather than *unfortunately* human. Our peccadillos are not mistakes. They are a function of who we are, and the world in which we live. Even Dr. Danny Kahneman understood the limits of his own prescriptions: "No one has ever made a decision because of a number," he said. "They need a story."

Dr. Rita Charon helped found the field of narrative medicine in 2000, after she became troubled by the way modern Western healthcare viewed—*objectified* is a better word—its patients and its practitioners.[18] Its systems-based approach wants to treat everyone involved as either the working or non-working parts of a machine, as almost unwitting bystanders to the real biological action unfolding around them. It felt to Dr. Charon as though our diseases themselves had become the most

---

18 Dr. Charon herself is careful to point out that no one person is capable of such wide-ranging reform, and change is a deeply collaborative process— see her article "The Shock of Attention" in *Enthymema* XVI, published in 2016. But despite her humility, she deserves credit for much of narrative medicine's founding ethos.

central, active characters, and the "best" treatments of them had become singular and universal, as though cancer were its own creation, as though diabetes existed in the world apart from us. Hospitals were too much like factories. Surgeries used to take place in operating theaters. Now they were performed by clinicians, in clinics.

Dr. Charon began thinking of herself as a more principal actor in the 1970s, when one of her patients, a man with cancer, saw her surname on her lapel. His eyes went wide. "So this is it," he said. In Greek mythology, Charon is the boatman of the underworld, ferrying doomed souls across the river Styx. The patient died two days later. Worried that she had given him fear rather than peace in his final hours, Dr. Charon nearly rushed to City Hall to change her name.[19] Instead she returned to school, to Columbia University, to earn her PhD in English literature. If she wanted to find a new way for us to understand sickness and its treatment, she first needed to learn something about structure. She developed a particular affection for Henry James: *Try to be one of the people on whom nothing is lost.*

Today, Dr. Danielle Spencer is the academic director of Columbia's Master of Science program in narrative medicine, which trains clinicians to apply some of the perspectives and techniques of the humanities in their practice, and encourages caregivers and patients to give greater voice to their experience. It was the only such program in the world when it began offering a master's degree in 2009; another has since been developed at the University of Southern California. Unlike Dr. Charon, Dr. Spencer is not a medical doctor. Her varied career includes ten years working as the art director for David Byrne,

---

19   Sigal Samuel, "This Doctor Is Taking Aim at Our Broken Medical System, One Story at a Time," Vox.com, March 5, 2020.

the famed artist, musician, and founding member of Talking Heads; together they collaborated on graphic design, fine art, and public art projects. Dr. Spencer learned to love Byrne's genre-busting, expectation-defying approach to his labors. "It was always interestingly difficult to explain in a nutshell what any given project was," she said. She was attracted to narrative medicine in part because of its interdisciplinary nature. "What happens when you bring different fields together in unexpected ways? Something interesting might happen."[20]

Dr. Spencer has a more personal reason for believing in a multifaceted approach to diagnosis and treatment. She coined the term "metagnosis" to describe the revelation of a condition that's been long present but undiscovered, like the slew of parents who realize they have lived their entire lives as people with autism, dyslexia, or ADHD when their children are diagnosed. For some people, the realization changes the stories of their entire lives and their roles in them. It reorders things. It clarifies and distorts. Dr. Spencer was diagnosed with a visual field defect that she had no idea she had, and no one else had detected. How could she have known she saw the world differently from others? She had never looked through anyone else's eyes, and no one else had looked through hers.

In the United States, medical education has remained largely unchanged since 1910, when an educator and critic named Abraham Flexner issued the *Flexner Report*, a wide-ranging collection of proposed reforms. In contrast to their peers in

---

20 I interviewed Dr. Danielle Spencer on August 20, 2020. She was indulgent of my generalized idiocy, and I appreciated her patience. She's the author of *Metagnosis: Revelatory Narratives of Health and Identity* (Oxford: Oxford University Press, 2020) and the co-author of *The Principles and Practice of Narrative Medicine* (Oxford: Oxford University Press, 2017).

more formalized Europe, North American doctors did not receive standardized training—leading to practicing physicians with wildly different competencies. Flexner wanted to close nearly 80 percent of existing medical colleges and have those that remained steep their students in hard science. "Flexnerian biomedicine" is, at its heart, modern medicine: using deep knowledge of physiology and biochemistry to treat disease and sickness. Although Flexner could have never foreseen the use of algorithms as diagnostic tools, they are the logical outcome of his recommendations more than a century after he made them.

Flexner's approach, and the work of his many acolytes, has yielded countless gains. He was a great believer in vaccines, for instance, and the number of former biological death sentences that have been commuted are too numerous to list. Such an unwavering focus on hard science was also accompanied, unfortunately, by the dehumanization of medical practice. Not only did doctors become standardized instruments; so, too, did patients. While Flexner wrote that physicians should behave ethically, America's newly rigorous medical education didn't always include training in ethics, which seemed to some too muddy and subjective a topic. How do you teach someone to be *good*? How do you embrace difference when the wrong kind of deviation can lead to death? Flexner's noble quest to rid the field of its charlatans and quacks meant that he also took a dim view of anything that resembled personality; fifteen-minute appointment blocks and the thirst for efficiency has rushed the rest of our character out through our doctor's office door.

Narrative medicine doesn't seek to diminish the importance of hard science in medical practice. "It's a corrective to the perceived dominance of biomedicine at the expense of humanistic values," Dr. Spencer said. In other words, it's about the more subjective, personal considerations that Flexner's reforms left out—like how a patient might react to seeing a doctor named Charon.

———

For many doctors, a patient's disease experience begins when he or she arrives in their ominous presence, complaining of symptoms. Practitioners of narrative medicine warn against writing such an unassailable version of events. There is no such thing. The moment of a patient's arrival is not the true start of any illness experience, or it's the start only in certain versions of its telling. (The acromegaly example I used in the previous chapter is based on a real case; the long road to diagnosis began with a balky hip, but the story of that patient's illness really began with the first unwelcome cells invading his pituitary gland.) There are multiple beginnings and so there are multiple ends, and each patient's journey between them varies as widely as the second act of every story ever told. Like Michael Lewis's respect for the role of luck in our lives, two patients could present the same disease in identical ways and receive parallel treatments and experience different results. Psychologists since Sigmund Freud have long understood the importance of narrative in their courses of treatment. Why should physical maladies be any different? Every sickness is its own drama.

There might be some biological reason for a spectrum of patient response, an unseen superpower or fault in their genes. (Remember how COVID-19 so dramatically affected some people while others were asymptomatic.) It might also be a hazier result of the rest of their lives, outside of their shared sickness—their socio-economic status, or whether they love and are loved. Narrative medicine asks that practitioners and patients become reciprocal partners in the joint experience of one getting better and the other helping them get better, both playing parts as speaker and receiver, as teller and listener. At bottom, it's about treating the patient as directly as the disease. Why did he or she get sick in the first place? If a sick person is "non-adherent" to prescribed treatments, why? An algorithm might tell one version of that story, and it could be a valuable account. "In many cases, I'm going to embrace that," Dr. Spencer said. But it isn't the only version of the story, nor the only relevant one.

Today's clinical practice in medicine too often presumes a collective agreement on means and goals, including a treatment's preferred outcome. "Getting better" can be defined so many ways—fixes are not universal, within medicine or without—and yet we enter the doctor-patient relationship assuming we're all on the same page. In virtually no other aspect of our lives do we believe everyone has identical desires. Pre-existing conditions might change the equation for some of us. Not everyone wants to live to be 100, or would give up bacon for an extra three years of good health. Narrative medicine asks us to remember that even when it comes to sickness and health, one person's blessing might be another person's curse. "That's certainly the case in end-of-life care," Dr. Spencer said. "Why shouldn't that be the case across the board?"

Doctors also suffer for our collective tunnel vision: Flexner's educational reforms have saved some of their most strange and unfortunate side effects for medical students. Numerous studies have shown that while they usually begin their training as devoted servants to others, they finish it cold and callused. Right about the time they begin seeing patients—exactly when we want them to care the most—they experience a kind of "empathy crash," becoming less compassionate than even the average human. Their suicide rates skyrocket; among those who survive the process, their souls may never recover.

Perhaps that hardening is a natural self-defense mechanism, the way a turtle lives in its own shell. Doctors must erect emotional walls between them and pain so that they don't themselves experience it. But it's also a partial result of their sleepless, harrowing educations—competitive past the point of degradation—and the hard-nosed, data-driven directives they've received. When you come to think of your fellow human beings as assemblies of cells, you, too, become less human. Dr. Spencer asked the obvious rhetorical question: "If you don't have wellness among providers, how can you expect them to be as compassionate and caring as we'd like them to be?"

During COVID-19's advance on New York City in the spring of 2020, the virus wrote and rewrote many thousands of stories. One of the more capable human chroniclers of that awful time was Dr. Craig Smith, the chair of Columbia University's department of surgery and surgeon-in-chief at New York–Presbyterian Allen Hospital. An expert cardiologist, Smith also has an enviable command of the English language. He began issuing written missives, distributed on Twitter, about the course and abatement of the pandemic. He sometimes included numbers. He almost always used language we don't expect from our doctors: evocative, poetic, crystalline. When a colleague was intubated on March 27, he wrote: "The enemy is inside the wire." On March 30, he wrote again: "It is time for battlefield promotions. Whether you're a frustrated leader-in-waiting, or a reluctant leader who needs to be catalyzed by events, this is your time. Dandelion seeds go nowhere without wind." On March 31, his message grew plainer: "We got this."

Did Dr. Smith save lives with his words? Perhaps not in the traditional sense; they pushed precisely zero air into collapsing lungs. But they did call heroes to action. They did give sufferers hope. Is that medicine? That seems indisputable to me.

He could not save everyone. One of COVID-19's many victims was among his fellow doctors at the Allen: Dr. Lorna Breen, a dedicated, almost pathologically driven emergency-room physician, killed herself on April 26.[21] She had told friends that she was "baffled and overwhelmed" by her pandemic experience. She had practiced considerable self-care over the course of her career—getting regular sleep, finding diversion in the mountains—but now she didn't have enough time or energy to look after her patients, never mind herself. A quarter of the Allen's COVID-19 sufferers died. "I couldn't help anyone," she had confided to a friend. "I couldn't do anything. I just wanted to help people, and I couldn't do anything." First she decided she could never be made better, and then she made one final decision.

By the coldest, strictest definition, she died of suicide. That's how her death would be recorded by an algorithm's accounts. But was that the sum of her experience? Was that the conclusion of the novel of her life? I suspect we would have acted differently, as a society, to the spread of COVID-19 if we'd seen the faces of the victims, if we had watched them die, instead of seeing the ends of their lives recorded as data points on a chart. If we'd seen what the doctors were seeing, maybe we would have been more careful, and more caring. What we saw from a remove—the distance of analytics this time acting

---

21 Corina Knoll, Ali Watkins, and Michael Rothfeld, "'I Couldn't Do Anything': The Virus and an E.R. Doctor's Suicide," *New York Times*, July 11, 2020.

as a comfort—they *felt*. What we deflected, they were forced to swallow. In certain versions of Dr. Lorna Breen's story, it's not hard to imagine that she drowned.

———

On March 12, 2009, a Sikorsky S-92 helicopter, delivering workers to an oil platform southeast of St. John's, Newfoundland, was forced to ditch in the Atlantic Ocean.[22] When dots disappear from radar screens, phones begin to ring. In the case of the missing helicopter, owned and operated by a company called Cougar, Rob Manuel was one of the first to receive a call. He's a tall, soft-spoken constable, posted at the time to the Major Crimes Unit of the Royal Canadian Mounted Police. He was called because accidents are not always accidents, and police decide whether a tragedy is the result of bad luck or something worse. In his work, Manuel has learned to be a fastidious note taker, and he began taking notes immediately that morning. He received the first call about the helicopter at 10:18 a.m. His notepad said so, and his notepad was one of the world's most unimpeachable sources.

That first wave of phone calls often relays information that is later proved untrue. (The same phenomenon happens in mass shootings, when first reports of multiple shooters almost always are found to be multiple sightings of the same shooter.)

---

22 I wrote about this accident and its investigation for *Esquire*: "The End of Mystery" appeared in the September 2009 issue. I spoke to several of the people involved, particularly Mike Cunningham, for years after. Accidents and their investigation became a strange obsession of mine. I couldn't explain why—there was just something about the people who try to find order in our most random-seeming experiences. Sitting next to them is like sitting next to someone who knows so much more about how the world really works than you do.

Manuel was told early on that rescuers had arrived at the site of the helicopter's ditch and found it floating on top of the water. He looked up from his notepad. "In hindsight," he said, "those reports were incorrect."

Other fragments of the reports he received were more accurate. A life raft was, in fact, found on the water, but it was empty. A survivor, a twenty-seven-year-old ice watcher named Robert Decker, was lifted from the surface. A body was also retrieved; it had belonged to a twenty-six-year-old cafeteria worker named Allison Maher. After some time, Manuel managed to determine that the helicopter had carried sixteen passengers and two crew. Some quick math told him that fourteen passengers and the two crew were still missing, along with the helicopter.

Not very long ago, those sixteen people would have been declared *lost at sea*. Newfoundland is wholly familiar with those three words and the sad mystery they represent. For centuries, fishermen took entire schools of cod where they now drill for oil, and in exchange, the ocean took hundreds and thousands of Newfoundland's fishermen. That was a rule of engagement with the North Atlantic—not only in Newfoundland, but for lost navies of mostly men in Massachusetts, and Ireland, and France. Those left behind struggled to explain why their loved ones didn't come home. Grief had a way—it still does—of opening imaginations wider than they might have been, especially when the twin objects of that imagination were a lost husband and the sea. Mermaids took them. Sirens sang to their hearts. They had passed through the gates of Atlantis and been greeted as kings; they were swallowed whole by vengeful white whales and giant squid.

Death could be magical then. Today, death is largely solvable. It's more knowable. Some people spend their lives trying to explain why people died when they did. In addition to Rob Manuel, Mike Cunningham, an accident investigator with the Transportation Safety Board of Canada, was called to St. John's. He summoned Allan Chaulk, his more mechanically inclined colleague, to join him.

Cunningham, a pilot who grew up next to the ocean, became an accident investigator in part because his father had crashed his own plane into the sea. He focused on the human side of the equation. Chaulk would attend to the potential failures of the machine. One couldn't complete his job without the other. Together they would first find the helicopter and its occupants, and then they would come up with a reason why it, and they, were at the bottom of the ocean rather than in the air, and then they would issue a report to try to prevent the same accident from happening again. Their job was a type of medicine; it was an antidote. But unlike typical physicians, they would never know the names and faces of the people they had saved, nor would those people know they had been rescued. Cunningham and Chaulk just had to believe that somewhere there was another helicopter that would not crash because of the time they spent inside one that did.

Chaulk led the team that used a camera-laden remote-operated vehicle (ROV) to find Cougar's lost Sikorsky. He was scientific about the search; the size of the ocean demanded he be methodical. He turned Robert Decker and Allison Maher into data points, along with the helicopter's blown-out door, a Pelican case, and some duffel bags that had been likewise recovered from the surface. He plotted the helicopter's flight path and measured the ocean's currents, and within a few hours, 540 feet beneath the waves, he had found a curled-up page torn from a flight manual anchored in the silt. The ROV nosed deeper into the darkness ahead, and Chaulk leaned closer to his monitor, until together they found the helicopter, turned almost inside out, lying on its right-hand side. They also caught flashes of orange survival suits and green rubber boots, perhaps as many as sixteen pairs.

Normally, aircraft accidents are not the result of one catastrophic failure. Investigators refer to such a mythical, singular source of blame as "the Golden BB." The human desire for definitive explanation can blind amateur detectives to more complex diagnoses, and veteran investigators fight against that same urge. Experience teaches them that accidents are most often the result of a series of mechanical shortcomings, compounded by pilot error. Usually, six or seven things have to go wrong, in a precise and cursed order, each breakdown feeding the other: what experts call "the chain of events." A lot of bad things have to happen without interruption for an aircraft to fall out of the sky. In their way, accidents are terrible miracles.

Even tragedies that *seem* to have one cause often have many. Malaysia Airlines Flight 17, shot down over Ukraine in 2014, would appear to have ended, along with the lives of its 298 mostly Dutch passengers and Malaysian crew, when it was hit by a surface-to-air missile. But that rocket was fired because of a war on the ground, and that plane was flying over that war because of poor choices and bad weather. Remove any of those factors from the chain of events, and that plane lands in Kuala Lumpur. Instead, it and however many families ended up in pieces on the farm fields of eastern Ukraine.

The distinction is similar to one that forensic pathologists make when they differentiate between the *cause* and *manner* of death. The cause of death is the immediate reason for expiration: In the case of someone murdered by gunshot, the cause of death is the bullet inside him. The manner is the larger explanation of how the bullet got there. The cause is often clear, a function of science. Constructing the manner, like linking the chain of events, is an art. It's not an invention of imagination; it's the fact that only imagination reveals.

Before Allan Chaulk lifted the helicopter to the surface, he brought up its passengers and crew, and he delivered them to shore, to the autopsy suite in the basement of the Health Sciences Centre in St. John's. A thin-faced man named Dr. Simon Avis was waiting for them. He had lost track of the number of bodies he had dissected over the course of his career. "Two, maybe three thousand" was his best guess. He had emptied and scrubbed every metal table he had at his disposal, and he stood in the suite with sixteen more bodies to visit with his experience and instruments.

The usual challenges of his job had been reversed. He knew the manner immediately: helicopter crash. The cause was what was missing.

"I have a good imagination," Dr. Avis said, "but it's a different type of good. I can think around things. Forensic pathology is just like any other type of medicine. It's not a black-and-white science, at least not always. Sometimes the answers aren't obvious, and sometimes the answers won't come to me until after the fact. I don't consciously think about these things, but I know I've sometimes been in bed, half asleep, and woken up saying, *That's why*." The same process that helped Peter Good design a timeless logo also helped Dr. Avis explain tragedy.

He began with an external examination of each body. He X-rayed some of them. He performed full autopsies on others. He found little evidence of trauma. There were few signs of impact, no broken bones or crush injuries. Nobody had been burned. There were no other signs of fire or explosion, no smoke inhalation. He stood in the middle of his suite and surveyed sixteen bodies that might have seemed perfectly healthy if they were not bodies.

Drowned, he wrote. For pathologists, death by drowning is a determination that requires a particular faith. For all our science, for all our technology, there remains no diagnostic test to prove that someone has drowned. There might be physical evidence, pink froth in the mouth or water in the sinuses, lungs, or stomach, but there isn't always. Sometimes, drowning is dry. It leaves no anatomical testimony. When a body is recovered from the water, and no other cause of death is apparent, the victim is presumed to have drowned. Drowning is the cause when it's the only cause left.

The families of the dead came to see Dr. Avis, and he told them what he believed the bodies of their loved ones had told him: The helicopter's fall had been so fast, and so steep, they had lost consciousness before impact; they had stayed strapped in their seats and sunk to the bottom of the ocean, and they had drowned. None of them had struggled. They had felt no pain.

"I'm still a doctor," he told me. "It's not only the sick who need healing."

Meanwhile, after the smashed helicopter had also been recovered and brought to shore, Mike Cunningham and Allan Chaulk stood in a hangar and stared at what was left of the mangled machine. They had already sent its black box in a cooler of water to Ottawa, where a man named Ted Givins had begun extracting its data and voice records. The first black boxes—today they're actually orange—were developed in the 1950s and tracked just five parameters: air speed, heading, altitude, vertical acceleration, and time. The flight-data recorder of the Sikorsky S-92 monitors 500 parameters. Voice recorders, by rule, are more horrifying, and they sometimes reveal surprising clues to expert ears: Givins once diagnosed a plane's death rattle from the sound of the stricken pilot's clipboard beating against the wall. But the data is often the source of more valuable information—as it so often is, particularly when it comes to reconstruction.

In the case of the helicopter, Givins determined that twenty-seven minutes into the flight, the pilots experienced a sudden and dramatic loss of oil pressure. They turned around and descended quickly, but still in control, to 800 feet above the ocean. The main rotor still turned. And then, forty-three seconds before the helicopter hit the ocean, something very bad happened. The voice recorder was silent from that point on. It was unusually silent, in fact, given the terrifying circumstances. Givins deduced that the helicopter had lost electrical power, its systems had shut down, and the pilots had no choice but to ditch.

Back in the hangar, Chaulk now wondered what had caused the devastating loss of oil pressure. He took apart the oil-filter bowl assembly, about the size of a flower vase. Another Sikorsky S-92 had made an emergency landing in Australia because it also had lost oil pressure, and the problem was found to be three titanium studs that bolted that oil-filter bowl to the main gearbox, which powered the rotors. Chaulk found those same three studs in the Cougar. One was broken clean through, and a second could be turned by hand. Further investigation with an electron microscope revealed significant metal fatigue. The first bolt had snapped, causing a loss of oil pressure, which eventually led to a full, fatal system failure; fifteen seconds before the crash, the tail rotor's gear had shredded in the absence of oil and stopped spinning. Mechanically speaking, at least, Chaulk had found his Golden BB. That single broken stud had caused everything else to fall apart.

Now Cunningham, the humanist, put himself in the cockpit. He is a man of rigor and method, but he also has an incredible capacity for dreaming. He had imagined himself crashing all sorts of aircraft over the course of his career. He had closed his eyes and delivered a Piper Navajo into the river in Fredericton, New Brunswick, after its engines had failed; he had piloted an MK Airlines 747 cargo plane into the trees at the end of the runway in Halifax, Nova Scotia, and been engulfed in flames. Now he put himself in the cockpit of a howling, bucking Sikorsky S-92 over the waters off Newfoundland.

"There's a danger of getting caught up in that—a personal danger," he said. "But I think if you really want to understand...If you don't go all the way to the wall, you might never understand what it's like to arrive there."

Most pilots in crisis situations revert to flying by hand and by gut. Without instruments, the pilots of the Sikorsky had no other choice. Their only hope was a single, long-shot out: a complex emergency landing called an autorotation. By pitching the helicopter to harness the wind, they could keep the main rotor spinning even if the tail rotor wasn't. They could cushion their impact by raising their helicopter's nose at the last possible second, shifting the worst of the concussive physics to the tail. That required them to intuit when the last possible second would be.

Cunningham dreamed. He looked out the helicopter's windows at the unhelpful ocean, a featureless sheet of blue, rising fast. Then he heard a terrible sound, the scream of shearing metal and grinding gears. He fought to maintain consciousness during the inevitable fall. There were scuff marks on the main rotor, so the pilot must have managed at least half the required heroics. It was still spinning at impact. But despite all his training, despite all the technology in his hands, his survival, his co-pilot's survival, and the survival of the fifteen men and one woman he had welcomed on board, would ultimately depend on luck and his best guess.

How fast was he falling? How close was the surface? When should he try to lift the nose? Nothing outside of himself offered a clue. He guessed his speed. He guessed his altitude and angle. He lifted the nose—just a half-second too late, and listing just slightly to his right. And his helicopter crashed and sank to the bottom of the ocean. It wasn't his fault.

———

"This accident might be one where every question gets answered," Mike Cunningham said when he was nearly finished with his work. He and his peers paint complete pictures more often than they once did, although mystery remains. Sometimes entire planes still disappear, and not a single question is answered: Malaysia Airlines Flight 370, for horrifying example. But in the case of the lost helicopter, Mike and his fellow investigators found some perfect union of hard data analysis and human imagination—ideal modern problem-solving—which allowed them to diagnose a sickness, and then to cure it. The three titanium bolts in the oil-filter bowl assembly of every Sikorsky S-92 in the world were soon replaced.

That fix represents the essence of the Eye Test to me. I don't think I'm proposing anything revolutionary; I'm suggesting only that we should stop and think about what the analytics revolution gives us and what it costs us, and where it leaves room for us and what only we can do. The world is not a laboratory; not everything can be quantified. Unexpected things still happen, and we call them accidents. Sometimes they're happy, and we should seek to take advantage of them.

Sometimes they're tragic, and we should try to prevent them. How? The way expert accident investigators do.

Data alone wouldn't keep other helicopters in the air. Data helped. Human creativity, human imagination, finished the job. Think of some of the people you've met in these pages. I hope that you saw something to admire in all of them, and in how they do their work. In the chapter on entertainment, I wanted to make the case for good taste. In sports, for passion. In weather, for adaptability. In politics, for curiosity. In crime, for humanity. In money, for inventiveness. And now here, in medicine, for reverence—for us to regard ourselves and each other with the same awe as we regard our most miraculous instruments. Do you see those attributes in yourself? Then you are capable of wonders. If not, then I believe you can improve those qualities in yourself, and you will become the creative superior to every machine on Earth.

Of course, sometimes you will make mistakes. And you won't be able to answer every question that existence poses. In truth, there was still one mystery that even Mike Cunningham couldn't solve, and he has a name: Robert Decker. On April 8, nearly a month after the crash that had claimed everyone but him, Decker walked into RCMP Headquarters in St. John's, and was brought into a small interview room, followed by whispers and furtive glances. He sat down with Constable Manuel, who pulled out his notepad. Most of what they said to each other was kept private, but Manuel confessed that interviewing Decker changed the way he thought about how the world worked. "It takes a lot to make an impression on me," Manuel said. "But I had a lot of admiration for him, the way he was able to keep it together."

There were theories about why Decker survived. His memory of the incident is imperfect, and so they will always remain theories. "Everything was normal," he recalled during a federal inquiry into offshore helicopter safety, the only time he has spoken publicly of the accident. "The sound was normal. The vibration level was normal." He had been asleep during the turn back toward land, and because the open water didn't offer much navigational aid, he had thought they were still flying toward the platform.

The pilots gave their passengers the call to brace. Decker was asked whether he braced the way he had been trained. "No, I didn't. I grabbed the seat in front of me." With both arms? "With both arms, yes."

He continued his testimony. "The next thing I remember was waking up in a submerged helicopter...It was instantly filled with water." He did not reliably remember much of his escape, nor his delivery to the surface. His memory flashed ahead to the downdraft of the helicopter that came to retrieve him, the spray of the salt, and the voice of the rescue swimmer.

Decker was the second youngest passenger on board, after Allison Maher. That might have helped both of them get out. (Dr. Avis ruled that Maher, like the others, had drowned, but he couldn't say when.) Perhaps they didn't fall unconscious during the descent; perhaps they did but woke up, unlike the others. Decker believed he'd forced his way through a broken window. Maher, alive or already dead—probably alive, because she was unstrapped from her seat—might have exited through the hole where the door used to be. Decker must have kicked toward the surface. She might have, too, but run out of air somewhere on her way up. Perhaps Decker's lungs were just a little bigger. Perhaps he'd taken a fuller breath before impact. Perhaps he had more air in his survival suit and risen faster. Perhaps he'd chosen, by chance, a better seat, the only seat that would contain a survivor.

"Sometime, it would be an interesting equation in physics to figure out how someone got out of a machine and someone didn't," Allan Chaulk said, speaking like a true engineer. That the helicopter landed on water made a difference. Aircraft that crash into land compress; water expands them. The surge creates cracks in the fuselage; the water blows windows and doors out rather than in. But planes that crash into the ground, or break up midair, can also offer transitory openings, and maybe one or more passengers will be tossed out of a fireball and into a cornfield in Sioux City, Iowa, or wake up on a Czech mountainside after falling 30,000 feet, or be found by her tiny cries next to the bodies of her mother, father, and brother, in the remains of a plane outside Detroit.

When Mike Cunningham's father crashed his own plane into the ocean, he survived. So did his infant son. His new wife, Mike's stepmother, did not, and neither did their three-year-old daughter, Mike's half-sister. Mother and daughter were buried in the same casket. Mike, who had not been on board, was a pallbearer, and he was haunted by the weight of his burden. Tears still came to his eyes when he remembered the last time he'd heard his little half-sister's voice, calling to him at home, through a closed bathroom door. He became determined to prevent other families from experiencing the wreckage that his did.

The baby boy, his half-brother, lived with ghosts as well. He grew up to be a man who didn't dream so much as he wondered. Why did he live when his mother and sister did not? The scientific, unsatisfying answer: Babies float. He had been in his mother's arms during takeoff. Perhaps his mother pushed him through an opening in the plane as it sank, or he was thrown through it. Either way, he had made his way out of the plane and bobbed to the surface, from which he was plucked, with a life left to live.

It was hard for him to think that something as sacred as life could depend on such randomness, on luck, on the uncontrollable and the unknowable, on dumb *circumstance*. Survivors often suffer through the same agonizing calculus. The sum, more often than not, is guilt. Why not them? Why me? Nobody really knows *why*. Maybe none of us is meant to know.

Humans have learned some incredible things. We understand gravity, rainbows, the internal combustion engine, static electricity, glassblowing, papermaking, satellite communication, photosynthesis, backgammon, and the written word. Sometimes we're also a little arrogant in our self-belief, too certain of our ability to end arguments. We invented numbers. We can always do the math.

No, not always. Riddles remain, and so, too, should our humility. We don't really know how a caterpillar becomes a butterfly, or whether a butterfly remembers when it didn't have wings. We don't understand how salmon know to return to the place they were born to give birth. We don't agree on the exact function of the human spleen. We don't know whether certain people with autism can see around objects, although apparently some can. We haven't made it to Mars. We don't have proof of other life in the universe. We haven't been able to build machines that can express empathy like we can or understand fairness or feel love.

We can't explain why our favorite song or movie puts a lump in our throats, or why some arms can throw a baseball 100 miles per hour. We can't predict precisely how much rain will fall on a given city block in a given day. We don't know why some people vote against their own self-interest, or who killed Jimmy Hoffa or the identity of D. B. Cooper, or whether Apple or McDonald's or the National Football League will exist in five or ten or twenty-five years. We don't know why COVID-19 kills some people and passes through others without their even knowing they had it. We don't know why Robert Decker is here when Allison Maher is not.

———

Every September 11 since Kenneth Feinberg completed his original task, a small box of candy or bouquet of flowers has arrived at his office. Feinberg does not know who sends them. He suspects they are from a woman, a widow, but that's only a suspicion. He really has no idea. That's what has changed the most about Kenneth Feinberg: He was once a man of certainty, a man of laws who saw the world in black-and-white, every choice like the choice between Martha's Vineyard or Nantucket. Now he is filled with doubt. He understands better than most of us that life is not linear. We can't know what the future will bring. Today represents the end of our understanding, the outer limits of the world of fact.

But it is within our power to prepare ourselves for to-morrow's uncertainty. Feinberg holds one truth with perfect conviction: On the anniversary of an unthinkable tragedy, someone who lost someone precious to them will thank him for his humanity and expertise, for his guidance through seem-ingly unnavigable chaos. No machine could have reconciled such a situation. Only particular people could, and can. Only a tasteful person, a passionate person, an adaptable person, a curious person, a mindful person, an inventive person, a care-ful person. That's the kind of person I aspire to be. I want to become one of the beholders. I hope this book has raised the

same desire in you. I want to stand beside them—beside you—
on a slowly advancing shore, looking out at an endless ocean.
We'll never know everything that's waiting for us on the other
side. But we can close our eyes and imagine the life we hope to
find there, and then open them and start making our way.

Acknowledgments

I'd first like to thank you, dear reader. I hope you enjoyed *The Eye Test* and it made you feel better about the world than you did before you read it. Our lives are full of challenges; our lives are full of wonder. It's up to us how we keep stock.

This book was made possible by two people thinking creatively: Sean Desmond, my publisher at Twelve, and David Black, my forever agent. The idea for the book was Sean's, because he's a man who looks at the world and asks *why*; he then talked to David, a man who looks at the world and asks *how*. I don't know why or how, but they decided that I was part of the equation. At the time, I'd recently left *Esquire* and was going through a divorce. I mostly asked: *What the hell just happened?* I was on a long drive to see some friends in Georgia for consolation when David called. I pulled into a roadside Panera for lunch and the time and space to talk to him. He told me the deal for this book was done, and everything was going to be okay. I had a little cry in front of too many innocent people who just wanted a cookie. Luckily, I had a giant bread bowl in front of me to catch my happy tears.

I'd like to thank everyone else at Twelve who has helped create the object you now hold. (Unless, of course, you have opted for the digital or audio versions, in which case, you're really missing out on this amazing new trend of printing ink on paper. It's wonderful.) Rachel Kambury was the assistant editor; Anjuli Johnson was the production editor; Elisa Rivlin provided the legal read; Jarrod Taylor designed the cover and didn't hate me, openly at least, for being picky about it; Marie Mundaca took care of the interior (Go, Team Garamond); Becky Maines did the copyediting; Megan Perritt-Jacobson helped get it into your hands. We all worked hard to make it as perfect as we could. If there are flaws, they are mine, and believe me, I am mortified by them.

Some of the stories you've read began as stories in *Esquire*, and I must thank my friends at my former work. In particular, David Granger, my editor-in-chief, indulged my wandering curiosity for fourteen years; Peter Griffin, my direct editor, honed every idea (and rejected many more of them), improved every story, and polished every sentence; Bob Scheffler and Kevin McDonnell fact-checked the hell out of every fact. Peter also laid his expert hands on this manuscript, for which I am grateful. The subjects of other stories first appeared in the *New York Times Magazine*, *WIRED*, and *ESPN The Magazine*. I'm indebted to the editors and fact-checkers who helped me there, too.

My sort of journalism is possible only when talented strangers agree to spend some of their precious time with me. To everyone who said *yes* to me over the years: I don't know why you did, but thank you. If you appear in these pages after having been in a magazine's, you made a good and lasting impression, and I am happy for the chance to know you. If we met because of this book, thank you for helping me understand something I was probably slow to understand. My questions were sincere, and I hope I conveyed your answers properly.

I also wish to thank all the journalists and writers whose

own research I've included here. Secondary sources can be tricky, as we've learned, but I trust all of you and your fine work and appreciate that you undertook it. I hope you feel well understood, summarized, and cited. I'd especially like to thank the hundreds of people who produce the *New York Times*, which has proved a constantly useful resource. You make a daily miracle.

My love and gratitude to my parents, John and Marilyn, and my children, Charley and Sam. I am fortunate to have my life bookended by yours.

And Ana. I love you so much. I will never take your belief for granted. Thank you for making me feel lucky every glorious day.

A Note on the Type

This book was set in Stempel Garamond, a typeface designed by D. Stempel AG foundry in 1925 and based on the original sixteenth-century Garamond font. It was written on a battered MacBook Pro with Word's version of Garamond. A lot of writers use generic fonts when they work, like Times New Roman or Courier or, Heaven forbid, Arial or Helvetica. Writing in an atypical, beautiful font can change how your words look on the page and affect how you treat them. Garamond slows you down. Garamond makes you careful.

About the Author

CHRIS JONES is a long-time journalist and short-time screen-writer. He has written extensively for *Esquire*, the *Atlantic*, *WIRED*, the *New York Times Magazine*, the *Wall Street Journal Magazine*, and elsewhere, and he has won two National Magazine Awards for his feature writing. He was also a producer on *Away*, the Netflix series starring Hilary Swank. He lives in Port Hope, Ontario, Canada, with his partner and two boys.

Index

INDEX

Las Vegas, 76–77
law enforcement. *See* criminal justice system
Leachman, Sancy, 228
Leaf, Ryan, 67
League City (Texas), 99–100
Lennon, John, 19
Leonardo da Vinci, 200
Levine, Lowell, 160
Lewis, Michael
  on Beane, 41, 74
  on luck, 37–39, 37n, 51
  Moneyball, 4–5, 39–42, 45, 52, 66, 74, 104, 193–94, 223
  on Morey, 43
  The Undoing Project, 223–26
Leyston Sixth Form College, 126
Lieberman, Joe, 145
lies, amplification of, 124–27
light, study of, 60
linen, 217
Liverpool F.C. (Reds), 43–44
Lloyd, Jessica, 174, 176–80
logos, 208–14, 213n, 241
London police, 155–56
Long, Terrence, 72–73
Los Angeles Dodgers, 52–53
lost at sea, 238–39
low-probability, high-impact events, 87
Loyal Friends and True, 81–82, 83, 151
luck
  baseball managers and, 67–68
  favorite songs and, 28
  in football (British), 44
  game shows and, 81, 89, 150–51, 154–55
  role of luck in life, 37–38, 37n, 51
  survivors and, 249
Luhrmann, Baz, 2

M

Machado, Manny, 58n18
Machine Gun Preacher (film), 6

Maddux, Greg, 49
Madonna, 24
magic performances, 29–36
Maher, Allison, 238, 239, 247
Malaysia Airlines Flight 17, 240
Malaysia Airlines Flight 370, 245
  manner of death, 240–41
Manuel, Rob, 237–38, 246–47
Marathon Man (film), 14
Martha's Vineyard, 182–83
Martin, Max, 19–23, 24–25
Martin's Method, 23
Masterminds (film), 8
Maurice, Paul, 54
Mayer, J. C. A., 157
Mayweather, Floyd, 103, 110n
McCain, Cindy, 140–41
McCain, John, 140–47, 141n
McCarthy, Cormac, 148n
McCartney, Paul, 19
McClaughry, M. W., 157, 158
McClaughry, Robert W., 157, 158
McGregor, Conor, 109–13, 110n
McIlroy, Rory, 212
McKee, Robert, 11–13, 14, 16, 18, 45
McNamara, Michelle, 175–76
media illiteracy, 103–4, 103n
Medical University of Vienna, 226–27
medicine, 215–51
  accident investigation comparison, 237–49
  currency design comparison, 215–19
  decision-making in, 223–29
  dehumanization of, 229–33, 235–37
  incomplete pictures and, 219–23
  medical diagnoses, 224, 226–28
  narrative medicine, 229–37
  reforms and, 231–33
  reverence and, 229–33, 235–37, 246
  training in, 232, 234–35
melodic math, 22
Merseyball, 43–44